Bibliografische Information der Deutschen Nationalbibliothek

Die Deutsche Nationalbibliothek verzeichnet diese Publikation in der
Deutschen Nationalbibliografie; detaillierte bibliografische Daten sind
im Internet über http://dnb.d-nb.de abrufbar.

ISBN 978-3-8325-4155-2

Logos Verlag Berlin GmbH
Comeniushof, Gubener Str. 47,
10243 Berlin
Tel.: +49 (0)30 42 85 10 90
Fax: +49 (0)30 42 85 10 92
INTERNET: http://www.logos-verlag.de

Management and Scheduling of Accelerators for Heterogeneous High-Performance Computing

Dissertation

A thesis submitted to the
Faculty of Electrical Engineering, Computer Science and Mathematics
of the
University of Paderborn
in partial fulfillment of the requirements for the
degree of *Dr. rer. nat.*

by

Tobias Beisel

Paderborn, Germany
June 2015

Supervisor:
    Jun.-Prof. Dr. Christian Plessl

Reviewers:
    Jun.-Prof. Dr. Christian Plessl
    Prof. Dr. Franz Rammig

Additional members of the oral examination committee:
    Prof. Dr. Marco Platzner
    Prof. Dr. André Brinkmann
    Dr. Jens Simon

Date of submission:
June 15, 2015

Date of public examination:
August 12, 2015

Acknowledgements

First of all, I would like to thank my advisor Jun.-Prof. Dr. Christian Plessl and my part-time advisor Prof. Dr. Marco Platzner for supporting my research and providing me with a research environment that left nothing to be desired. Their advice, guidance, and experience has been a great benefit and support for my work on this thesis and during my PhD.
Furthermore, I would like to thank:

- Prof. Dr. Franz Rammig for serving as reviewer for my dissertation.

- Prof. Dr. Marco Platzner, Prof. Dr. André Brinkmann, and Dr. Jens Simon for serving on my oral examination committee.

- Prof. Dr. André Brinkmann for supporting my research and initiating the BMBF ENHANCE project that was of great value for me.

- My colleagues Andreas Agne, Jahanzeb Anwer, Stefan Biedemann, Alexander Boschmann, Stephanie Drzevitzky, Heinrich Giebler, Heiner Giefers, Mariusz Grad, Tobias Graf, Markus Happe, Nam Ho, Server Kasap, Paul Kaufmann, Tobias Kenter, Tanja Langen, Enno Lübbers, Achim Lösch, Björn Meyer, Antoniou Paraskewi, Lars Schäfers, Tobias Schumacher, Gavin Vaz, and Tobias Wiersema for valuable discussions and making my working environment a very pleasant place.

- Bernard Bauer for always being available for any kind of request and his kind organizational help in any situation.

- Axel Keller, Andreas Krawinkel, and Holger Nitsche for patiently and perseveringly considering my consecutive requests and their technical support.

- The colleagues of the Paderborn Center for Parallel Computing for a motivating and enjoyable working atmosphere.

- The Bundesministerium für Bildung und Forschung (BMBF) for funding the "Enabling Heterogeneous Hardware Acceleration Using Novel Programming and Scheduling Models (ENHANCE)" project under project grant 01|H11004 in the "HPC-Software für skalierbare Parallelrechner" program.

- My collaborators in the ENHANCE project for making it an exiting project with interesting and fruitful discussions on my work.

- The Bundesministerium für Wirtschaft und Energie (BMWi) for funding the "Tumordiagnose" project under the project grant KF2159003FO9 and Dr. Dirk Iwamaru and Dr. Toni Vomweg for the collaborative work in the exceptional project and for giving me very interesting insights to breast cancer diagnosis.

- The Bachelor, Diploma, and Master students, as well as student assistants that I have supervised for helping me implement and supporting my research.

- All the very helpful proofreaders of this dissertation.

Finally, I would like to thank my family. In particular, I would like to thank my parents and parents-in-law for their continuous support, my wife Anna for her outstanding care, encouragement, and patience, and my sons Karl Maximilian and Paul Konstantin, who are my greatest motivation and inspiration.

Abstract

In recent years, single-core CPU processing systems have evolved over homogeneous multi-core processors to manycore computing systems in order to accommodate the ever-growing demand for computational power while limiting the power consumption. Furthermore, accelerator technologies, like Graphics Processing Units (GPUs) and Field-Programmable Gate Arrays (FPGAs), achieved increasing interest by providing specialized processor and memory architectures that allow custom solutions for a wide range of application domains. Combining different kinds of hardware resources to a heterogeneous computing node allows to provide remarkable computational performance and energy efficient resources that serve a wide range of scientific and industrial computations. The use of such heterogeneous systems has received great attention and has been subject of numerous research endeavors since their advent. Moreover, semiconductor industry nowadays shows increasing interest in combining heterogeneous computing resources to on-chip heterogeneous solutions.

However, the benefits of heterogeneity come with several challenges: The heterogeneity in architectures involves a diversity of programming models and languages. In addition, each accelerator type requires a specific instruction set architecture and dedicated binaries, as well as vendor-specific drivers and runtime environments. Many efforts have been undertaken to simplify the usage of such systems. Programming frameworks like OpenCL, OpenACC, and OpenMP provide an abstracted view on the underlying hardware. They allow to target heterogeneous resources by a common application programming interface and a compilation and execution infrastructure. However, there still is a major lack of execution environments for concurrent and automatic execution of applications on available resources, especially in operating systems.

In this thesis, novel techniques for run-time management of heterogeneous resources and tasks that are capable to execute on diverse resource types are proposed. The major focus of this work is to enable these tasks to be scheduled like CPU tasks in current operating systems. Most accelerators do not inherently support preemption of task execution, which limits the flexibility of task execution in heterogeneous systems. Therefore, cooperative multitasking is used in this work instead, which allows tasks to voluntarily offer writing a checkpoint that unambiguously defines the applications state. This thesis proposes a programming pattern that defines such states, which are mappable to arbitrary computing resources. On top of this programming pattern, two schedulers are provided: one located in user space and one extending the Linux Completely Fair scheduler in kernel space. Both perform task scheduling and execution based on tasks cooperatively yielding resources and task migration among resource types. Several scheduling and load balancing algorithms are defined that aim at increasing the performance, reducing the total energy consumption, and allowing for fair execution of a set of tasks. This thesis shows that the presented approaches are superior to state-of-the-art approaches and improve on the metrics for heterogeneous task execution.

Furthermore, a novel approach is presented in this work that allows for transparent acceleration of binary applications by using a technique called *shared library interposing*. In many situations it is not possible to modify an application for execution on heterogeneous resources, e. g., when using binary applications. The shared-library-interposing technique is used to redirect library calls of (binary) applications to an alternative library providing an accelerated implementation with the same functionality. To this end, a framework called *liftracc* is provided that intercepts and redirects library calls to a wrapper library, which acts as a gateway to accelerator-specific versions of the original library. With different library selection methods being encapsulated in the wrapper library and a mapping of the original library interface to the interface of the target library, the approach provides transparent acceleration of single library calls. An evaluation based on the BLAS library for linear algebra shows that this approach is feasible. Overheads of a library call redirection are in a range that allow for speedups to be achieved.

Zusammenfassung

In den letzten Jahren haben sich Einkern-Prozessor-Systeme über homogene Mehrkern-Prozessor-Systeme hin zu Vielkern-Prozessor-Systemen weiterentwickelt, um der ständig wachsenden Nachfrage nach Rechenleistung gerecht zu werden und den daraus entstehenden Energieverbrauch zu begrenzen. Des Weiteren haben Beschleuniger-Technologien, wie z.B. Grafikprozessoren und Field Programmable Gate-Arrays (FPGAs), ein gesteigertes Interesse erfahren, da sie maßgeschneiderte Lösungen durch spezialisierte Prozessor- und Speicher-Architekturen in einer Vielzahl von Anwendungsbereichen ermöglichen. Die Kombination von Prozessoren mit einem oder mehreren Beschleunigern in einem heterogenen Rechnerknoten stellt eine enorme Rechenleistung sowie energieeffiziente Ressourcen bereit, die einer breiten Palette von wissenschaftlichen und industriellen Berechnungen dienen. Die Verwendung solcher heterogenen Rechensysteme hat enorm an Bedeutung gewonnen, die sich auch in einer Vielzahl von Forschungsvorhaben widerspiegelt. Zudem zeigt auch die Halbleiterindustrie ein zunehmendes Interesse an der Kombination heterogener Rechenressourcen auf einem einzelnen Chip integrierten Lösungen.

Das Ausnutzen der Vorteile heterogener Systeme beinhaltet jedoch auch einige Herausforderungen: So bringt die Vielfalt der Architekturen auch ein großes Spektrum von Programmiermodellen und -sprachen mit sich. Darüber hinaus erfordert jeder Beschleunigertyp die Nutzung eines bestimmten Befehlssatzes und dedizierter Binärdateien sowie die Verwendung herstellerspezifischer Treiber und Laufzeitumgebungen. Es werden umfangreiche Anstrengungen unternommen, um die Verwendung solcher Systeme zu vereinfachen. Programmier-Frameworks wie OpenCL, OpenACC und OpenMP bieten eine abstrahierte Sicht auf die zugrunde liegende Hardware. Sie ermöglichen es, heterogene Ressourcen durch eine einheitliche Programmierschnittstelle und eine integrierte Übersetzungs- und Ausführungsumgebung zu nutzen. Allerdings besteht weiterhin, insbesondere durch Betriebssysteme, ein großer Bedarf an maßgeschneiderten Ausführungsumgebungen für die nebenläufige und automatische Ausführung von Anwendungen auf verfügbaren Ressourcen.

In der vorliegenden Arbeit werden neue Techniken für die Verwaltung heterogener Rechenressourcen sowie für die Ausführung von Prozessen, die Implementierungen für verschiedene Ressourcentypen bereitstellen, vorgestellt. Der Schwerpunkt dieser Arbeit ist, diese Prozesse durch aktuelle Betriebssysteme möglichst gleichartig zu den Prozessen auszuführen, die ausschließlich auf der CPU ausgeführt werden. Aktuelle Beschleuniger-Architekturen unterstützen allerdings meist keine native Unterbrechung der Ausführung von Prozessen zu beliebigen Zeitpunkten, wodurch deren flexible Ausführung eingeschränkt wird. Stattdessen wird in dieser Arbeit kooperatives Multitasking verwendet. Prozesse bieten dabei freiwillig ihre Unterbrechung zu einem bekannten Ausführungszeitpunkt an, zu dem der Prozesszustand eindeutig ist und — bei einer Unterbrechung — in persistentem Speicher abgelegt werden kann. Ein zu diesem Zweck neu entwickeltes Programmierschema definiert diese Hardware-unabhängigen Zustände und wird in zwei Prozess-Schedulern genutzt: in einem separatem User-Space Scheduler und in einer Erweiterung des Linux Completely Fair Schedulers im Kernel Space. Beide realisieren das Scheduling und Ausführen von Prozessen unter Nutzung einer kooperativen Unterbrechung und der anschließenden Migration von Prozessen zwischen Ressourcentypen. In dieser Arbeit werden mehrere Scheduling- und Lastbalancierung-Algorithmen definiert, die eine Verbesserung des Durchsatzes, eine Reduzierung des Gesamtenergieverbrauchs und eine faire Ausführung mehrerer Prozesse anstreben. Es wird gezeigt, dass die vorgestellten Ansätze zur Ausführung von heterogenen Prozessen aktuellen Vergleichsansätzen überlegen sind und die genannten Metriken verbessern.

Diese Dissertation präsentiert zusätzlich einen neuen Ansatz, der transparente Beschleunigung von Binäranwendungen mit Hilfe einer Technik namens *shared library interposing* ermöglicht. Oft ist es nicht möglich, bestehende Anwendungen für die Ausführung auf heterogenen Ressourcen anzupassen, z.B. wenn sie lediglich als Binärdatei vorliegen. Mit shared library interposing können Aufrufe dynamischer Bibliotheken beliebiger (Binär-) Anwendungen an eine alternative, beschleunigte Bibliothek gleicher Funktionalität umgeleitet werden. Zu diesem Zweck wird ein Framework namens *liftracc* eingeführt, das Aufrufe zu bestimmten Bibliotheken abfängt und an eine sogenannte Wrapper-Bibliothek umleitet, die als Schnittstelle zu Beschleuniger-spezifischen Versionen der ursprünglichen Bibliothek dient. Die Wrapper-Bibliothek kapselt verschiedene Auswahlmethoden zur Bestimmung der Zielbibliothek und bildet die Eingangsdaten des originalen Aufrufs auf die Schnittstelle der Zielbibliothek ab. Damit ermöglicht der Ansatz die transparente Beschleunigung einzelner Bibliotheksaufrufe. Eine Auswertung zeigt, basierend auf der BLAS-Bibliothek für lineare Algebra, dass dieser Ansatz praktikabel ist. Die Kosten einer solchen Umleitung von Funktionsaufrufen liegen in einem Bereich, der eine Beschleunigung der Aufrufe erlaubt.

Contents

CHAPTER 1

Introduction

1.1 Motivation

Heterogeneous computing, that is computing on systems providing non-uniform computing resources like Central Processing Units (CPUs), Graphics Processing Units (GPUs), and Field-Programmable Gate Arrays (FPGAs), has experienced a remarkable boost in the 2000s. The driving force behind the use of these systems has been the flattening growth of CPU clock frequency caused by challenges in semiconductor design, beginning in the early 2000s. Moore's law from 1965 [121] predicted an increase of chip density roughly doubling every year. With an update in 1975 [123] that increased the predicted doubling time to 18 month, his prediction had already been met for nearly 40 years in the 2000s. The so-called power wall describes the major reason why the design of single-core chips reached a limit resulting in the the redesign of chips to combine multiple processors on a single chip. The power wall arises through a polynomial increase of power consumption for a linear increase of processor clock frequency. The continued technology miniaturization resulted in an increasing leakage current at the same time. The so-called Dennard scaling [55] states that power density stays constant with ongoing transistor scaling, i. e., power consumption stays in proportion with used chip area. However, Dennard scaling no longer holds, as transistor gate oxides became too thin to avoid current to leak out into the underlying substrate. As a result, static power losses have increased that led to rising chip temperatures again further increasing the power loss. In the mid-2000s, semiconductor industries turned toward replacing single power-inefficient processors with many power-efficient processors on a single chip to keep up with Moore's prediction. Approaching the power wall went hand-in-hand with the fact that the cost efficiency of improving the architecture of a single processor has begun to decrease due to increasing costs in the production process and, thus, costs finally outweighed the benefits in performance. While improvements in single-core scaling could still be reached through innovations, like multiple instruction issue, out-of-order execution or deep pipelining, these were limited by the so-called ILP wall, i. e., limits in instruction level parallelism (ILP). Therefore, the semiconductor industry declared parallel computing to be the future allowing for the parallel execution of several tasks on multicore processors.

Turning chip design toward placing multiple cores on a single chip allowed for different ways of combining processing cores. Manycore systems combine up to 100s of cores and GPUs even combine 1000s of cores on a die, while multicore systems combine only a few complex processors on a single chip. The complexity of the cores decreases with an increased number of cores. With 1000s of very simple cores, GPUs are especially suited for data-parallel tasks computing a single instruction on multiple data (SIMD). FPGAs in contrast are freely configurable logic circuits, which may be individually configured to the need of applications and even allow to further decrease the core complexity and increase the count of cores accordingly. These and other emerging parallel architectures can be combined with a single- or multicore CPU in a heterogeneous system and define a solution to overcome the described limitations in semiconductor design. Today, heterogeneous systems come with many different designs ranging from Systems-on-Chip (SoC) solutions with specialized hardware accelerators to hybrid CPU/GPU architectures. Heterogeneous multicore systems with different core types but with a single instruction set architecture (ISA) are used as well as heterogeneous multicore systems including different core types that implement different instruction set architectures. Moreover, computing devices that make use of heterogeneous architectures are diverse, ranging from embedded systems in mobile devices to high-performance computing (HPC) systems used in data centers. Heterogeneity is accepted as the future microprocessor and system design, both by industry and academic researchers.

The spread of use of heterogeneous computing resources is mainly based on the power-efficiency of these architectures and their flexibility to be used across diverse application domains. Heterogeneity allows customization of used architectures to the growing and diversifying requirements of applications. Moreover, many accelerator resources provide high performance potential for a rather low cost, which does not limit the use of high-performance computing to only a few markets any more. Today, many libraries, tools, and programming languages are available for accelerators that lower the threshold for application developers to get started with using these resources. However, while the benefits in performance and energy have been discussed, many important challenges are yet to be investigated regarding the architecture, hardware/software interfaces, programming models, compilation, run-time systems, and performance-evaluation and -estimation.

A lot of research has been undertaken in these fields that I roughly summarize to three areas: 1. heterogeneous architectures, 2. programming frameworks, and 3. execution environments. Research on architectures includes the ongoing development of single accelerator resource types but also their combination in integrated heterogeneous systems. While accelerator manufacturers, like NVIDIA and Advanced Micro Devices (AMD) for GPUs, and Altera and Xilinx for FPGAs, provide new and improved models of their existing product series, the general trend goes toward the on-chip combination of architectures. Currently, the focus lies on integrating CPU and GPU into a single processor device. All major competitors in the CPU and GPU market already provided or announced systems that shall make use of the advantages of both CPU and GPU while reducing communication overheads through shared on-chip memory. In embedded systems, heterogeneous system design is already the norm. For instance, current smartphones are equipped with both a multicore CPU and a GPU.

Programming frameworks for heterogeneous architectures aim at providing both high-level abstractions for programming diverse architectures and the automation of the compilation tool-flow to generate binaries for multiple target resources. This research area is also mostly driven by industry today. With OpenCL, OpenACC, and OpenMP 4.0, several programming standards have arisen that aim at heterogeneous systems and are already widely used. OpenCL moves toward being the major standard for developing portable applications for CPUs, GPUs, and FPGAs from scratch and is supported by an increasing number of processor vendors. OpenACC and OpenMP in contrast focus on extending given applications by code annotations and using compiler directives for automatic code translation as an input to the proprietary compilers of the hardware manufacturers. In addition, many libraries, like BLAS (Basic Linear Algebra Subprograms) or FFT (Fast Fourier Transform), exist for different target resource types, which allow for function-level acceleration of applications and enable application developers to leverage the power of accelerators while abstracting the details of the architecture. Moreover, academia has its stake in this field through research on extensions of existing programming standards for supporting additional architectures and cross-compilers for different programming languages. These try to bridge the gap of transferring existing applications to current systems equipped with specialized hardware.

Regarding execution environments two general approaches can be stated. The first is provided through batch systems, like HTCondor [162] or TORQUE [150], that allow for configuring available computing resources and dynamically mapping tasks to these resources. These systems abstract from the used programming model, as they map binaries and their inputs to computing resources. They aim at, but are not limited to distributed systems and allow checkpointing and migration of tasks. However, they only allow migration between architectures of the same ISA and matching resource parameters. A second approach deals with execution environments that are either used on top of an existing programming model or provide an equivalent programming model itself. Although there are approaches for checkpointing and task migration among heterogeneous resources, these are generally limited to migration between architectures of the same ISA. Moreover, run-time systems mostly follow a run-to-completion approach that provides a resource to an application until it completes its computation on the resource. This limits the flexible use of available resources and the ability to react to dynamically changing system states.

This thesis touches the field of programming frameworks but focuses on execution environments for heterogeneous systems. It aims at filling the gap in heterogeneous execution environments for transparent, dynamic and flexible task management at run-time with task migration between arbitrary computing resources. It also investigates the use of library interposing as a technique for transparent accelerator usage for binary applications at a function-level.

1.2 Claims of this Thesis

In the 2000s, we have seen the rapid emergence of heterogeneous computing in the general purpose and high performance computing domains. Today many of these systems employ heterogeneous nodes that use accelerators, such as GPUs, Xeon Phis, or FPGAs, in addition to CPUs. The most suitable resource for a certain application depends not only on the application itself, but on application parameters such as data size and, in addition, on the objective for task execution, for example, maximizing performance or minimizing energy consumption. Nevertheless, it also depends on the availability of given resources. If the best suited resource is not available, using a less suited resource may be beneficial, but also waiting for the best suited resource may be the better choice in other situations. Preemptive multitasking and task migration between CPU cores has been a cornerstone of operating systems for decades. However, accelerators today are typically used with a run-to-completion model. This paradigm poses a severe limitation to the flexibility of task management, which leads to suboptimal overall performance and energy consumption for a set of tasks. There exist no automated tools today that exploit the potential of heterogeneous computing outlined above through migrating tasks based on their suitability for certain resource types, the current set of tasks in the system, and resource availability. Preemption of tasks mapped to accelerators and migration of tasks between heterogeneous resources have hardly been investigated. The main challenges are the lack of a common instruction set across resources, finding a suitable representation of the application state, and defining an applicable programming model for heterogeneous resources. Considering the rapid adoption of accelerators in general purpose and high performance computing, I argue that enabling preemption on accelerators and migration between different resource types is not only crucial for improving the performance and energy consumption, but also for enabling novel uses of heterogeneous compute nodes.

> Claim 1: Enabling operating systems to manage heterogeneous hardware resources and enabling both preemption and migration of tasks between resources allows for performance- and energy-efficient scheduling of a set of tasks at run-time.

Scientific users frequently do not only program and run their own custom applications, but also use proprietary domain-specific software or simulation frameworks like MATLAB, for which no source code is available. This prevents modifying the applications to target different accelerators. As a result, missing hardware and programming knowledge and the unavailability of source code keeps many scientific users outside the field of computer science from exploiting the possible advantages of heterogeneous computer systems. But how may these applications benefit from acceleration or energy savings anyway without modifying the binary itself?

Many scientific applications make extensive use of highly optimized libraries for computationally intensive operations. Examples of frequently used libraries are the BLAS library for linear algebra, the GNU scientific library (GSL) for numerical calculations, or the Vector Signal Processing Library (VSIPL) for embedded signal processing platforms. These numeric libraries are typically installed as shared libraries, which are dynamically loaded by the applications at runtime.

Shared library interposing provides a mechanism for modifying existing applications without requiring access to the original source code by intercepting and replacing calls to shared library functions with different accelerated functions. I argue that shared library interposing may be used to leverage the performance of heterogeneous computers transparently through using a fully flexible and even dynamic mapping of library functions to hardware accelerators without requiring any programming effort from the user's side.

> Claim 2: Library-interposing techniques allow for transparent run-time application acceleration on heterogeneous hardware resources without the need to adapt the original program.

1.3 Contributions of this Thesis

To show the validity of the claims, I provide a task scheduling framework that enables tasks to voluntarily release a resource, i.e., yield a resource, at preemption points for possible subsequent migration to a different resource, independent of the underlying ISA. I use a set of example applications from different application domains to evaluate the profitability of the approach with regard to different scheduling objectives. In addition, I provide a library-interposing framework to redirect and remap library calls of binary applications to accelerators and show the potential benefits of the approach. Thus, I both explore thread- and function level acceleration of applications on heterogeneous systems.

In particular, I provide the following contributions:

- I enable applications for yielding and possible subsequent heterogeneous migration. For achieving this, the main challenges are the lack of a common instruction set across resources, finding a resource-independent representation of the application state, and defining a programming model for heterogeneous resources. To tackle these challenges, I define a programming pattern that allows for checkpoint-based multitasking of applications. This novel approach enables preemption at preemption points through applications releasing a resource cooperatively and additionally enables heterogeneous migration of tasks in systems equipped with accelerators. Applications still remain with the use of the accelerator vendor's drivers and APIs, as provided in the original application, which makes the approach applicable to many given applications. I show the feasibility and the low complexity of the approach by discussing an example application.

- I provide algorithms for heterogeneous scheduling of tasks that support task migration. I define scheduling parameters and decision policies to assign tasks to resources, perform task switches, and migrate tasks based on their suitability for a resource, their priority, and expected overheads. I define task scheduling policies that aim at reducing the total runtime and the total energy consumption of a set of tasks, or strive for a fair distribution of computation times among tasks. Load balancing policies are combined with the scheduling policies to distribute tasks among available resource types with respect to the scheduling objectives.

- I present a Linux kernel extension for a kernel-space scheduler that enables task scheduling on heterogeneous resources. Particularly, I provide an extension to the Linux Completely Fair Scheduler (CFS) that provides awareness of installed accelerators, enables scheduling of specific tasks to accelerators, and allows time-sharing and task migration using a cooperative multitasking and checkpointing approach. The scheduler's hardware selection decision is based on meta-information provided by the applications. The scheduler integrates with the CFS approach to increase the fairness among tasks, but also increases the performance for a set of tasks. I use a set of applications to demonstrate the approach to be beneficial in both respects, despite the overheads introduced by yielding tasks and task migration.

- I provide a user-space scheduler named *HetSched* for task scheduling on heterogeneous resources, which is a completely refined multithreaded and modularized implementation of the previous kernel-space scheduler. The programming pattern used is further simplified. It even enables automatic checkpoint determination and translation of the original application code to match the pattern in certain cases. I include new load balancing and scheduling policies that not only allow for fair time-shared scheduling of tasks on accelerators, but also aim at performance-only or energy efficiency optimizations. The scheduler's benefits are evaluated by providing and comparing different state of the art scheduling approaches.

- I propose shared library interposing as a mechanism for transparent application acceleration and present an extendable library-interposing framework for transparent acceleration of applications by redirecting library calls to accelerators at run-time. The framework allows for the implementation of different policies to map functions to available computing resources. I present a case study, which allows to evaluate the benefits and the overheads of the approach on the basis of the BLAS library for linear algebra.

1.4 Thesis Structure

The thesis is structured as follows:

Chapter 2   provides background information on the emergence of heterogeneous computing, its characteristics, and current technologies in the field. It also discusses advantages and challenges in heterogeneous computing.

Chapter 3 outlines concepts and key ideas for enabling dynamic task management in heterogeneous systems. It defines parameters that influence scheduling decisions and defines a task model that includes an affinity of tasks toward target architectures. Moreover, cooperatively yielding of resources at preemption points is discussed as a solution for flexible heterogeneous run-time systems.

Chapter 4 makes the case for heterogeneous task migration. It describes the inevitable changes in the lifecycle of a task and the required changes to an application that enables its migration between arbitrary instruction set architectures. A programming pattern is derived and proposed for the use with a heterogeneous scheduler.

Chapter 5 proposes scheduling policies for heterogeneous task migration. I define possible scheduling objectives and parameters that influence the mapping of tasks to available computing resources and derive corresponding scheduling policies.

Chapter 6 describes two experimental schedulers that make use of the concepts introduced in Chapters 3 to 5. I provide a user-space and a kernel-space solution for integrating the scheduler into the operating system. While the user-space version provides an independent scheduler implementation to be used with Linux operating systems, the kernel-space scheduler integrates heterogeneous resources and task management into the Linux operating system scheduler. Both approaches are evaluated through sets of tasks comprising multiple applications and the profitableness for targeted scheduling objectives is shown.

Chapter 7 describes a novel approach to transparent application acceleration through the use of library interposing. I discuss feasible solutions to intercept library calls and describe a framework that uses decision policies for transparent use of available resources. As a proof of concept, the results include a runtime and overhead analysis of selected functions of the BLAS library as candidates for acceleration.

Chapter 8 summarizes the contributions and results of this thesis and discusses lessons learned during the technical preparation of the contributions.

CHAPTER 2

Background

Transitioning from traditional parallel computing on CPUs to heterogeneous computing resources for small and large scale applications has experienced a rapid growth in recent years and has been boosted by different developments in both software and hardware. This chapter gives an overview of the historical emergence of heterogeneous computing, the current state-of-the-art, and future trends. Additionally, potentials and challenges of heterogeneous computing are discussed.

2.1 The Emergence of Heterogeneous Computing

Heterogeneity has been exploited previously for different types of CPUs, e. g., with multiple clock speeds. Heterogeneous computing nowadays defines a rather architecture-based diversification of computing resources, i. e., combining CPUs with accelerators like Graphics Processing Units (GPUs) or Field-Programmable Gate Arrays (FPGAs). The birth and the increased usage of accelerator equipped systems has been driven by application demands for increased or customized computational power as discussed in the following sections.

2.1.1 Semiconductor Design - CPU Design Reaching Limits

Semiconductor technology has shown a remarkable evolution from the first single transistors in 1959 to billions of transistors in current CPUs. In 1965, G.E. Moore has observed a trend in chip development that turned out to be valid, with certain reinterpretations, until today [121]. According to Moore's law, the number of components per chip would double every year. While this originally included resistors and capacitors, not only transistors, Moore revised his observation in 1975 [123], and 1995 [122]. The first revision clarified the doubling to be associated with increasing number of chips, and increasing number of transistors per chip in a yearly manner, while eliminating nonfunctional chip area, which would double rather every 2 years [113]. The second revision corrected the pessimistic prediction to chip density doubling roughly every 18 months [142]. Besides density, memory and logic evolution were regarded separately after late 1970s, as microprocessor chips developed faster than memory chips [113] eventually leading to the *memory wall* [177], i.e., memory access limiting the overall microprocessor performance.

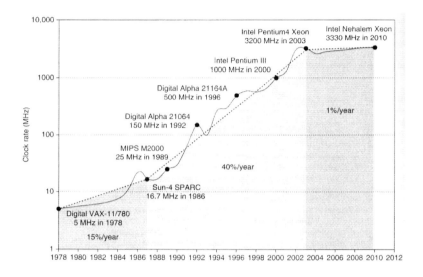

Figure 2.1: Uniprocessor clock rate (MHz) increase since 1978. Increase has slowed down massively since 2003. Image from [80].

Standardized roadmaps were established to predict the future development of memory and logic chips resulting in the foundation of the International Technology Roadmap for Semiconductors (ITRS) in 1999 [74]. While Moore's prediction has often been seen as a self-fulfilling prophecy [119], chip production reached limits in several aspects requiring the chip design to change. In the 2000s, the increase in uniprocessor performance began to flatten due to limited leakage of the chips. With the 90nm production process, gate oxide leakage was increasing exponentially. It became a meaningful percentage of the chip's power consumption [30] and defined the *power wall*. Additional power dissipation requires additional cooling and, therefore, further increases operation expenses. Although the clock rate increase of single processors factually came to a standstill in 2003 (see Figure 2.1), the microprocessor performance continually increased (see Figure 2.2) due to performance increasing innovations that maintained the transistor count and power, such as multiple instruction issue, out-of-order execution or deep pipeline [14]. On-die caches allowed an additional performance boost without compromising energy efficiency [31]. Nevertheless, these innovations were also limited through the *ILP wall* limiting single chip performance by a limited instruction level parallelism (ILP), i. e., by the inability to keep functional units busy while waiting for memory accesses. As a result, performance increase was reduced from 52% per year to 22% per year from 2003.

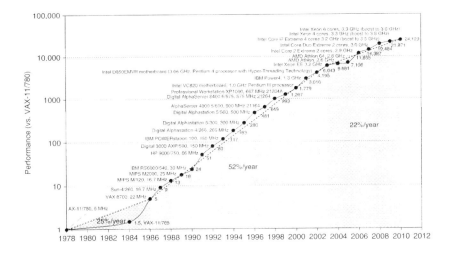

Figure 2.2: Performance growth of uniprocessors since 1978 relative to the VAX 11/780 measured by the SPEC benchmarks [81]. Image from [80].

With frequency ceasing as the driving force behind pushing microprocessor performance forward, new ways to preserve the ever-growing performance of CPUs had to be found. Shrinking a processor die by advanced fabrication processes reduces the size of the microprocessor circuits and the current used by transistors while maintaining their clock frequency. As an effect, it reduces cost and saves space that is required for a chip on the underlying silicon wafer. The semiconductor manufacturing advances became more important due to the limitations in increasing single processor performance introduced by the power wall in the 2000s. From 2004 to 2015, the production process has been reduced from 90nm to 14nm, seeing a forecasted shrink to 5nm in 2026 [44]. The reduction of size ultimately led to the advent of multicore microprocessors that place two or more processors on a die. After all, reducing the production process has physical limits and predictions of the ITRS are usually not met any more in the 2000s and corrected with each new roadmap for semiconductors. Esmaeilzadeh et al. [61] already depicted a noticeable slowdown in improving the production process in 2011 and predict the end of the multicore era.

2.1.2 From Parallel Computing to Heterogeneous Computing

With the pervasive use of computing and increasing size of datacenters all over the world, the interest in sustainable computing has increased considerably. "Green Computing" has emerged as the name for a strong consideration of energy efficiency as a major aim in computing in the 2000s. In recent years, the emphasis on maintaining transistor performance while supporting higher operating frequencies has actually shifted to an emphasis on delivering lower leakage power and improved energy efficiency [30]. This paradigm shift is also pushed by the need for power efficient embedded systems, e.g., to increase the battery lifetime of mobile devices. In the mid-2000s, the semiconductor industry declared parallel computing to be the future [14] by replacing single power-inefficient processors with many efficient ones on a single chip. Brodtkorb et al. [34] state a "rule of thumb" that decreasing the voltage and frequency by one percent decreases the power density by three percent and the performance by 0.66%, i.e., dual-core designs running both 85% of frequency and supply voltage offer 180% better performance than single-core designs while keeping the power demands stable. With increasing number of processors, or cores per chip, multicore microprocessors were introduced that represent a new era of computing and introduced many new challenges in hardware and software by relying on application or task parallelism.

Introducing multicore processors allows various chip designs, making it feasible for customization of chips toward the requirements of the applications assigned to it. One may combine only few, complex, and powerful cores to achieve computational throughput, or increase the number of cores to a large number of less powerful cores, i.e., providing a low frequency, but also low power dissipation and voltage, and, thus, increasing the energy efficiency. Even introducing on-chip heterogeneity is possible by combining different sized processors as motivated in [13] and, e.g., implemented in the IBM Cell-Broadband-Engine Architecture (CBEA) [92] (see Figure 2.3).

The Heterogeneous Era The use of multicore CPUs has been growing rapidly since their advance along with an increase in the number of cores over time. Multicore CPUs use thread-parallel processing on shared memory regions and generally follow the multiple instruction, multiple data (MIMD) taxonomy class partly being extended by vector processing units allowing data-parallel single instruction, multiple data (SIMD) instructions. Multicore architectures with a large number of cores (loosely defined as tens to hundreds) are referred to as manycore CPUs and are typically connected by a network-on-chip. The best known example is Intel's Many Integrated Core (MIC) Architecture known as Intel Xeon Phi [49]. It actually is a coprocessor and, thus, uses a distributed memory model and defines a heterogeneous system in combination with a regular CPU connected via PCI Express (PCIe). See Table 2.1 for a comparison of architecture types.

CPUs are generally not tailored to a particular task, which causes inefficiencies in terms

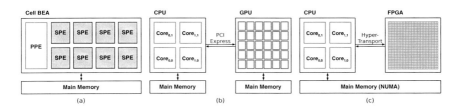

Figure 2.3: Examples for Heterogeneous Architectures: (a) Cell BE Architecture combining a Power Processor Element (PPE) with Synergistic Processing Elements (SPE) (b) combining a CPU with a GPU and (c) combining a CPU with an FPGA. The FPGA may be connected via PCIe too. Image based on [34].

of chip area and power consumption and increases the design complexity of the chip. Scalability of multicore systems might actually be limited by power constraints [62] and, thus, require customized solutions instead. Further increasing the number of cores to 1000s while reducing their complexity defines the idea used by modern general-purpose Graphics Processing Units (GPUs). GPUs are accelerators that are optimized for SIMD data-parallel computations and extend a single- or multicore CPU system via PCIe or on-chip interconnects for specialized computations. Although the number of cores is increased by a large factor, power drain on full utilization of current GPUs is only slightly higher (typically less than a factor of 2) than that of CPUs. While GPUs are optimized for specific applications, Field Programming Gate Arrays (FPGAs) are accelerators that use arbitrarily designable processing elements while allowing massive parallelism. They provide freely programmable logic blocks, allowing a large number of basic logic elements. FPGAs usually follow a data-flow computation model and, thus, are especially well suited for applications that are applicable to pipelined execution to achieve a high data throughput. As algorithms are synthesized in hardware, they are often very fast in comparison to software implementations on a CPU or GPU and have low latencies. However, their fully customizable design allows implementing soft-core processors on the configurable chip area.

All of these architectures have experienced a boost in the 2000s, showing the trend toward customization as the solution to the CPU scalability limitation. Customization sacrifices generality and increases development efforts for increased performance or energy efficiency through customized computing resources and interconnects, and a custom level of parallelization. Customization also may constrain the type of parallelism and thereby optimize the execution, as, e.g., done by GPUs that require defining sets of threads to be executed efficiently in parallel [31].

Besides above mentioned GPU and FPGA accelerator types, as well as the mentioned Xeon Phi and Cell BEA architectures, several less commonly used architectures have crossed the High Performance Computing (HPC) market, sometimes disappearing again after a certain period of interest. ClearSpeed Technology Ltd [42] aimed for very low energy parallel array processors, provides a fast on-chip network designed for SIMD execution.

Property	Multicore CPU	Manycore CPU	Graphics Processing Unit (GPU)	Field-program-mable Gate Array (FPGA)
cores	$\sim$ 2-8	$\sim$ 10-100	$\sim$ 1000	$\sim$ 100000
core complexity	very complex	complex	simple	very simple
computation model	MIMD + SIMD	MIMD + SIMD	SIMD	data-flow
parallelism	thread + data parallel	thread + data parallel	data parallel	arbitrary
memory model	shared	shared/ distributed	distributed	distributed
power	$\sim$ 150 W	$\sim$ 225 W	$\sim$ 225 W	$\sim$ 50 W
programming languages	high-level languages (C/ C++/Java/...)	high-level languages	C/C++-extensions	HDL / C/C++-extensions

Table 2.1: Classification of current parallel computing architectures. The values shown are exemplary for typical high-end processors or accelerator cards and shall only give an idea of architectural differences. *Power* values provide typical singe-chip power drain numbers. *Cores* shall not be understood as processor cores when regarding GPUs and FPGAs, but rather as compute cores on GPUs that are mostly usable for parallel SIMD computations only and processing elements in the smallest extent, i. e., basic logic elements on FPGAs.

In addition, fixed-function accelerators, e. g., media codecs or cryptography engines sacrifice programmability toward optimization in hardware and are likely implemented on application-specific integrated circuits (ASICs). While these are generally suited for combination with other architectures in a heterogeneous environment, this thesis will focus on the widely used GPU and FPGA architectures as discussed before.

Generally, there is not a single and always applicable optimal solution for all kinds of applications any more, which introduces both opportunities and challenges for a heterogeneous combination of parallel architectures. All architectures have strength and weaknesses for certain kinds of applications, making a combination of architectures a valuable approach.

2.1.3 Application Diversity

The pursuit of both faster and complex computing resources is based on an interdependency with a growing demand for computational power by applications and algorithms. More powerful traditional CPUs allowed for more complex mathematical models in scientific and industrial applications while demanding advances of the hardware by exploiting current architectures to their limits. This is true till today. Models for scientific or industrial problems are still getting more and more complex to further improve their correctness, accuracy, and precision.

According to "2014 HPC User Site Census: Applications", report published by Intersect360 in September 2014 three of the top five HPC usage categories (chemical research, fluid dynamics, weather/environmental modelling) make extensive use of numerical methods. These kind of applications are still scaling to large-scale CPU-parallel computing clusters and exploit their potential best.

Applications today not only demand computational power, but also rely on fast interconnects for data communication and fast access to large sets of memory, which can not be met by CPU-based systems any more. New application domains arose in recent years that have different demands and characteristics, e. g., bioinfomatics, molecular dynamics, or system's biology. While many applications of high-performance computing have been compute-bound, i. e., limited by the speed of the used CPU, applications today often work on a large data, i. e., are also memory-bound and, thus, require fast access to large sets of data. *Big Data* [114] is currently pervasively discussed as a general term especially in the area of high-performance computing. Analysis of ever-growing amounts of data using data-mining approaches is not only computationally intensive, but also requires to store and work on enormous amounts of data. These applications require the used hardware to be adapted to their needs, i. e., provide customized solutions for fast memory access, and do not scale well to large CPU cluster solutions.

A well known classification of applications into algorithmic methods that capture patterns of computation and communication has been presented in [13]. Applications are classified to 13 *dwarfs*, each defining an algorithmic method that captures a pattern of computation and communication. Different ways of parallelization are required for each of these dwarfs and, therefore, differently well suited for parallel execution. Their list not only depicts the complexity of providing parallel algorithms, but also shows the diversity of application domains implying the application's different demands to the used hardware. Feng et al. [63] show an overview of the suitability of example applications for each application domain on diverse hardware using OpenCL [75]. While the success of parallelizing an application is generally limited by Amdahl's law [10], i. e., by the non-parallelizable parts, many other characteristics determine the suitability for parallelization in general and also the suitability for parallelization on CPUs or other architectures. These include the degree of parallelization, memory access patterns (ordered or random) or intra-application dependencies within the control- or data-flow. New hardware architectures experienced a growing interest that is also based on this diversity of application demands.

2.1.4 Diverse Hardware Requires Diverse Software

The advent of parallel computing not only broke with traditional CPU design, but also required to adapt the used programming models to match and efficiently use parallel architectures. Threads have been introduced to programming languages long before multicore processors emerged but focussed on concurrent rather than parallel execution. However, first programming APIs for threading on CPUs, like POSIX Threads, and OpenMP, allowed fast adaptation to parallel computing requirements for shared memory systems.

While concurrency means performing computations logically at the same time, parallelism means performing them physically at the same time. Thus, parallel programming encounters problems like cache coherency, i. e., keeping local caches consistent despite of parallel execution on different cores. Many libraries, like Intel Threading Building Blocks [48], have been introduced that simplify multiprocessing on shared memory systems.

Extending parallelism from shared to distributed memory systems introduced further challenges, especially the distribution of required data over the used local memories and synchronization. Message passing has been used for communication over network structures enabling distributed execution of programs. Concurrent distributed computing has a much longer history than parallel processing and has already been applied in the 1960s. With the launch of the Message Passing Interface (MPI) [65] in 1992, today's most used message passing protocol had been introduced that further promoted distributed computing. Combining message passing with shared memory thread parallelism enabled large-scale parallel cluster systems. Extending cluster nodes with accelerators further introduces heterogeneity, also in terms of used software, e. g., using Graphics Processing Units.

Graphics Processing Units   The driving force behind GPUs becoming more powerful computing resources, equipped with a growing count of cores and an accordingly large number of parallel threads has been the need to render high-resolution 3D scenes in games in real-time [129]. Rendering high-resolution graphics is inherently suited for massive parallel execution, as each pixel in an image can be computed by a separate thread. In fact, a GPU runs the same thread on each pixel to be rendered, thus, working data-parallel in SIMD instruction mode. Today GPUs are suited for more general computations, making rendering graphics only a special case for GPU computation.

Rendering graphics is the historic reason for performing computations on a graphics processor. First steps toward general-purpose GPUs (GPGPUs) have been made with introduction of the first graphics accelerators by the Nvidia Corporation (NVIDIA) in 1997 (RIVA 128), which provided fixed-function pipelines and was designed to accelerate Microsoft Direct3D and OpenGL. In 1999, the first GPU (GeForce 256) was introduced, which integrated a transform and lighting entity resulting in the first vertex shader programmable GPU in 2001 (GeForce 3). Shaders were small programs that introduced lighting and shading to pixels, later vertices. In 2002, the next generation GPUs (GeForce FX) introduced computing with Cg [50], DirectX 9, and OpenGL, were executing a thread for each pixel and, thus, already highly multithreaded. Using Cg, each thread executes a Cg program rendering a single pixel or vertex. For the first time in GPU history, Cg allowed to be used for general-purpose computations, although Cg was not designed for that purpose and, therefore, difficult to use. GPGPUs in the common sense were introduced with the launch of the NVIDIA Compute Unified Device Architecture (CUDA) [51], a software and hardware architecture that enables the GPU to be programmed with high-level programming languages, in 2006. C for CUDA is based on the C programming language and allows to integrate processing NVIDIA GPUs in C and C++ applications and enabled GPU computing to become widespread and obtain a large interest in the high performance computing (HPC) market. NVIDIAs strongest competitor is semiconductor company Advanced Micro Devices, Inc. (AMD), who acquired ATI Technologies Inc. (ATI), a microprocessor producer specialized in graphics chips, in 2006 to access the GPU market and, thus, the heterogeneous CPU-GPU market. However, AMD never had a strong stake in the market for general purpose computing on GPUs with their AMD Stream SDK [84] and, thus, early focussed on OpenCL for future CPU-GPU integrated systems. AMD Stream SDK later was replaced by the AMD APP SDK [85] that also targets the Heterogeneous System Architecture (HSA) [66] introduced by the HSA Foundation and provides a shared memory bus for CPU and GPU.

Field-programmable Gate Arrays In contrast to application-specific integrated circuits, ASICs, whose functionality is (partly) fixed to a special purpose, Field-programmable Gate Arrays (FPGAs) are integrated circuits, whose logic blocks and interconnects are freely configurable. First FPGAs were introduced in 1985 by Xilinx. Today, although being slightly ahead, Xilinx shares marked lead with Altera [125].

FPGAs consist of a very large number of configurable logic blocks (CLBs), which internally contain a number of programmable basic components: flip-flops (FFs) and look-up tables (LUTs). These basic elements are connected by a programmable interconnect network, which allows to configure a routing network on a grid-layout and provides large flexibility in using the FPGA. Basic components are, therefore, configured to represent logical circuits. They are combined to a large array of logic elements implementing complex operations or a set of similar circuits that are usable in parallel. More recent FPGAs additionally include specialized components like BRAM configurable memory or embedded hard digital signal processing (DSP) blocks.

FPGAs are configured using a hardware description language (HDL) allowing a formal definition of digital logic circuits. HDLs abstract from the very low layer details of the electronic circuits and enable their description, simulation and synthesis with a high-level description language. Two major approaches were introduced in the 1980s that are still mainly being followed today. VHDL [82] was introduced in 1983 and is based on Pascal and Ada languages. Verilog [152] was introduced 1984 and standardized in 1995 and is a C-like language. Both approaches still coexist and are both supported by major FPGA vendors. Circuits designed in a HDL are subsequently simulated with vendor-specific tools and, on success, synthesized on the FPGA board for execution. The major difference to developing applications for CPU and GPU is the way of thinking about the implementation of the desired algorithms. FPGA developers think of their algorithms as logic circuits rather than traditional algorithms based on control statements, which makes the design of FPGAs complicated for CPU developers. The barrier to entry thus seems higher, which made FPGAs lag GPUs in their spread of use. Custom computing engines on FPGAs requires deep hardware and application knowledge to achieve highly efficient circuits. Despite that, programming FPGAs has become simpler by later developments. SystemC [88] is a modeling language combining hardware and software descriptions by extending C++ with a new library. Maxeler Technologies [118] enables the description of dataflow models of FPGA kernels and their communication with the CPU in Java language. Recently, both Xilinx and Altera introduced software development kits to compile OpenCL applications for their FPGAs [86, 46].

2.2 Heterogeneous Computing Today

Computational resources and tools used in HPC have a very broad range, historically and also in terms of functionality, as discussed in Section 2.1. Applications have varying requirements on computational power or memory that may be mapped on available kinds of architectures providing different strength and weaknesses. Heterogeneous computing is a promising way of exploiting the strength of diverse architectures and hiding their weaknesses. However, the world of heterogeneous computing is complex, as it requires a lot of knowledge on architectures and tools. A major current and future objective in heterogeneous computing is, therefore, to simplify both architectures and tools.

2.2.1 Heterogeneous Systems

Heterogeneous architectures, as introduced in Section 2.1, are employed in heterogeneous systems using different system topologies. Figure 2.4 shows how accelerators are typically combined with host CPU systems.

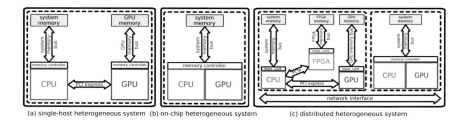

(a) single-host heterogeneous system (b) on-chip heterogeneous system   (c) distributed heterogeneous system

Figure 2.4: Topologies of heterogeneous systems.

The most common appearance of a heterogeneous system extends a single- or multicore CPU system with an accelerator, e. g., a GPU or an alternative, as shown in Figure 2.4 (a). Data transfers need to use the system provided interface to the accelerator, typically PCI express (PCIe), in today's systems. Accelerators have their own memory space and can only access host memory through data transfers. Data consistency has to be ensured by the executed program. This kind of topology may as well integrate several accelerator types, as shown in Figure 2.4 (c).

Figure 2.4 (b) shows an on-chip combination of a CPU with an integrated GPU presented by all major microprocessor vendors. AMD calls their integrated CPU-GPU processors Accelerated Processing Unit (APU) while Intel (IvyBridge and Haswell microarchitectures) and NVIDIA ("Project Denver" microarchitecture) present according architectures. CPU and GPU share the same physical memory and, thus, do not require explicit data transfers.

Data transfers use on-chip bus systems and, therefore, remove the bottleneck of CPU-GPU communication via peripheral interconnects. On the other hand, these System-on-Chip (SoC) solutions compromise in certain dimensions, which limits performance. As an example, current discrete AMD GPUs (AMD FirePro S9150 Server GPU) provide a highly optimized 512-bit memory interface to GDDR5 memory that allows a theoretical off-chip bandwidths of 320 GB/sec while current AMD APUs (AMD "Kaveri" A10-Series A10 PRO-7850B) are slow by almost a factor of 9 (34.1 GB/s). Furthermore, CPU and GPU are competing for this bandwidth, so a parallel use of CPU and GPU for data intensive computations might limit the peak performance [97]. In addition, limited performance is a matter of the chip size. An on-chip combination of architectures limit the size of both CPU and GPU. On the other hand, integrated CPU-GPU systems increase the power efficiency in contrast to discrete use of CPU and GPU [144]. Due to high density, power efficiency, and low cost, integrated GPUs are promising candidates for next-generation microservers and datacenter workloads [97]. Heterogeneous execution on integrated GPUs and SoCs will therefore be a key feature of future architectures [95]. In embedded systems, e. g., in smartphones, on-chip integration of CPU and GPU is already state-of-the-art.

Alternatively, FPGAs and CPUs can be integrated as a SoC. Xilinx partnered ARM Ltd. to announce the UltraScale MPSoC Architecture [87], which extends Xilinx's UltraScale FPGA to enable heterogeneous multiprocessing. In addition to the FPGA, it attaches 64-bit quadcore processors, dualcore Real-Time Processors, and an OpenGL conformant GPU for graphics acceleration, all designed by ARM.

Single-server systems, as discussed above, could additionally be combined to heterogeneous clusters as shown in Figure 2.4 (c). Network interfaces, like Ethernet or InfiniBand, are used for inter-server connection of heterogeneous nodes. The TOP500 list [165], which provides a list of the 500 fastest supercomputer sites of the world, shows a considerable trend toward systems including heterogeneous computing resources, as shown in Figure 2.5. While the performance share of accelerator-equipped systems was only 5.17% in November 2009, the November 2014 list shows an increased share of 34.42%. Among the top 10 systems, 50% of the systems are equipped with accelerator technology. The system ranked 1st (Tianhe-2 [164]) integrates 48,000 Intel Xeon Phi accelerators, while the system ranked 2nd (Titan [132]) provides 18,688 Nvidia Tesla K20X GPUs, showing the importance of heterogeneity in supercomputing.

2.2.2 Programming Heterogeneous Applications

Programming frameworks for heterogeneous architectures today provide an abstracted view on the underlying hardware while providing binaries for multiple target resources. OpenCL [75], OpenACC [133], and OpenMP 4.0 [29] are already widely used programming models and are driven and supported by the hardware manufacturers. Broadly speaking, the current approaches can be classified in two groups: The first group provides a programming API that is used to develop corresponding applications. The second group uses code annotations without modifying the application code massively. The first approach is followed by OpenCL, which is becoming a major pillar of the heterogeneous computing world,

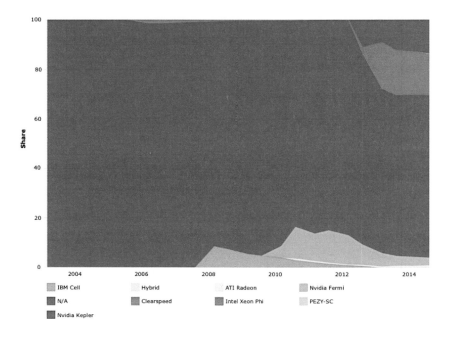

Figure 2.5: Performance share of systems with accelerators/coprocessors in the Top500 list (November 2014) [165].

but requires applications to be rewritten according to the OpenCL API. OpenACC and OpenMP extend given applications by pragmas and use compiler directives for automatic code translation that again is used as an input to the proprietary compilers of the target resources. In addition, many helpful libraries available for function-level acceleration are utilized via a variety of programming models and target architectures.

Research on programming heterogeneous architectures is mainly twofold. On the one hand extensions of existing programming standards are followed for supporting additional architectures [20, 21, 96, 153] and on the other hand many cross-compilers for different programming languages have been developed [11, 72, 104, 173] that help to transfer existing applications to systems equipped with specialized hardware.

2.2.3 Runtime Systems

Regarding execution environments, two general approaches exist. First, there are batch systems, like HTCondor [162] or TORQUE [150], that allow to configure available computing resources and dynamically map tasks to these resources. Using distributed heterogeneous systems requires data partitioning and distribution among compute nodes via message passing, but also embraces the need to efficiently use every single heterogeneous server node internally while providing workload to all available computing resources. Today, management systems for job scheduling on cluster have been adapted to support heterogeneity. HTCondor, TORQUE, Bright Cluster Manager [33], etc., support CPU and GPU job scheduling while some support Intel Xeon Phi and FPGA as well. These systems abstract from the used programming model, as they map binaries and their inputs to computing resources. Nevertheless, these are batch systems that aim at cluster computing and are thus not optimized for the use of single heterogeneous nodes. Moreover, each job typically needs to provide a specific description of required hardware and an expected maximum execution time.

Additionally, there are execution environments that are either based on an already given programming model [116, 155, 161, 174] or provide a suitable programming model to be used with it [15, 17]. These mostly aim at single-node systems and provide a better integration with the programming of heterogeneous architectures. One of the best known examples is StarPU [17], which is widely used today. It performs scheduling of tasks provided through a Directed Acyclic Graph (DAG) and does not closely integrate with the operating system. Heterogeneous runtime systems from the operating systems point of view are still subject to research.

2.3 Potentials and Objectives of Heterogeneous Computing

As already discussed, heterogeneity is one possible answer to the *brick wall* [13], illustrating the combined limitations of *power wall*, *memory wall*, and *ILP wall*. Defining heterogeneous computing only to counter given semiconductor design problems is insufficient. The need for changes in semiconductor design has been an opportunity for heterogeneity to prove its benefits in several different domains:

- **Custom computing**: The diversification of architectures allows to make use of strengths of specific resource types, i. e., use the best suited architecture for specific applications. It even allows to use application-specific architectures.
- **Desktop supercomputing**: Speeding up application by making use of massively parallel architectures is not limited to a minority having access to supercomputers any more, but may be accessed by everybody.
- **Ecological acceptance**: Supercomputing has become extremely thirsty for energy with some compute centers consuming enough energy to power a small town. Heterogeneous architectures provide a chance to reduce the used energy while sustaining performance. This has become a public interest, e. g., manifested in the Green500 list [45] listing the top 500 supercomputers by energy efficiency.
- **Limit expenses**: With reduced energy consumption and low acquisition costs for some architectures, e. g., consumer GPUs, the costs for high performance computation has become affordable for a larger group of people.

While above list includes the most significant benefits of heterogeneous computing, its major objectives are well known:

- **Performance**: Increasing the achieved performance of executed computations enables faster and better computational results.
- **Energy efficiency**: Decreasing the energy consumption for executed computations or increasing their energy efficiency reduces costs.

The heterogeneity can improve these objectives depending on the executed application. A heat distribution example is shown in Figure 2.6. The optimal resource usage for an application varies depending on the scheduling objectives and input size. A heterogeneous system thus introduces the flexibility to choose the best computing resource for execution of the application.

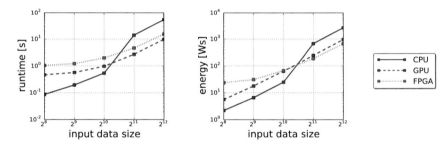

Figure 2.6: Runtimes and energy consumption values for a heat distribution example application executed with different input data sizes. Best target resource depends on input data size (one dimension of input matrix).

2.4 Challenges and Limitations of Heterogeneous Computing

The greatest challenge of heterogeneous systems is that they are heterogeneous in many domains. Heterogeneity not only allows individual solutions through custom computing, it also requires individual solutions and increases complexity. While there are many efforts for standardization, there are still many open challenges, from architecture level to runtime systems. The major challenges and limitations can be categorized in the following areas:

- **Architectural diversity**: As shown in this chapter, there is a large architectural diversity in computing resources with varying strengths, which will probably remain in future, even if partially solved. However, the outcome of this diversity is a difference in instruction set architectures (ISAs), application binary interfaces (ABIs), and interconnects. Developers need to know about architecture details and how to make use of them for best performance and energy efficiency. For instance, efficient use of accelerator internal memory stacks is essential for performance reasons, but requires deep knowledge of the memory architecture. Moreover, different ISAs or even integrated circuits used on FPGAs prohibit migrating tasks from one architecture to another seamlessly, which is a key requirement for flexible use of heterogeneous systems. Most accelerator architectures do not support preemption but assume a run-to-completion execution model. While computations on CPU cores can be easily preempted and resumed by reading and restoring well defined internal registers, most hardware accelerators do not even expose the complete internal state nor are they designed to be interrupted.

- **Interconnects and memory locality**: Accelerators typically do not have autonomous access to the shared memory space of the CPU cores. Explicit data transfers of inputs and outputs are required. Different memory address spaces additionally require synchronization and cache coherence protocols. Diverse interconnects, e. g., PCIe, Hypertransport, or other on-chip bus systems have different implications on performance and energy efficiency of executed applications through provided bandwidth and interconnect saturation. Data transfers can have large impact on their runtimes and, thus, need to be considered both at development and execution time. This diversity will also most likely remain in future, although already being abstracted by programming models today and becoming less important due to increasingly fast interconnects.

- **Programming models and development tools**: The heterogeneity of architectures resulted in a large variety of programming languages, compilers and debuggers, mainly for historic reasons. This introduces a considerable complexity to application developers. A lot of effort has been undertaken on this limitation in recent years, already making things easier for developers nowadays. With OpenCL [75], OpenACC [133], and OpenMP 4.0 [29], three programming standards for CPU/GPU systems have been introduced, which already have a wide acceptance among developers. Moreover, standard debuggers, like GDB, are extended to support accelerator code, e. g., CUDA-GDB. Although resulting applications are executable on different resources, they do not inherently allow to be preempted or migrated among these by runtime systems. Moreover, each of these programming standards is limited to a subset of target computing resources. For instance, FPGA support is only in the beginning with OpenCL and not yet given for OpenACC and OpenMP.

- **Runtime systems**: Heterogeneity is already widely used, but operating systems still lack mechanisms for managing and optimizing the use of heterogeneous resources. While there is a lot of research conducted on runtime systems for heterogeneous systems, no standard tools have emerged for executing multiple tasks on multiple resources from an operating system type of view. Even OpenCL lacks an execution model that allows to automatically and transparently execute multiple applications on multiple resources. Operating systems should manage accelerators [134], as well as apply common CPU scheduling schemes on heterogeneous resources. This would require unrestricted scheduling that allows both preemption and migration, which is limited by current architectures and programming models.

2.5 Chapter Conclusion

This chapter established a background on the history of heterogeneous computing and todays heterogeneous computing technologies. We have shown that heterogeneous computing is not only a trend that is used in a niche of high-performance computing, but rather a solution to limitations in traditional CPU design. In addition, we depicted that heterogeneous computing is not just a possible solution to keep up with todays computational demands, but the only available solution that provides energy- and cost-efficient high performance computing. Integrated GPUs and other SoC-integrated accelerators will be a key feature of future architectures [95], which is confirmed by current and prospective hardware architectures of the major hardware semiconductor manufacturers. "The Future Is Heterogeneous" is a popular phrase used in various resources, e. g., [148]. It expresses the belief of both leading semiconductor industry and academia. The International Exascale Software Project roadmap [59] states that heterogeneity is a key requirement on the extreme-scale/exascale software stack.

At the same time, we showed that heterogeneous computing is challenging for several reasons. While a lot of work has already been done on programming models, with OpenCL being a key technology that is pushed forward by both industry and academia, run-time systems for heterogeneous systems have not yet established a standard and have not been integrated with operating systems till today. Hence, the International Exascale Software Project roadmap [59] states heterogeneity to be one of the challenging research topics on the recommended research agenda for runtime systems. Exploiting distributed heterogeneous systems includes not only scheduling tasks over network connected hardware resources, but also requires runtime systems on each single heterogeneous node. We have discussed a variety of different architectures and their combination to a heterogeneous system. Combining several accelerators within a single workstation is attractive for solving medium sized scientific computing problems in a cost-effective and energy-efficient way without accessing large and expensive supercomputing systems. This enables nearly every scientific and industrial institution to access significant computing power to address increasingly complex numerical simulations. This underlines the necessity to find solutions for better integration of heterogeneous runtime systems with the operating system. Our work, therefore, focuses on the operating system point of view on schedulable hardware resources and tasks to be executed through an operating system connected scheduler. We, thus, aim at single-node system topologies with dedicated hardware resources.

CHAPTER 3

Basic Concepts and Ideas

This chapter introduces the major ideas and basic concepts for energy- and performance-efficient task execution. We first narrow the field of heterogeneous computing to our main focus of runtime systems for heterogeneous computing and give an introduction to the major objectives of heterogeneous task execution. We then define a model of heterogeneous task execution as a basis for this thesis' contributions including a system model, a task model, and a task execution model. This chapter discusses the field of thread acceleration rather than the acceleration of functions, which will be discussed on Chapter 7.

3.1 Towards the Efficient Use of Heterogeneous Resources

As already shown in the previous chapter, heterogeneous computing in the form of systems comprising different, often specialized computing resources has a long history. In particular, for embedded systems with tight performance and energy constraints the integration of heterogeneous resources into one node or a system-on-chip is widespread. In the last decade we have also seen a rapid emergence of heterogeneous computing in the general purpose and high performance computing domains. Today many of these systems employ heterogeneous nodes that use accelerators such as GPUs, Xeon Phis, or FPGAs in addition to CPUs. The driving force behind this rapid adoption is the opportunity to significantly improve the performance and energy efficiency of applications by executing them on the most suitable computing resource. The most suitable resource depends not only on the application but also on its parameters such as data size and on the scheduling objective, for example, to maximize performance or to minimize energy usage.

This defines a scheduling problem of matching tasks to resources and executing tasks in a well defined and orderly way. We approach the challenge of performing scheduling decisions at runtime and treat hardware accelerators as peer computation units that are managed by the operating system (OS) kernel like CPU cores. The aim of scheduling tasks in the context of heterogeneous systems is to assign tasks to computing resources in order to increase performance or save energy.

Figure 3.1 validates the idea of using heterogeneous resources. The figure presents our measurements of execution time and energy consumption for four example applications and varying input data sizes taken on a heterogeneous node equipped with CPU, GPU, and FPGA (cf. Chapter 6.3). The graphs show that the relative benefit of different resource types is highly application-dependent. Moreover, the optimal resource type changes when increasing the data size. For instance, the correlation benchmark in Figure 3.1(d) shows that offloading the computation from the CPU to the GPU only pays off at data sizes larger than 2^{10} when optimizing for performance; when optimizing for energy efficiency the threshold is already at data size 2^8.

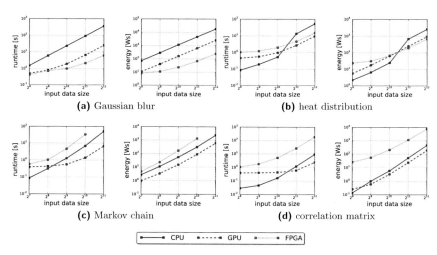

(a) Gaussian blur   **(b)** heat distribution

(c) Markov chain   **(d)** correlation matrix

CPU   GPU   FPGA

Figure 3.1: Runtimes and energy consumptions of four example applications, executed on different resource types with variable data input sizes (matrix size in 1 dimension). The figure shows measured runtime and energy for (a) a Gaussian blur image processing algorithm, (b) a 2-dimensional heat transfer simulation, (c) a Markov chain steady state computation and (d) correlation matrix calculations.

3.1.1 Heterogeneous Computing is Fast

The performance of an application on a certain computing resource is represented by the required runtime to fully compute the complete application or a certain part of it. Different runtimes are compared through their speedup over a reference runtime. Speedup is most commonly defined as the ratio between the runtime T of a task p on a resource r_i and the runtime T of p on the reference resource r_j, independent from the resource type of r_i and r_j:

$$S(p, r_i, r_j) = \frac{T(p, r_j)}{T(p, r_i)} \qquad (3.1)$$

However, as the speedup is limited by Amdahl's law [10] and computing a task on an accelerator involves overheads through required data transfer times, it is not self-evident that acceleration may be achieved for any type of application. Nevertheless, the power of heterogeneous resources to achieve speedups in contrast to CPU-only execution has been shown for many years [34, 64, 91].

In particular, numerous works have provided examples that accelerator resources may speed up single applications [12, 35, 37, 108]. In addition, few applications have been adapted to efficiently use more than one accelerator type in parallel [179]. Multiprocessing on heterogeneous systems has also been evaluated, but is limited in its effectiveness, as we discuss later in this chapter. Despite that, schedulers enable multiprocessing and thereby allow parallel use of available computing resources, i.e., achieving speedups compared to single-resource execution too [18, 38, 105].

We do not intend to provide an exhaustive list here, but the above selection shows the verifiable and wide-ranging performance benefits in using heterogeneous systems. We further discuss related work on multiprocessing in Section 3.5.

3.1.2 Heterogeneous Computing Saves Energy

Regarding the emerging field of "Green Computing" [126], it appears only natural to consider energy efficiency in addition to performance in parallel and high-performance computing. While it is quite obvious that accelerators allow to speed up computation, it is not instantly clear that they allow energy-efficient execution of applications too.

Knowing about the estimated power consumption and execution time of a task on a certain resource type is essential for performing scheduling decisions that target energy-efficient task execution. In serial computing, the possibilities to save energy were more or less limited to minimizing execution time and resource usage, which are general assets of quality programming. Now, with the continuous spread of multicore systems, new possibilities arise to exploit parallelism to save energy rather than just for speedup [39]. As already discussed in the previous chapter, power density scales with both clock frequency and the supply voltage to the square, leading to a polynomial relationship between power consumption and clock frequency:

$$P = C \cdot \rho \cdot f \cdot V_{dd}^2 \qquad (3.2)$$

P is the power density in watts per unit area, C the total capacitance, ρ the transistor density, f the processor frequency, and V_{dd} the supply voltage [25]. Hence, parallelizing software over multiple cores bears the potential to reduce the total power required to solve a given computational problem. For example, instead of running two parallel cores at full speed to achieve a speedup of 200%, one might want to consider reducing frequency and voltage by 15% for a speedup of 180%, but at half the power consumed per arithmetic operations [34]. Whereas these numbers already show a major benefit of multicore processing, heterogeneity even introduces an additional chance for energy reduction. Heterogeneous systems comprise different arithmetic units that usually have strong differences in how much power they consume per operation. This is especially true for systems with massively parallel, SIMD-style accelerators like GPUs. These resource types dedicate far fewer transistors to non-arithmetic functionalities, so arithmetic operations are done with much less circuitry being involved, and consequently, less energy per operation.

Lastly, the way the parallel application itself is implemented allows for optimization regarding power consumption. Reducing code redundancy and balancing data-transfers with the computational effort might reduce energy. Data transfers also consume power and might even require more switching activity than arithmetic computation, so there remains a tradeoff, which requires in-depth knowledge of the underlying resource type. For example, in [172] it has been shown that sometimes it even pays off to reduce the number of cores involved in solving the problem to reduce distribution of data and, hence, energy-expensive data traffic. There are ongoing efforts toward development of "green algorithms" that optimize power consumption down to the instruction level, often supported by experimental measurements to estimate energy cost of specific operations [171]. From a scheduling point of view, an application could even offer multiple implementations of a task that have different energy consumptions on the same resource type.

With reducing the processor frequency in multicore processing, introducing heterogeneity and code optimization toward the use of heterogeneous resources, there are least three levels on which heterogeneous parallel computing can be used to save energy. Thus, enabling heterogeneous scheduling toward this objective in a heterogeneous multicore system is not only feasible, but even allows to reduce costs.

3.1.3 Heterogeneous Scheduling May Achieve More

Increasing performance and decreasing energy consumption are well-defined and commonly followed objectives. But task execution on heterogeneous systems should not be limited to these objectives, as it is capable to achieve even more.

With the increasing dissemination of heterogeneous systems and the increasing interest in integrated solutions for heterogeneous resources, operating systems for heterogeneous systems become more important. Several works follow the approach of managing accelerator resources within the operating system [8, 24, 94, 139, 161], but do not integrate with the approach of traditional CPU scheduling. These approaches are further discussed in Chapter 6, in direct comparison to our approach.

We consider the scenario of using accelerators not only as an extension of a computing system for executing special tasks, but as peer computation resources that may be scheduled by the operating system almost equally to CPUs. Through more and more upcoming System-on-Chip heterogeneous systems, accelerators are provided a shared memory space with the CPU and use on-chip buses to load data into the local accelerator memory regions. Thus, data transfers are de-emphasized from being a major bottleneck, allowing also smaller portions of computations to be accelerated. We, therefore, consider accelerators being used similarly to CPUs as a valid scenario and to become more important in future. The mainline Linux operating system uses the Completely Fair Scheduler (CFS) [120] for CPU scheduling. The general scheduling principle of the CFS follows the objective to treat all tasks fair, i.e., to provide all tasks with the same share of CPU-time within a time period. This not only increases fairness, but at the same time increases interactivity, as long running tasks do not block short running tasks. Moreover, extending the operating system to be fully aware of accelerators and their tasks enables a scheduler to quickly react on system changes and, thus, keep utilization of available resources high. Transferring this idea to the heterogeneous case is new and has so far not been thoroughly examined.

Including these additional aims and objectives we derive a model for heterogeneous systems, their tasks and task execution in the following.

3.2 Heterogeneous System Model

Currently, scheduling tasks to heterogeneous resources follows a run-to-completion model, i.e., assigning an application to a resource until its computation on the resource is completed. We believe that scheduling is limited by this model, as it is less flexible as current CPU scheduling. CPU scheduling, as implemented in the current Linux kernel, i.e., by the Linux Completely Fair Scheduler (CFS), allows to transparently preempt and migrate tasks among CPU cores and enables time-sharing of available CPUs. This is not possible when using accelerators due to hardware limitations, as discussed in Section 2.4. Thereby, the efficient use of available resources by given tasks is limited, as dynamic changes of the system state may not result in immediate revisions of the current task-resource assignment. This thesis will show that this actually limits performance.

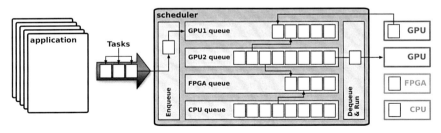

Figure 3.2: Scheduling on a heterogeneous system in a scenario that allows preemption and migration.

We consider a general scheduling scenario as shown in Figure 3.2, by enabling tasks to be interrupted in their execution for later continuation or even for being migrated to a different resource. Benefits and costs of task preemption and migration are further discussed in Section 3.4, while our approach to enable tasks for preemption and migration will be described in Chapter 4. Within this chapter, we assume tasks to be preemptive and to be even migratable between different resource types.

Let R_{het} be the set of all computing resources used by a heterogeneous scheduler. Each non-CPU resource is counted separately, while all CPUs together are considered a single computing resource. For an example testbed composed of 2 CPUs, 1 FPGA and 1 GPU, we define R_{het} as:

$$R_{het} := \{R_{CPU}, R_{GPU_0}, R_{FPGA_0}\} \tag{3.3}$$

$$R_{CPU} := \{R_{CPU_0}, R_{CPU_1}\} \tag{3.4}$$

A computing system R however consists of several computing resources $r_i \in R$, where each computing resource has a dedicated resource type $a \in A$:

$$R := \{r_0, ..., r_n\} \tag{3.5}$$

$$A := \{CPU, GPU, FPGA\} \tag{3.6}$$

where $r_i = a$ can be true for several i. Thus, each available resource type may be represented by one or several resources, which may be of the same design or slightly differ, but represent the same class of accelerator. A here represents a simplified example set of resource types. In practice these would be more diverse, e. g., a *GPU* resource type would be split into several resource types, for instance an NVIDIA GPU with compute capability 2.0, an NVIDIA GPU with compute capability 3.0, and an AMD APU. However, without loss of generality, we remain with the simplified definition of A in this thesis, e. g., assuming all GPUs in the heterogeneous system to be exchangeable.

If a resource runs idle at a certain time, a scheduler should be able to run another suited task on the resource as soon as possible. Therefore, the scheduler in a heterogeneous compute environment R is queueing tasks p on certain run queues for later execution on dedicated resources of different resource types a, as depicted in Figure 3.2. Hence, heterogeneous scheduling includes providing a set of queues to sort application-provided tasks to, perform load balancing between queues, i. e., migrating tasks between queues, dequeuing tasks for execution, and reenqueueing tasks if they are preempted. Certainly, one queue per computing resource is not the only possible solution, as further discussed in Chapter 6.

3.2.1 Responsibilities of a Heterogeneous Scheduler

We transfer the idea of preemptive scheduling and unrestricted task migration to the heterogeneous case as depicted in the general scenario for heterogeneous scheduling above. We, therefore, can derive the following responsibilities for a heterogeneous scheduler, as shown in Figure 3.3: it needs to

1. manage available hardware resources, e. g., represented by task queues,
2. accept/decline tasks during task registration and assign accepted tasks to matching task queues,
3. sort available queues with respect to a well defined scheduling policy,
4. dequeue tasks for execution if a resource runs idle,
5. stop and reenqueue a task, i. e., trigger a preemption of a task,
6. perform load balancing between resources through task migration, both before and during execution of the tasks without losing its state, and
7. integrate with the operating system to perform decisions on a well known decision base.

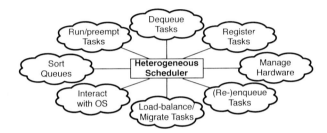

Figure 3.3: Overview of the responsibilities of a heterogeneous scheduler.

In Section 3.4, we discuss how such a scheduler can have positive impact on the system performance and cost-effectiveness. Next, we discuss possibilities to integrate our proposed scheduler into the operating system.

3.2.2 Operating System Integration of a Heterogeneous Scheduler

Dynamically selecting an appropriate resource type for a task to be scheduled at runtime is a non-trivial problem that has to be performed by a scheduler. This scheduler can be located at different locations within the system, either in the application, in user space or in the system's kernel. The decision for one of these locations is not obvious. We here discuss advantages and disadvantages of each of these possibilities.

Scheduling of homogeneous CPU cores is currently done within the kernel, as all needed input information for the scheduling decision is available to the system, such that the scheduling problem can be completely hidden from the application programmer. The heterogeneous scheduling problem is more complicated, as more decision parameters have to be taken into account, which are partly not available to the operating systems scheduler component. Parameters include the systems state, i. e., the current load on available computing resources, but especially also tasks that may be suited differently well for execution on available computing resources.

Application-internal Scheduling   Performing scheduling for heterogeneous components is still commonly done by the application developer from within the application. The major advantage is that the developer knows the application best and, thus, may implement the best possible scheduling for the specific application. Nevertheless, such scheduling is limited to a single application and does not provide any support for multitasking on accelerators. In addition, it usually ignores any information on the system state, thus, incurring significant inflexibility. We advance the view that the operating system should generally be responsible to not only manage accelerators but also be in charge of managing all workloads on the available resources.

User-Space Scheduling   A second way of performing scheduling decisions is to provide a user-space library, which performs scheduling decisions for accelerator tasks in cooperation with the operating system. Generally, user-space scheduling abstracts from the details of the operating system and hardware, but can provide access to operation systems internals through given kernel interfaces. Task execution on accelerators currently relies on the accelerator APIs that have to be executed from user space. Thus, executing tasks from a user-space scheduler does not require additional kernel-space/user-space switches. As we do not intend to use a second CPU scheduler and also do not intend to implement a completely new CPU scheduler replacing the comprehensive and highly optimized functionality of the CFS, a user-space scheduler would have to cooperate with the CFS for CPU scheduling. To perform adequate load balancing it needs to include the load of all CPU tasks in its decision. Collecting such detailed load information by accessing the kernel's CFS data structures is complex and expensive from user space, especially if the data has to be accurate and up-to-date. Retrieving according scheduling information from the *proc* filesystem, a pseudo-filesystem which provides an interface to kernel data structures, trades this complexity for reduced accuracy. Our approaches to this challenge are presented in Chapters 5 and 6.

Kernel-Space Scheduling   The third approach to heterogeneous scheduling is to extend the operating systems scheduler within the kernel to provide the ability to schedule threads for diverse hardware components. This allows the scheduling process to be completely hidden from the application developer and a holistic view on the current system status. It can, therefore, perform global decisions including all the utilization of managed computing resources, such as the load of the CPUs and I/O resources. In case of heterogeneous systems this would be a consequent continuation of the traditional CPU scheduling approach that is performed within the kernel. This approach leads to the inverted problem of the first approach, such that the scheduler does not inherently know any details about the application. Moreover, the kernel logic grows depending on the sophistication of the scheduling algorithms.

This thesis provides both a scheduler solution for the kernel space and the user space. While the kernel-space scheduler provides a proof of concept for the actual integration of the scheduler to the kernel, the key advantages of the user-space approach are the easy use of a library during development, test and at runtime, as well as the avoidance of an extension of the Linux kernel and adaptations to each new release of the kernel. As the major aim of this thesis is to provide mechanisms for effective scheduling on heterogeneous resources, the user-space solution, to be presented in Chapter 6, has achieved a greater focus and provides the majority of the scheduling mechanisms. Nevertheless, we believe that a scheduler generally should be part of the kernel. This is especially true when assuming automatic preemption on accelerators to be possible in future. Preemption enables the kernel to have full control without requiring applications to cooperate, if task execution shall be intercepted. The need for tasks to be cooperative is discussed in the subsequent Section 3.4. We, thus, designed the user-space scheduler with the goal to ultimately integrate it into the Linux kernel and thereby making it part of the operating system. To make this step easier in a future work, we base both of our implementations on the general structure of the CFS and use data structures as given by the kernel.

3.3 Heterogeneous Task Model

With the objective of performing task scheduling, the need arises to define what the entity to be scheduled, i. e., a task, actually is. We here specify our definition of a task and how we may rate it with respect to its execution on a certain resource type.

3.3.1 Specification of a Task

The CFS is responsible for scheduling *tasks*, which are either threads or processes. A process again might consist of one or several threads that are handled as individual tasks in the CFS. The CFS, therefore, does not differentiate between a thread and a process internally. Within the scheduler a task is represented as a *scheduling entity*, which additionally includes scheduler relevant information about the task.

We adopt the use of threads for easier integration with the CFS and their lightweight handling. Since a scheduler has no internal representation of the program executed on hardware side, threads to be scheduled on a heterogeneous systems have to be managed indirectly via a representative thread. We call these representatives *delegate threads* as they are a delegate of the application thread to the scheduler. Figure 3.4 depicts the idea of managing delegate threads in a queue handled by a scheduler.

Generally a thread may embrace every kind of program, from a single command, to a function, through to a full program. It, thus, does not limit the generality of the approach. Function scheduling as used in Chapter 7, therefore, can be considered a special case of thread scheduling. However, a function is more specific, as each function usually has a well known interface, i. e., the function header, to be called for execution.

Runtime and Speedup The runtime of a task is related to a certain resource, i. e., $T(p, a)$ defines the wall-clock execution time of task p on resource of resource type a. We limit the runtime and speedup to be defined for a certain resource type instead of each resource, so we define $T(p, a)$ to be the time task p executes on resource type $a \in A$. Speedup, as introduced in Equation 3.1, is a measure to evaluate the performance of a task on a

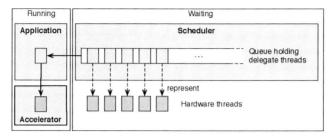

Figure 3.4: Delegate threads being enqueued for execution on an accelerator resource. Delegate threads represent a hardware thread to the scheduler.

certain computing resource compared to a reference resource. Speedup values are only used to number runtime differences of a single task on different resource types and, thus, may not be directly used to compare different tasks with each other. Therefore, the reference resource type, as stated in Equation 3.1, is of minor importance and may be selected differently for each task. This also makes the speedup independent from the supported resource types of a task.

Task Execution Phases   For a task p to be executed on a resource type a, we define cost $C(p, a)$ of execution as the sum of costs according to three execution phases as

$$C(p, a) = copy\_in(p, a) + compute(p, a) + copy\_out(p, a), \tag{3.7}$$

where $copy\_in(p, a)$ defines the costs to copy all required input data for executing on resource type a, $compute(p, a)$ defines the costs for the actually performed task execution, and $copy\_out(p, a)$ relates to the cost of transferring execution results back to the main memory of the host that is containing resource a. No direct data transfer costs are generated for the $copy\_in(p, a)$ and $copy\_out(p, a)$ phases for tasks being executed on a resource only using shared memory. When neglecting data loaded on cache misses, we can limit the costs for execution on a CPU to $compute(p, R_{CPU})$. The costs of a task execution may, e.g., be defined by the task runtime or its energy consumption.

Energy Consumption   While the runtime of a task can be measured easily, measuring the energy consumption of a task relies on possibilities provided by the used hardware. The best way to obtain meaningful energy consumption values is to actually measure how much energy is consumed in the course of processing a task implementation on each otherwise idle target resource. This can either be achieved by hooking into the power supply lines of the processing platform or through hardware vendor given interfaces that allow to retrieve power or energy values. In this thesis, we use dedicated hardware components that allow to precisely measure power and energy values of the different components as described as part of the evaluation in Section 6.3.5. If the used hardware resource does not inherently support the measurement of energy consumption values, we need to think of alternatives.

If we know how much power each resource dissipates under load, we can make a first estimation of how much energy a task implementation might consume. Precise data on this is not always available, but hardware manufacturers usually reference a value in their hardware specification called *thermal design power (TDP)*. The TDP represents the maximum thermal power (in Watts) that the cooling system of a processor is required to dissipate and can be used as an estimation of how much energy is consumed per second under full load. However, TDP vales are very rough estimates, as they assume full utilization of the resource and hardware vendors have different opinions on how pessimistic their TDP indications should be.

Nonetheless, even by enabling accurate energy value measurements, we have to differentiate the energy consumption that is rooted on the task itself and energy consumption that is produced by system and background tasks, as well as idle power consumption of currently unused resources. We define an affinity model next, which incorporates these differentiations.

3.3.2 Affinity Model

In general, the affinity defines a value expressing the quality of the execution of a task p on an resource type a, for example, in terms of overall performance or energy consumption. Again, we limit the expression of an affinity to resource types instead of single resources. Thus, we define an affinity of a task for a certain resource type a.

Runtime Affinity As the performance of a task p on a certain resource type a is commonly defined by its speedup over a reference resource of resource type $a_r \in A$, we will simply transfer the speedup to define the affinity:

$$Aff_{runtime}(p, a, a_r) := S(p, a, a_r) \tag{3.8}$$

The speedup here is defined on a resource type a rather than on a single resource r_i as defined in Equation 3.1.

Energy Affinity In order to evaluate an energy-related affinity, we adapt the idea of the speedup metric. The energy ratio considers the energy consumption of all resources available in the execution environment while executing a task p on a resource $r_i \in R$ and the energy drain of all resources while executing this task on a reference resource type $a_r \in A$, as energy is not only consumed on the currently executing resource and, thus, influences the system energy consumption. According to this, the energy which is spent at runtime of task p on an resource type a ($E_{total}(p, a)$) is the sum of the energy consumed by every single resource $r \in R$ ($E_{r,total}(p, a)$):

$$E_{total}(p, a) = \sum_{r \in R} E_{r,total}(p, a) \tag{3.9}$$

This implies that task p is responsible for the total energy consumption $E_{total}(p, a)$. In fact, this assumption is just partly correct. Each resource has an almost constant idle power dissipation, which is independent from a concrete task execution. We subtract the energy consumption of all available and at the same time idle resources from the measured runtime-related energy consumption. Thereby, we determine a more task related energy consumption to define the energy affinity:

$$
\begin{aligned}
E_{task}(p,a) &= \sum_{r \in R} E_{r,total}(p,a) - \sum_{r \in R} E_{r,idle}(p,a) \\
&= E_{total}(p,a) - \sum_{r \in R} E_{r,idle}(p,a) \\
&= E_{total}(p,a) - \sum_{r \in R} \int_{T(p,a)} \underbrace{P_{r,idle}(p,a,t)}_{\text{nearly constant}} \mathrm{d}t \\
&\approx E_{total}(p,a) - \sum_{r \in R} P_{r,idle} \cdot T(p,a) \\
E_{task}(p,a) &\approx E_{total}(p,a) - T(p,a) \cdot \underbrace{\sum_{r \in R} P_{r,idle}}_{=:E_{idle}(p,a)}
\end{aligned}
\tag{3.10}
$$

Finally, we can define the energy affinity by the following equation:

$$
Aff_{energy}(p,a,a_r) := \frac{E_{task}(p,a_r)}{E_{task}(p,a)}
\tag{3.11}
$$

By including the idea of subtracting the energy consumption of idle resources, we expect to improve on the information value of a task's energy criterium. However, we can not differentiate background load that is executed during energy measurements. We currently see no way to actually identify which tasks have added which fraction of the consumed energy in a reasonable complexity. Our approximating approach to this problem is to measure energy values to be used for affinity assignment only in case the according resource is idle otherwise. While this is easily achievable on non-CPU resources, background tasks on the CPU can only be minimized rather than excluded. This leads to a small but acceptable uncertainty factor to be minimized by an increased number of energy measurements.

Figure 3.5 illustrates the runtime and energy affinities of the same example task as shown in Figure 2.6. For the input data sizes of 2^8 to 2^{10}, the task has highest runtime and energy affinity to the CPU. However, the preferred computing resource differs between runtime and energy affinity for larger data sizes. On the one side, we can gain the best performance if we execute the task on the GPU, but on the other side, we can minimize the energy consumption if we assign the task to the FPGA. Thus, we may use these values as an indicator for choosing an execution resource, depending on our aspired objective.

While runtime- and energy-aware scheduling approaches for heterogeneous resources have been discussed in several related works (cf. Section 5.4), defining an affinity value, as a general metric to rate the suitability of a task toward an architecture adapted by the underlying scheduling policy, has not been considered yet.

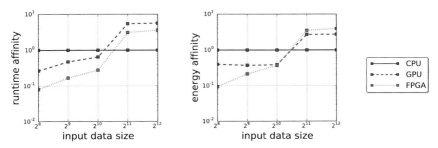

Figure 3.5: Affinities according to Figure 2.6. Affinities are computed with respect to the reference resource CPU ($a_r = R_{CPU}$)

3.4 Heterogeneous Thread Execution Model

Allocating a resource for a task for a certain time comes with resource type dependent overheads, in particular overheads introduced by the *copy_in* and *copy_out* phases of the task. This increases complexity compared to CPU-only task execution as performed in the CFS. This section analyzes the impacts of transferring the ideas of preemption and migration to the heterogeneous case to derive a task execution model for heterogeneous systems.

3.4.1 Completely Fair Scheduling

Without disqualifying the extension to large-scale distributed systems, we currently aim at scheduling heterogeneous resources in single-node systems. We, therefore, give a brief introduction to CPU scheduling in the CFS, i.e., the state-of-the-art in scheduling CPU-only single-node systems, as a basis for extending the concepts to accelerator-based systems. The current Linux CFS follows the goal of fair scheduling, i.e., providing all tasks with an equal amount of CPU time with respect to their priorities. This increases the interactivity and responsiveness of the system (see Figure 3.6). To this end, it manages a *virtual runtime (vruntime)* for each task p, which is a task-specific execution time that is normalized by the task's *weight*. Both the *weight* of a task, which is defined by its priority, and its *vruntime* are detailed in Chapter 5. The CPU queues of the CFS scheduler are sorted by the current virtual runtime of the tasks included in the queue, so that the task with the lowest *vruntime* is executed next. It is provided a timeslice that is defined as the task's weighted fraction of a *sched_period*, in which every of the n tasks should run once:

$$sched\_period = max\{sysctl\_sched\_latency,$$
$$n * sysctl\_sched\_min\_granularity\} \quad (3.12)$$

In this definition, *sysctl_sched_latency* (6ms, in the Linux 3.8 kernel) is the minimum targeted preemption latency for CPU-bound tasks and *sysctl_sched_min_granularity* defines the minimum preemption granularity for CPU-bound tasks (currently 0.75ms, Linux

3.8 kernel). In addition, the CFS performs load balancing between queues based on the *load* of the queues, i.e., the sum of its tasks' weights.

With the 2.6.24 kernel, Linux introduced group scheduling, which was an adaptation of the initial fairness idea toward the fact that tasks often spawn other tasks internally. With introducing task group scheduling, the CFS accounts for these task structures by maintaining a virtual runtime for task groups while each single task in a task group still maintains its own virtual runtime. That way tasks spawning several subtasks will be treated fair as a group and not on task level and, thus, large groups will not block other tasks or task groups from receiving a fair share of the computation time. This is, e.g., useful to provide a fair amount of CPU time to all users of a system and applicable to several scenarios, e.g., cloud nodes that share resources between different users based on their requirements, or SMP machines used by several users in research or in small businesses.

As mentioned before, tasks are represented by a *scheduling entity*. Tasks are held in sorted run queues, which in CFS are implemented by self-sorting red-black trees. Using such a tree, enqueuing and dequeueing tasks can be performed efficiently, i.e., both dequeueing a task before dispatching it to its associated CPU core and enqueueing a tasks, e.g., after execution was preempted, can be performed in $O(\log n)$, where n is the number of nodes (tasks) in the tree. Enforcing tasks groups, tasks are structured hierarchically within the red-black tree, where the root node is a scheduling entity not representing a process itself, but a group of tasks instead. With group scheduling, each scheduling entity has its own run queue, which is a subtree of the red-black tree representing all tasks and task groups within one of the CFS queues.

Scheduling, therefore, is a two-step algorithm: 1. choosing the task group to be run based on the share of CPU time defined via the *cgroup* interface used by system administrators, and 2. running the leftmost task from the task group's rbtree. Internally a task group schedules the tasks of the group according to the CPU time provided to the top-level scheduling entity. All tasks within the group are essentially removed from the primary run queue and enqueued to the run queue of the top-level scheduling entity of the group. The hierarchy may consist of several task groups, while each actual task is only part of a single group.

Generally task groups can and should also be supported by a heterogeneous scheduler. For instance, in a cloud scenario nodes might be equipped with heterogeneous resources that might have to be shared among different users. Moreover, these users might be sorted to specific groups, e.g., to "supreme users" and "normal users" groups, where supreme users may gain a higher share of computation time. Nevertheless, we focussed on general concepts of heterogeneous task execution and left group scheduling in our heterogeneous scheduler to be implemented in future work.

3.4.2 Preemptive Multitasking Versus Run-to-completion

As mentioned before, current heterogeneous systems use accelerators such as GPUs and FPGAs with a run-to-completion execution paradigm, i.e., a task started on an accelerator stays there until termination. However, this paradigm poses a severe limitation to the flexibility of task management, which may lead to suboptimal overall performance and energy consumption for a set of tasks. There exist no automated tools today that exploit the potential of heterogeneous computing outlined above through migrating tasks based on their suitability for certain resource types, the current set of tasks in the system, and resource availability.

However, several methods have been discussed that enable preemption of tasks running on GPUs or FPGAs that rely on roll-back mechanisms, full memory checkpoints, or virtualization. These are further discussed in Section 3.5. Generally checkpointing tasks on accelerator resources may be useful in several ways, with a common selection being:

- *Fault-tolerance*: Checkpointing can be used to build fault-tolerant systems by periodically storing checkpoints to non-volatile memory. In the case of a failure, aborted tasks can be restarted from the latest checkpoint on the same resource or even, in case of a hardware fault or a busy resource, on a different resource type.

- *Real-time*: Most real-time scheduling methods require preemption, which is in conflict with the current run-to-completion execution model for accelerators. Our approach enables preemption on heterogeneous resources and, thus, allows to adapt existing real-time techniques.

- *Fair time-sharing*: Preemption of tasks allows for time-sharing of heterogeneous resources, that is, each user or application is assigned a fair share of the execution time of the resource.

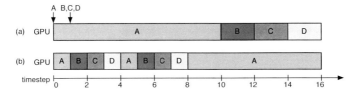

Figure 3.6: Example scenarios executing 4 tasks with and without time-sharing on a GPU. Gantt chart (a) executes the task sequentially. Chart (b) uses time-sharing enabled by preemption for fair task execution. It reduces both average turnaround times and average response times.

The focus of this thesis is on task execution in heterogeneous environments. One aim is to evaluate the fair time-sharing approach followed by the Linux CFS for heterogeneous systems. Figure 3.6 shows how preemption on heterogeneous resources improves both average turnaround times and average response times of tasks through the use of fair time-sharing.

In this example scenario, we examine a single GPU and 4 tasks to be executed. Task A requires a computation time of 10 time units (TU), tasks B, C, and D each execute 2 TU on the GPU and arrive 1 TU after task A. In a non-preemptive scenario (a), the tasks are executed sequentially. If all tasks are enabled for preemption, the tasks may be executed in an interleaved way for providing fair execution times to tasks, as shown in scenario (b). In addition, it increases the task response times and interactivity and it reduces the average turnaround time of tasks, as long running tasks do not block short running tasks. The average response time, that is the average time that the tasks needs from their submission to starting their computation on any supported resource, is reduced from 9 in (a) to 1.5 in (b). The average turnaround time is the average time the tasks need to complete their computation from their submission time. It is reduced from 13 in (a) to 9.25 in (b).

3.4.3 Heterogeneous Task Migration

The exertion of preempting non-CPU tasks is the basis for a subsequent task migration. Transparent task migration is a standard procedure executed in the Linux kernel for scheduling tasks on CPUs. A context switch for moving a task from one CPU core to another is cheap in comparison to a heterogeneous context switch. This is due to fact that CPUs use shared memory, so that a context switch includes, in worst case, writing cached data to main memory and moving the thread context to a different core.

Migrating a task between heterogeneous resources is far more complex. When a task is migrated from one resource to another with a separated memory space, the task's context that represents its full execution state must be copied to the target resource as shown in Figure 3.7. Once the context is copied, the control flow of the according task continues execution on the target resource. The context is required to be interpretable from both the source resource and the target resource.

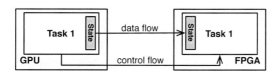

Figure 3.7: A task migration between heterogeneous hardware resources is composed of two steps: 1) transferring the task's state from the source to the target resource and 2) hand over the control flow to the new resource.

The example shown in Figure 3.8 demonstrates the benefits in terms of performance if scheduling of hardware accelerators with enabled task preemption and migration is performed by the OS. In this example scenario, we consider a system providing one CPU and one GPU. 3 tasks can execute only on the GPU (A,B,C), their execution time is 2 time units (2 TU). Task D can execute on the CPU (duration 50 TU) or on the GPU with a 5× speedup (total execution time on GPU: 10 TU). It is assumed that task D can create and

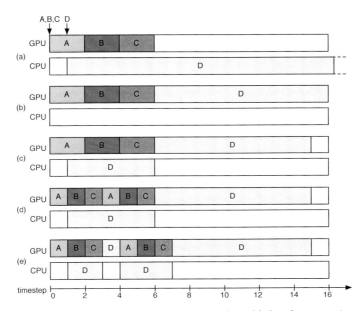

Figure 3.8: Scheduling in heterogeneous systems with enabled task preemption and migration reduces the total runtimes of a set of tasks.

read checkpoints of its state, which enables the migration of D from the CPU to the GPU and vice versa. Tasks A, B, and C are released at time 0, task D is released at time 1. This motivating example neglects management and migration overheads that are involved to accentuate the potential benefits.

The Gantt charts depict five scenarios. Figure 3.8(a) shows the case where scheduling is part of the applications and no time-sharing is supported. Since only one GPU resource is available and the tasks A, B, and C can execute only on the GPU, their execution is sequential. When task D is released at time 1, it finds that the GPU is not available. Assuming that the scheduler integrated in task D is work conserving, i. e., assigning tasks to idle resources immediately, then it will start execution on the CPU although execution on the GPU is much more efficient. The turnaround time for all tasks is 51 TU. Figure 3.8(b) shows a scenario, in which the scheduler used is non-work conserving, that is, it may decide to delay the execution of task D until the GPU resource becomes available. In this case, the turnaround time for all tasks is reduced to 16 TU, but the response time for task D has been significantly increased due to the execution of A, B, and C. The CPU is not used in this case. The case in Figure 3.8(c) illustrates a schedule that uses work conserving scheduling with preemption and migration of tasks enabled. Here, task D also utilizes the CPU resource while the GPU is busy with other tasks, but is migrated to the GPU, as soon as it becomes available. By the parallel use of available resources, the total runtime of the regarded set of tasks is reduced by 1 TU compared to case (b). The case in Figure 3.8(d) illustrates the cooperative time-sharing approach we are additionally aiming at with this work. If several tasks are ready for execution on the GPU, each task is executed for a timeslice of 1 TU. This approach not only utilizes all available computing resources, but also minimizes the response time of all tasks. The case in Figure 3.8(e) illustrates an approach slightly different to (d), which uses a different interpretation of fairness. Here, fairness means that every task gets a fair share of computation time on its best resource, i.e., the GPU. Thus, it requires to be non-work conserving.

In addition, one could enforce priorities when performing scheduling decisions. Assuming task D to be of higher priority would run D directly after A in cases (b) and (e). In cases (c) and (d) in contrast, a prioritization of objectives would be required, either in favor of task priority, or in favor of performing work-conserving scheduling.

This thesis aims at dynamic runtime systems in the scope of operating systems. Thus, planning systems that consider all remaining tasks for computing an efficient schedule ahead of execution are not matching the general execution scenario. The system state including the number and type of running tasks changes constantly. Moreover, estimated runtimes of tasks may be inaccurate requiring to permanently recompute an according schedule. We, therefore, do not specifically target non-work conserving scenarios, removing scenarios (b) and (e) from consideration. The remainder of thesis therefore focuses on scenarios shown in Figure 3.8(c) and (d).

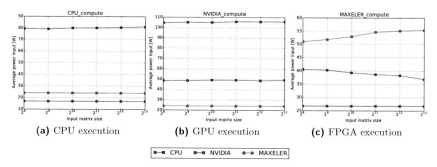

(a) CPU execution   **(b)** GPU execution   **(c)** FPGA execution

Figure 3.9: Average power input of the compute phase of an example Gauss blur application for different input matrix sizes (one dimension of quadratic matrix). The
figure shows measured average power consumption values for (a) CPU execution, (b) GPU execution, and (c) FPGA execution in a system with 2 CPUs,
1 GPU and 1 FPGA. Devices not used have an idle power consumption.

These scenarios can be reinterpreted for energy-related scheduling. Preemption and migration of a task theoretically make sense also, if a task is not running on most efficient

resource in terms of energy consumption. Nevertheless, energy related scheduling is much more complex, as costs are also generated through idle resources, as already discussed before. Energy consumption additionally depends on different other aspects, e. g., the total system load, or resource dependent dynamic frequency scaling on high or low load. The higher the total system load, the higher is the temperature of the available resources, which again leads to higher energy consumption values. We generally assume that preemption and migration are also beneficial for total energy consumption based on the fact that the energy consumption of a task is mostly highly correlated to its runtime.

Figure 3.9 shows the average power drain of the compute phase using a Gauss blur example with varying input sizes on different resource types. Summing up the energy consumption of all three resource types involved in a single measurement, we can see that the total power consumption differs by a factor $\phi < 2$ between the execution on different devices. For example, executing Gauss blur with input size 2^{11} on the CPU (Figure 3.9 (a)) results in average power inputs of about $121W$ (GPU: $17W$, FPGA: $24W$, CPU: $80W$), while executing the same task on the FPGA (c) results in a total power drain of roughly 119 (GPU: $27W$, FPGA: $54W$, CPU: $38W$). On the GPU (b), the power input sums up to about 180 (GPU: $107W$, FPGA: $24W$, CPU: $49W$), which is the highest value, but still only approximately 1.5 times higher than on the FPGA. Even if we exclude the power inputs of the resources currently not used by the task, i. e., just comparing the power inputs of the actually used resource type, the factor ϕ roughly remains the same.

This means that, unless a task has a runtime difference lower than ϕ, the runtime will also dominate the energy. Therefore, the energy consumption on a resource a will most likely be lower compared to a second resource b, if the speedup of a over b is higher than ϕ. Certainly, this is a simplified model, as it neglects power consumption of data transfers, but it is valid for all of our example applications, even if including the energy consumed by the data transfers. Additionally, Figure 3.1 shows that the best resource in terms of energy and runtime only differs for small input sizes and accordingly small total execution times. Thus, we may conclude a large correlation between runtime and energy consumption for our example applications.

Task Migration Overheads   Task preemption and migration between CPUs can be performed with very low overhead. Saving a process- or thread-context does not require to copy a full representation of the data, as it is accessible in main memory to all CPUs. Assuming data to be interpretable by involved resources, task migration between accelerators requires two additional steps: 1. a $copy\_out(R_A)$ phase for current resource R_A and 2. a $copy\_in(R_B)$ phase for target resource R_B. Neglecting management costs, the migration cost for a migration from resource R_A to resource R_B can then be defined as:

$$mig\_cost(R_A \rightarrow R_B) := copy\_out(R_A) + copy\_in(R_B) \tag{3.13}$$

The effect of this migration cost in terms of runtime is depicted in figure 3.10, showing example migrations of a task from a resource R_A to a faster resource R_B. Without migration the task may either choose R_A or R_B depending on the resource availability or wait on R_B. Including according $copy\_in$ and $copy\_out$ phases, $T(R_A)$ denotes the execution time on

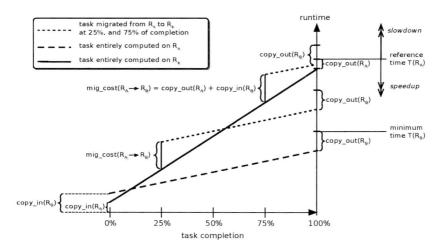

Figure 3.10: Example illustrating the performance benefits of migrating a task from a resource R_A to a faster resource R_B. The earlier the task is migrated, the higher is the achieved speedup. A late migration might raise the overheads over the benefits, resulting in an overall slowdown.

reference resource R_A and $T(R_B)$ defines the execution time on R_B, which is the minimum achievable execution time in our example. A migration may result in a speedup, as well as a slowdown depending on execution progress of the task. While a migration at 25% of the execution results in a speedup, migrating the task at 75% experiences a slowdown, as $mig\_cost(R_A \rightarrow R_B)$ exceeds the absolute benefit in execution time.

3.4.4 Cooperative Multitasking

As discussed before and further evaluated in Section 3.5, preemption and especially migration on accelerators is a possibility of software rather than hardware. While non-voluntary preemption on FPGAs is possible, GPUs currently do not directly support it yet, even if it has been planned for a long time already [159]. Preemption currently still relies on full-memory images or hardware virtualization.

This thesis aims at preemptive multitasking that additionally enables tasks to be migrated independently of the underlying architecture. We, thus, require preemption of tasks with low overheads, as otherwise overheads may exceed the performance or energy consumption improvements, especially when aiming at time-shared fair scheduling. Thus, above stated current approaches to preemption and migration are not utilizable.

Checkpointing can be performed when the application can safely interrupt its execution and store its state in main memory and, thus, be used for preempting a task. Nevertheless, even enabling preemption on accelerators does not solve the migration problem. The major difficulty is to find a way of mapping the current state of a computing resource to an equivalent state on a different computing resource. To allow preemption and subsequent migration of applications on accelerators, their delegate threads need to be in a state, which can be interpreted by other accelerators or by the CPUs.

As it is not possible to interrupt an accelerator at an arbitrary point of time and to assume that it is in such a state, we propose to use a cooperative multitasking approach asking tasks to yield resources at preemption points to resolve these limitations. After reaching a preemption point, an application voluntarily hands back the control to the OS, which then may perform scheduling decisions to write a checkpoint and migrate a thread at these points. We, therefore, require applications to provide periodically reached preemption points that are unambiguously defined by a set of data structures that are storable as checkpoint data and mappable to different resource types.

Checkpointing We define a checkpoint as a set of data structures that unambiguously defines the state of the application. The checkpoint data structure can either be defined by the application developer or inserted by a compiler. A checkpoint has to identify a preferably small set of data structures that is readable and translatable to corresponding data structures of other computing resources. While in a simple case a checkpoint only needs to store the current loop index, more complex data structures used in, e. g., image processing algorithms require to store the complete intermediate results that might be of large extent. In general, a checkpoint is implemented as a combination of a set of data structures that define the current content of all data structures that have been modified up to the current execution progress and the progress of the execution itself. In addition, a checkpoint is of larger value for a multitasking approach, if possible preemption points to write the checkpoint data are reached several times during the execution of the task.

Identifying possible preemption points and the checkpoint data, therefore, includes to identify the hotspots of an application. Hotspots of applications that are subject to acceleration are often found to be surrounded or even defined by a loop. Today, many profiling tools, like Intel VTune [89] or Valgrind [127], provide comprehensive analysis to identify hotspots in sequential or CPU-parallel programs. In addition, the LLVM Compiler Infrastructure [102] is often utilized for automatic hotspot detection [53, 141]. Moreover, automatic preemption point and checkpoint data extraction for task migration has been shown to be possible [67].

Preemption points may be introduced at arbitrary points of execution time, for instance, before and after calling a function. Of course, automatic extraction of preemption points gets more difficult if the according application code does not follow conventional code patterns like loops. Automatic definition of preemption points and extraction of corresponding checkpoint data is not part of this work. Chapter 4 shows details on how preemption points and checkpoint data structures are integrated into an application manually. We used an automatic checkpoint extraction mechanism shown in [67] for a subset of our test applications to show the possibility for an automation.

Task Granularity Task switches on CPUs are very cheap compared to a task switch on an accelerator. As introduced in Section 3.3 *copy_in* and *copy_out* phases have to be considered for a task execution on a non-CPU resource. Depending on the data transfer bandwidth to the resource and the size of the input and output data of the task, these data transfer phases can have significant influence on the tasks execution time. Tasks switching on heterogeneous resources, therefore, not only introduces additional data transfers, but also limits the achieved speedup, as overheads become more significant, the shorter the execution time is. With time-shared execution, task are given a certain timeslice they are allowed to compute on the allocated resource. We call this time period the *task granularity*, which defines the frequency a task should be requested to yield. In the CFS, CPU tasks are granted a timeslice of at least 0.75*ms*. Depending on the system load, a task may only compute a single timeslice, but remains with the full extent of data transfers, so that the relation of data transfers to execution time gets worse and speedups are limited. Figure 3.11 shows how checkpointing overhead may influence the total runtime of a set of tasks. We compare a GPU-only schedule without time-sharing in (a) with granularities of (b) 1 TU, and (c) 0.5 TU with each *copy_in* and *copy_out* phase requiring 1/2 of a TU for four tasks with different execution times. We can see that the total execution time of the set of tasks may be increased significantly, which may even completely consume the benefits for the average turnaround times.

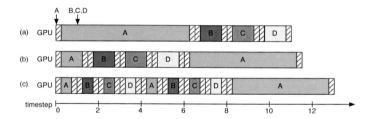

Figure 3.11: The influence of the task granularity on the overheads and total execution time. Striped areas denote *copy_in* and *copy_out* phases. While case (b) decreases the average turnaround times of (a) from 8.75 time unite (TU) to 6.25 TU with only a total runtime increase of 0.5 TU, (c) decreases the average turnaround time only by 0.25 to 8.5, while increasing the total runtime by 2 TU. The improvement on average response times is hardly touched by the overheads here.

Therefore, the minimum CPU timeslice of 0.75*ms* obviously does not match the architecture of coprocessors, as data transfer times are rather in the seconds than in nanoseconds or milliseconds. Useful values are determined in our evaluation, depicting results for granularities with an extend of 100s of milliseconds to several seconds. Knowing the expected execution times of the different task phases even allows a dynamic adaptation of the granularity.

With cooperative multitasking, the frequency a task returns control to the scheduler may depend on the granted granularity, but does not have to. A task may also return control at each possible checkpoint and request further computation time. If the granted timeslice has not yet been completely consumed, the task should be notified accordingly. Returning control at each preemption point enables a scheduler to react dynamically on a changing system state, e. g., if a task with higher priority is waiting for execution. Ignoring the granularity does lead to less reactive scheduling. We, therefore, assume tasks to be cooperative and, thus, return control to a scheduler on a regular basis, i. e., as often as a checkpoint may be written at a preemption point. Non-cooperative tasks reduce the quality of scheduling results regarding both fairness and performance. We either need to accept this "misbehaviour" or alternatively force the task to stop.

A task that runs on a certain resource type a is provided a timeslice that it may use for its computation. With global execution time steps t_k and t_l on resource type a, we define a timeslice as the execution granularity of task p on resource type a:

$$granted\_exec\_period(p, a) = [t_k, t_l], \text{ where } t_k < t_l \text{ and } t_k, t_l > 0 \qquad (3.14)$$

$$granularity(p, a) = t_l - t_k \qquad (3.15)$$

We expect a task to always start its computation with the start of a $granted\_exec\_period$, i. e., at time t_k, but we can not expect a task to finish exactly at time t_l.

Extending the Task State Model We have introduced the idea of delegate threads to represent hardware counterparts to a scheduler. These delegate threads are normal CPU threads that underly the execution through the CPU scheduler. The introduction of multitasking to heterogeneous resources extends the task's state model as shown in Figure 3.12.

The left hand side of Figure 3.12 shows the well known task states used within the Linux operating system. A task that is executed on an accelerator resource with being enabled for yielding a resource and task migration through the use of checkpoints requires an additional state machine. Once a delegate thread is submitted to a scheduler for execution on any of the available resources (`schedule()` function), it traverses a separate state diagram, as shown on the right hand side. These states must be represented in the delegate thread to be known to the operating system and the heterogeneous scheduler and are valid until the task completes (`exit()` function). A delegate thread thus has two separate states, one for being represented as a CPU task to the CPU scheduler and a second state that represents the state of execution through the heterogeneous scheduler. The following states are introduced:

- **TASK_HET_CLEANED**: In this state the complete context of the task is available to the host, i. e., no data has been modified by any computing resource that has not been subsequently transferred to the main memory. In this state, the task has either not started computation or has written a checkpoint before releasing a resource (`yield()` function).

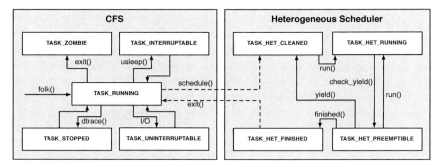

Figure 3.12: Extended state model for heterogeneous task execution with tasks yielding resources.

- **TASK_HET_RUNNING**: The task has been assigned a resource managed by the heterogeneous scheduler and may start or continue its computation.
- **TASK_HET_PREEMPTIBLE**: The task has reached a state where it may write back the checkpoint data and release the resource on request or due to having finished computation. We call this a preemption point. It now may either continue execution (`run()`), if the current execution timeslice is still valid or a new timeslice is assigned, or free the resource in case of yielding (`yield()`) by writing the checkpoint data. In case it has finished computation, its state changes to TASK_HET_FINISHED (`finished()`).
- **TASK_HET_FINISHED**: This state is reached in case the task is completed the computation. It then transfers all result data to the host and releases the resource.

Note that if the execution on a resource has reached a state where it needs to be triggered for further computation (e.g., at a preemption point), the delegate thread needs to get CPU time first to actually trigger a state transition for the resource computation. Thus, through blocking a delegate thread, the hardware counterpart is blocked as well, as soon as it requires any action of the delegate thread. On the other hand, once a computation has been started on an accelerator, the delegate thread may be blocked, but without effecting the thread executing on the accelerator hardware immediately.

3.4.5 Scheduler Evaluation Scenario

Based on the general discussions above we here conclude our general scheduling and evaluation scenario for heterogeneous task scheduling. The following conclusions can be summarized:

- **Set of Tasks:** We use multitasking rather than multithreading, while each of the used tasks may be multithreaded internally. In contrast to many related work approaches, we, thus, do not aim on utilizing resources through single tasks that possibly have a set of subtasks, but through a set of independent tasks. We assume task dependencies to be resolved before tasks are submitted to a scheduler for execution on heterogeneous devices. Task sets used for our evaluation are composed of up to 4 different applications, each of them being used with up to 5 different input data dimensions (see Figure 3.1). Each of the used tasks has an initialization phase that is executed on the CPU only, before reaching the kernel provided for multiple target resources.

- **Resource Utilization:** CPU tasks are executed by the operating system CPU scheduler and, therefore, are executed concurrently. They are possibly multithreaded and, thus, executed on several CPU cores in parallel. Tasks that are executed on accelerators are currently assumed to utilize the resource completely. Hence, we do not allow several tasks to be executed concurrently or even in parallel on an accelerator resource. Moreover, tasks may only request execution on a single resource, so we concider a 1:1 relation of tasks and accelerator resources. We do not assume a planning system, but rather make dynamic decisions on the current system state. Therefore, we generally consider work-conserving approaches instead of waiting for a resource to become available.

- **Task Submission Time:** We submit all tasks of a task set at the beginning of a task set execution. However, as our schedulers are not planning tools, each task that arrives is handled individually. Therefore, our examined schedulers are also able handle dynamic situations, i.e., they can efficiently deal with any task arriving at any point in time. Tasks have no initial order. They are ordered by scheduling policies that include the task priorities inherited from the operating system.

- **Performed Evaluations:** We mainly evaluate the results of our schedulers through three measurements: 1. The makespan is the complete execution time of the set of tasks, i.e., from the beginning of the first task execution to the completion of the last task. 2. The total energy consumption is the system wide energy consumption during the makespan of the set of tasks, i.e., including the energy consumption of all used and unused resources. 3. The average turnaround time of the set of tasks is a measure for the tradeoff between time-sharing for fairness reasons and the overall performance of the set of tasks, i.e., the makespan.

3.5 Related Work

This chapter discusses the general approaches of this thesis to perform heterogeneous task management and discusses implications given through the inability of hardware accelerators to provide task preemption and subsequent migration mechanisms inherently. We limit the discussion of related work on approaches that enable preemption or migration for non-CPU resources and leave the discussion of related work on task execution, i.e., programming and scheduling frameworks to the following chapters.

Preemption, which is a basic requirement for multitasking and migration, has already been studied for GPUs and FPGAs. The main challenges are the lack of a common instruction set across resources, finding a suitable representation of application state and defining a programming model for heterogeneous resources.

Early work has shown that migrating the state of an application between heterogeneous CPU cores is possible. In [151], a technique is presented that allows objects and threads to be migrated between machines using heterogeneous nodes at native code level. The authors introduce so called "bus stops" as machine-independent formats to represent program points. We extend this idea to current hardware resource types like FPGAs and GPUs.

Task preemption and multitasking on coprocessors have been investigated since their use has been growing in the 2000s. Early work on FPGAs already explored the possibilities of sharing hardware resources for parallel execution of multiple tasks on a single FPGA [169, 140], by performing full context saves and restores for multitasking [147] and rolling back a task in favor of another task [140]. Checkpointing has been further examined in several works over the following years, proposing state machines for a well-defined and storable state [98], or adding on-chip monitoring for retrieving the context information [143] build on the Berkeley Lab Checkpoint/Restart (BLCR) library [79].

With GPUs gaining more and more attention as computing resources for general purpose computing in the mid-2000s, sharing GPU resources among several tasks follows three general approaches. First, tasks share GPUs by spacial multitasking, i. e., by subdividing GPU resources and assigning several tasks simultaneously [7]. This even enables "fair" sharing of GPU resources among tasks [9]. A different approach that has been followed is performing checkpoint/restart on GPU tasks. The authors of [157] also use the BLCR to write the state of an application process to a file without code modifications. Transparent migration of OpenCL processes requires an interception of OpenCL calls to use an API proxy, which shows substantial overheads, even without writing checkpoints. A corresponding approach has been provided for CUDA applications in a previous work [158]. Similarly, [101] also uses a 2-step (copy-to-host, write checkpoint) mechanism on GPUs that uses a Virtual Cluster Checkpoint (VCCP) approach instead of the BLCR. In [145], checkpointing within the GPU kernel is enabled but limited to CUDA applications. Tanasic et al. [160] enable preemptive multiprogramming on GPUs through two preemption mechanisms. While the first is a context switch storing the complete memory image to the main memory including registers and shared memory regions, the second, called "SM draining", stops issuing additional work to the GPU and waits for the completion of the current execution of a Streaming Multiprocessor. A third general approach is GPU virtualization. vCUDA [146] virtualizes a CUDA GPU to allow multiple guest operating systems in virtual machines to access the CUDA functionality, one at a time. Significant overheads are introduced by redirecting API calls to the host OS via RPC and keeping track of manipulated data for later migration. In [178] a virtual OpenCL framework is presented that supports migration of virtual GPUs through decoupling physical GPUs as migratable virtual resources. The state of a virtual GPU is migrated between virtual proxies, each connecting a physical GPU.

While above mentioned approaches are useful when running one or several tasks on single or multiple homogeneous accelerators, migration between heterogeneous resource types is not supported. Thus, utilization and efficient use of highly heterogeneous systems is still limited. We identified two recent approaches that allow task migration in multi-ISA heterogeneous systems and, thus, approach toward our objective of unrestricted task migration among arbitrary computing resources. DeVuyst et al. [56] use compiler modifications to identify large portions of the program that may be kept in an architecture-independent representation to minimize state transformation at migration time. To avoid performance loss through unoptimized code, state equivalence is only guaranteed at points representing function call sites. Nonetheless, immediate migration is allowed through binary translation at other points of execution and demonstrated to be possible at acceptable cost. Their approach is limited to multi-ISA CPU architectures and neither is binary translation applicable to FPGA bitstreams nor can the state of a GPU execution be read at any point in time. Venkat et al. [168] recently presented a similar approach to [56] with optimizations on migration overheads. Either of these approaches aims at multi-ISA CPU systems that provide shared memory regions. Although these approaches generally may be extended to accelerator resources, this comes with increased effort, especially if distributed memory space is used. Moreover, the question of providing a state representation that is valid for all target resources including non-CPU resources is not inherently solved by these approaches. Summarizing the discussed approaches, we can conclude that task preemption and migration is a topic that has been examined by many researchers already. However, all of the approaches have been limited to a single type of resources until now. Therefore, our aim to target at arbitrary resources has not been followed by other approaches yet.

3.6 Chapter Conclusion

This chapter introduced basic concepts we follow throughout this thesis to achieve unrestricted, performance- and energy-efficient task execution on heterogeneous resources. We provided a heterogeneous system model, a task model and a heterogeneous task execution model.

In our heterogeneous system model, we discussed the general approach of scheduling tasks to heterogeneous resources. We aim at single-node heterogeneous systems that extend a single- or multicore CPU with additional accelerators like GPUs or FPGAs. We transferred the idea of preemptive multitasking and unrestricted task migration to the heterogeneous case. Our aim is at providing a scheduler that manages available hardware resources through queues, assigns and dispatches tasks for execution on given resources using scheduling policies, and enables load balancing through task preemption and migration at runtime. We discussed the benefits of a kernel-space integration of such a scheduler, but also pointed out major benefits for a user-space scheduler, especially on the ease-of-use during development and evaluation. We, therefore, provide a twofold solution in the remainder of the thesis, both evaluating a user-space and a kernel-space integration with the operating system.

In addition, we defined a task model for tasks to be executed on heterogeneous resources. We defined a task to be represented by a thread, which does not limit the granularity of executed entities. We identified runtime and energy consumption to be the major assessment criteria for the execution of a task on a certain resource and introduced an affinity model that allows us to rate the suitability of a task-resource combination through two affinity values: a runtime affinity representing the possible speedup of using a certain resource type over a reference resource type to evaluate task performance and an energy affinity that evaluates a task concerning energy consumption.

Finally, we provided a task execution model relying on the possibility of tasks yielding resources and migration of tasks between arbitrary computing resources. Preemptive multitasking and migration between cores of the same instruction set architecture is standard in CPU systems. A novelty of our work is that we approach preemption also for accelerator tasks by applying cooperative multitasking for yielding resources at preemption points, albeit at a coarser granularity than CPU-based mechanisms. We additionally discussed migration across different instruction set architectures or even customized hardware as used on FPGAs through the use of resource independent checkpoints. We showed the theoretical benefits of such a task scheduling mechanism, including increasing performance- and energy efficiency for scheduling sets of tasks, but also the possibility to enable time-sharing for fair task execution. The latter additionally bears the potential to reduce the average turnaround time and the average response time of tasks in a set of tasks. We concluded the chapter with a discussion of related work showing the absence of task migration solutions that allow heterogeneous task migration on arbitrary architectures, which, therefore, is a major contribution of this thesis.

CHAPTER 4

Programming Pattern for Heterogeneous Task Scheduling

Preemption of tasks mapped to accelerators and migration of tasks between arbitrary heterogeneous resources have hardly been investigated, as discussed in the previous Chapter (cf. Section 3.5). As mentioned before, major challenges are the lack of a common instruction set across resources, finding a suitable representation of a task's state and providing a programming model for heterogeneous resources.

Current programming models that allow execution of tasks on multiple architectures typically require source code annotations and a specialized compiler or major changes to the code, e. g., when using a complete framework like StarPU[18]. A major aim of our work, therefore, is to keep the changes to be undertaken by the application developer as small as possible, regarding changes in the code and the compilation toolchain.

To tackle these challenges we define a programming pattern that allows for checkpoint-based multitasking of applications.

4.1 Lifecycle of a Task

Despite the increasing spread of on-chip integrated accelerator solutions, most accelerators still require executed tasks to explicitly copy required input data to the dedicated resource memory regions and transfer results back to the host memory after task execution. Typically the developer implements these task functionalities in separate phases (*copy_in*, *compute*, and *copy_out*) of an application's task, as already introduced in Section 3.3.1. We assume the developer to implement these phases by providing three functions. The function `init_resource()` transfers the data required for computing the task to the selected resource. Accelerator resources also need to load the code to be executed to the resource. On GPUs this usually is done automatically by the device driver. Bitstreams for different applications are dynamically reconfigured on the FPGA on their first call to init_resource(), if not already loaded. For immediate execution and using the FPGA for multitasking, all bitstreams need to have been synthesized beforehand. The function compute_resource() then performs a computation on the transferred data, before the task releases the current resource after copying the result data back to host memory in the free_resource() function.

If preemption is not possible, these phases are simply executed in sequential order, as depicted in Figure 4.1. While releasing the resource normally is performed by the resource driver, initially choosing the architecture to be used may be part of the application or performed by an external decision making entity, e. g., a scheduler.

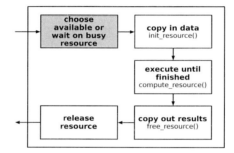

Figure 4.1: Lifecycle of tasks without preemption. A task executes three phases that 1) init the task for execution on a computing resource, 2) performs the computations, and 3) stores the results and releases the resource. Choosing the resource is performed by the application itself or a scheduler.

We propose a programming pattern that allows for checkpoint-based multitasking by organizing the computations of tasks into blocks. At the end of each block, a task reaches a preemption point at which its progress and working data set can be extracted in a form that can be interpreted by all targeted computing resource types. At the preemption point, a task can either write back the checkpoint data and possibly be migrated, or continue processing the next block.

Figure 4.2 shows the lifecycle of a task that follows this pattern. After an initial assignment to a resource type, a task proceeds with computing its blocks in the compute_resource() function until it is finished, it yields the resource in favor of another task, or it is migrated to a different resource. The function compute_resource() thus only continues computation from the last state of the transferred data to the next preemption point, where it either continues with the next block or yields the current resource by copying the checkpoint data back to host memory in the free_resource() function. Task management decisions are highlighted as grey boxes in Figure 4.2 and can be taken at the initial assignment and every time a preemption point is reached. The actual policies driving yield requests and migration decisions are outside the programming pattern. Therefore, our approach works with arbitrary decision mechanisms.

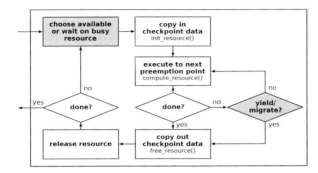

Figure 4.2: Lifecycle of tasks enabled for yielding at specific preemption points and heterogeneous migration. A task's main functionality is captured in a loop that allows for checkpoint-based preemption after each iteration. The checkpoint data needs to be resource-independent to enable heterogeneous migration. Grey boxes denote task management decisions.

4.2 Programming Pattern for Applications

We introduce a programming pattern that enables the depicted multitasking approach to work with any type of component taking decisions on how to assign a resource to a task. Subsequently we show details of our programming pattern through the stepwise porting of an example application.

4.2.1 Generic Application Example

Figures 4.3 to 4.5 depict the necessary steps to make an application ready for heterogeneous migration. We start from an application comprising a kernel on an accelerator and code on the host that copies input data to the accelerator, calls the kernel and finally reads back the results. For most applications, the host code will include a sequence of such copy-in, kernel execution and copy-out phases due to limitations of accelerator memory and dependencies between different kernels. We assume applications to generally provide this kind of structure.

Figure 4.3 (1) shows such an application example. Although we are very specific in parts of the example pseudocode that is loosely based on C language syntax, we consider this example to be generic enough to match most applications targeting accelerators. We additionally assume that an accelerator kernel performs computations within a loop or nested loops for step (1), which is common for many applications, especially for scientific code.

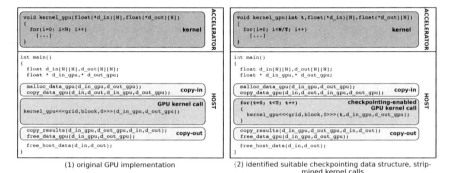

(1) original GPU implementation

(2) identified suitable checkpointing data structure, strip-mined kernel calls

Figure 4.3: Programming pattern step 1: Applying our programming pattern to a generic GPU example application. If required, a hardware kernel is strip-mined to enable checkpointing.

Step (2) of Figure 4.3 prepares the original code (1) for checkpointing. While in-kernel preemption has been shown to be possible [145], our approach requires preemption points outside the kernel that is executed on an accelerator resource, especially as task migration demands to be performed on a well-known and resource-independent state. Thus, if necessary, we apply strip-mining to the kernel. For that purpose, the original loop with N iterations is split into a number of iterations moved to the host (T) and the remaining iterations on the accelerator (N/T). With this approach, T actually restricts the minimum granularity for reaching preemption points. We call the distance between two preemption points the preemption distance. The larger T is defined, the more often a preemption point is reached, which increases responsiveness, but decreases performance by introducing overheads for checking each time, whether actually writing a checkpoint is requested. However, not every preemption point requires to write a checkpoint. In addition, kernel call overheads are introduced, as a large kernel is separated into small kernels. Although these overheads are quite small (significantly lower than 100 microseconds on average for OpenCL kernels [163]), too many additional kernel launches introduce an overhead, which needs to be considered when performing strip-mining.

Figure 4.4 shows step (3), which unifies the copy-in, kernel execution and copy-out code for all supported resources (here only GPU is supported) using newly defined functions init_resource(), compute_resource(), and free_resource(). While these encapsulations of course come with the overheads of function calls, they enable the application

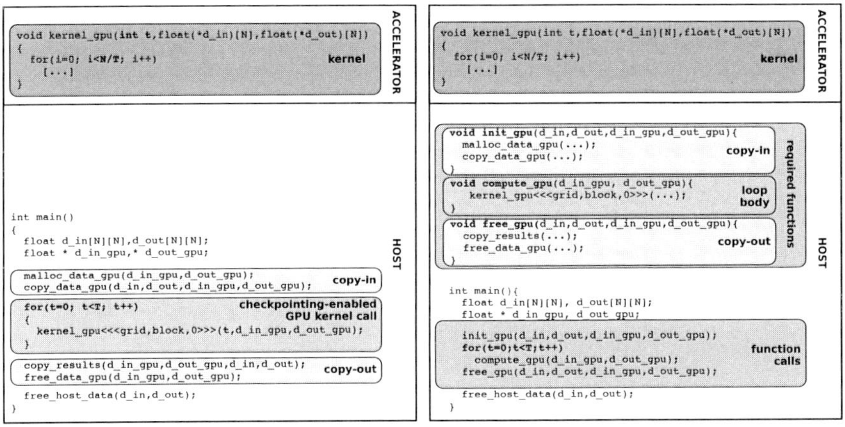

(2) identified suitable checkpointing data structure, strip-mined kernel calls

(3) transformed to programming pattern by encapsulating init, compute, and free phases into dedicated functions

Figure 4.4: Programming pattern step 2: Encapsulate kernel executions phases to functions. Copy-in, kernel execution and copy-out phases are each represented by a function, so that they may be triggered by a decision mechanism located outside the programming pattern

phases to be triggered by an entity located outside the programming pattern.

Figure 4.5 depicts step (4), which defines the checkpoint data structure that saves the task state. After the checkpoint is defined by an encapsulating data structure, we finally need to modify the `init_resource()`, `compute_resource()`, and `free_resource()` functions to work on data included in the checkpoint data structure only. This makes the functions independent from their callers and assures that the checkpoint data includes the complete task state. Finally, we need to transform the host main loop to reach preemption points frequently, where it can check for the need to actually write a checkpoint.

4.2.2 Checkpoint Example

The basic concept of our preemption and migration mechanism bases on is the introduction of preemption points and a resource independent checkpoint data structure. Listing 4.1 shows the checkpoint data structure introduced in Figure 4.5 (4) in a fully implemented version for a heat distribution example, as actually used in our evaluation. As proposed before, the checkpoint data includes the progress information (here: t, as the counter of the outer loop) and the data pointers that define the intermediate results. In particular, we need data pointers for each supported architecture, including the CPU, to enable copy-in and copy-out functions to transfer data between the CPU and the according accelerator resource. The example shows a task enabled for GPU execution and Maxeler FPGA execution, thus, providing data pointer for the CPU and the GPU, as well as a pointer to

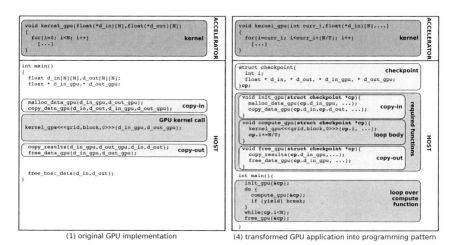

(1) original GPU implementation

(4) transformed GPU application into programming pattern

Figure 4.5: Programming pattern step 3: Add a checkpoint data structure that is valid on all supported architectures and base the task execution on it by handing it to the functions implementing the init, compute, and free execution phases.

the data structure embracing the FPGA checkpoint data (`max_engine`). The `max_engine` field points to a data structure that includes all information on the Maxeler FPGA: a file with the FPGA configuration bitstream and other data used to access the accelerator at runtime, e.g., the id of the FPGA the bitstream has been loaded to. We additionally include a maximum value (`t_max`) to define the termination condition of the outer loop.

Listing 4.1: Example checkpoint data for a heat distribution application.

```
struct heat_checkpoint {
    //outer loop variable, task progress (timesteps)
    int t;

    //maximum loop index for loop termination condition
    int t_max = TMAX;

    //CPU host data pointers
    double *datapoints_g, *datapoints_h;

    //GPU device data pointers
    double *datapoints_g_d, *datapoints_h_d;

    //Pointer to Maxeler FPGA configuration struct
    void *max_engine;
} heat_checkpoint_t;
```

4.2.3 Discussion of Practicability

Our approach is efficient and highly flexible. Efficiency means that the overhead for actually writing a checkpoint is very low since the checkpoint data includes minimal progress information and data structures defined to be used by the kernel anyway. As can be seen in the final main loop on the host (see Figure 4.5 (4)), there is no data transfer between host and accelerator if yielding a resource is not requested by a scheduler at a preemption point. Flexibility is established by the fact that the checkpoint data is completely resource-independent.

Another noteworthy advantage is that we can utilize computing resources with fundamentally different programming models. Our programming pattern provides a smart way to include CPUs and GPUs, as well as non-ISA-based architectures such as Maxeler FPGAs. For instance, applications written in Maxeler's Java-based MaxJ language have to be considered as data flow graphs (DFG) with significant restrictions in control flow. Our initial CPU implementations are written in C. Usually, they are based on control flow statements such as count-controlled loops. Furthermore, there is no C to MaxJ compiler available, so that a programmer has to port the tasks manually to the FPGA. That implies a high programming effort, since the porting includes a fundamental redesign to match Maxeler's programming paradigm. The additional programming pattern-related effort for programmers to adjust their implementations is small compared to actually port the application to the FPGA.

Many computationally intensive applications, in particular in scientific computing, spend the major part of their work in loops and, thus, match our approach well. Moreover, many scientific applications provide loop nests in their most time-consuming parts, which reduces checkpoint data determination to the pattern shown in Section 4.2. However, our programming pattern does not limit tasks to a loop-based design. Any kind of task providing the required encapsulation to the three introduced functions may be used for checkpointing and migration. For instance, a simple switch-case structure may be used to subdivide a kernel into parts. Using a progress counter as a switch condition, each case includes the code to be executed at a certain progress of execution.

Currently, transforming an application to our programming pattern is a manual process. Due to the fact that many scientific applications follow the described structure, automatic hot-spot analysis and checkpoint data determination may be applied. In fact, we used automatic checkpoint definition as presented in [67], allowing us to determine minimal checkpoint data for some of our benchmark applications and even partly restructure the given code toward our programming pattern automatically. This has been limited to GPU and CPU implementations.

While a lot of applications already are strip-mined in the sense that kernels executed on accelerators are called several times during execution, it may sometimes be necessary to enable preemption points within an accelerator kernel through the use of strip-mining. As discussed before, this comes with certain kernel launch overheads that have to be accepted as a tradeoff to the approach. Furthermore, the choice of a common checkpoint data structure and strip-mining may limit the compiler's ability to optimize the implementation on certain resources. For example, FPGA implementations generally profit from unrolling loops into deep pipelines for latency hiding. This is at odds with frequent preemption points and short blocks and may jeopardize performance in such cases. Chapter 6 analyses the overheads through the use of our programming pattern. To this end, we ported a correlation matrix example application to our programming pattern that had to be strip-mined to match the needs of our programming pattern.

4.3 Application to a Heterogeneous Scheduler Scenario

Our programming pattern permits an application-internal or -external decision mechanism to suspend a task for later continuation. We aim at using a scheduler for taking decisions on task execution. To allow application-provided tasks to be mapped to different architectures, we allow the application programmer to provide multiple implementations for a task to our scheduler. As specified by our programming pattern, each task provides references to these implementations and a matching and resource-independent checkpoint data structure. In addition, a task may optionally provide an affinity value expressing the suitability of the task for each supported architecture, as described below.

4.3.1 Affinity Information on Tasks

In our affinity model introduced in Section 3.3.2, we define affinities of tasks toward certain architectures based on the task performance or a task's energy consumption. As an extension to the general programming pattern presented before, we enable a task to provide such affinity information itself for each supported resource type. This has several benefits: First, it allows the application developer to enable or disable certain target architectures on purpose or put a larger emphasis on a certain architecture by increasing the affinity. Second, the scheduler does not have oracle knowledge about a task that has never been executed before. An initial affinity value improves on the scheduler's first decision where to execute the task. Lastly, these values may be used for limiting the supported architectures to a single one, which is especially useful to build up a history of runtimes and energy consumptions for a certain task as a basis for affinity computations in a profiling phase. The user-space version of our scheduler obtains according values through measurements, relieving the application programmer of the responsibility to provide meaningful values.

The kernel-space scheduler requires some additional values, which have been removed to minimize the scheduler interface in the later user-space version. Listing 4.2 shows a function that defines values of data struct members to provide according data to the kernel-space scheduler. This example is extracted from an example application used with our scheduler. It defines additional values to the affinity, so we call the struct *meta-information* on a task. The `taskMetaInfo` method implemented by a task, sets the mandatory values for the meta-information, which ensures that only compatible computing resources are assigned to the task. The meta-information can be individually set for an application, e. g., it is possible to set `parallel_efficiency_gain`, a rating of how much a task benefits from data-parallel execution, dynamically depending on the input data. The example `type_affinity` defines the GPU to be twice as suitable for the worker as the CPU in terms of performance. Setting an affinity to zero tells the scheduler that no implementation for the specific computing resource exists. The application developer does not have to know the exact performance difference between implementations. The affinity only gives an approximate hint of how much the implementation for one computing resource outperforms the other.

Listing 4.2: Example implementation for `taskMetaInfo` function to provide affinity information on a task.

```
void taskMetaInfo(struct meta_info *mi){
    mi->memory_to_copy=0;              // in MB
    mi->memory_consumption=1;          // in MB
    mi->parallel_efficiency_gain=5;    // 0 to 5
    mi->type_affinity[CU_TYPE_CUDA]=2;
    mi->type_affinity[CU_TYPE_CPU]=1;
}
```

4.3.2 Delegate Threads

Tasks that execute on heterogeneous resources may have no access to main memory and use a completely different instruction set or execution model than the same task running on a CPU. In order to schedule and manage these tasks without requiring a major operating system rewrite, we need to expose the tasks to a scheduler as known schedulable entities. Therefore, we represent each task executing on a hardware accelerator as a thread to a scheduler. As already introduced in Section 3.3.1, we denote each thread representing a task on a hardware accelerators as a *delegate thread*. The general idea of delegate threads has already been discussed likewise by other works [8, 26, 130]. A task executing on the CPU does not have a corresponding hardware counterpart. However, the delegate thread is used as a schedulable entity, too, and executed the same way as on non-CPU resources. Apart from serving as a schedulable entity, the delegate thread also performs all operating system interaction and management operations on behalf of the task being executed on the accelerator, such as transferring data to and from the computing resource and controlling its configuration and execution. The delegate threads must be spawned explicitly by the application to be submitted to a scheduler that performs a scheduling decision.

As implemented through the introduced programming pattern, a scheduler needs to be provided with all necessary information to perform a reasonable decision on where to execute a task through the delegate thread, i. e., the supported resource types, a checkpoint data structure and, if intended, additional meta-information as shown in Figure 4.6. As introduced before, supported resource types are represented through the `init_resource()`, `compute_resource()`, and `free_resource()` functions. Executing an according function is triggered by the scheduler by providing a time slot on a certain resource. In order not to limit the used ISAs and APIs and avoid additional dependencies on these in a scheduler, the scheduler shall not have the responsibility to copy input data or results and execute the tasks. It shall only provide a computing resource to a task for a certain amount of time.

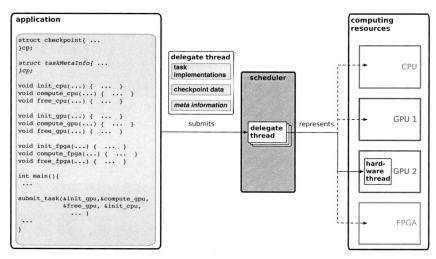

Figure 4.6: Task are handled as delegate threads that provide information on available implementations and a checkpoint data pointer. A heterogeneous scheduler assigns the task to a computing resource based on this information and the system state. The delegate executes its corresponding hardware counterpart.

4.4 Related Work

Delegate threads have also, e. g., been used by Bergmann et al. [26], who present an approach using "ghost processes" to make reconfigurable System-on-chip (rSoC) hardware processes appear like software processes in a Linux environment. Software ghost processes are associated to hardware processes, used to control these, and allow communication with the associated hardware threads. The authors use processes combined with inter process communication (IPC) instead of threads to encapsulate hardware processes. This makes the handling of hardware tasks less lightweight and more complicated for OS integration. Kosciuszkiewic et al. [99] use an existing Linux OS kernel and regard hardware tasks targeting FPGAs as a dynamic drop-in replacement for software tasks, such that tasks are universal (indistinguishable) for soft- and hardware and appear as regular threads to the OS kernel. The interaction between software threads and hardware tasks was limited to FIFO communication for streaming applications. We do not set restrictions toward the implementation used in our init, compute, and free functions. In ReconOS, Lübbers et al. [109] extended the Linux and eCos operating systems by a uniform interface for software threads on the CPU and hardware threads on FPGA accelerators. They extended the multithreaded programming model to heterogeneous computing resources. Every hardware thread is associated with exactly one software thread, which allows communication between FPGA threads and OS data structures. ReconOS' delegate threads forward any OS call sent to the delegate also to the associated hardware-thread. That is, they delegate OS calls from the OS to hardware and vice versa. Our delegate threads do not forward any standard OS calls, but only our custom calls to change the task state in the heterogeneous scheduler. All of these example implementations aim at FPGA hardware. The scope of used architectures is much broader with our delegate threads, by aiming at arbitrary architectures.

Besides OpenCL, OpenACC, and OpenMP, several works have proposed programming models for task execution on heterogeneous resources. We examine approaches that provide multiple implementations of a task for different target resources next. We may differentiate between approaches that use compilers to enable tasks for heterogeneous execution and approaches that extend known programming models to the heterogeneous case. Cross-compilers allow code transformation from a high-level language to specific accelerator resources, e. g., [23] for C to CUDA compilation, or even from a language extension like OpenMP [104]. While these approaches generally enable execution of tasks on an additional resource, the result is not portable. Cross-compilers that target OpenCL further push toward a heterogeneous use. In [72], OpenMP code is transformed to OpenCL and, thus, enables heterogeneity. Automatic compilers usually limit the quality of the results, as general transformation rules are applied that only rarely provide best possible solutions. Therefore, a focus is set to optimize intermediate results during compilation. E. g., in [11], sequential C code is used as input to automatically produce CUDA, OpenCL and OpenMP code, including a polyhedral loop optimizer in the compilation toolchain. OpenACC allows automatic code generation for CUDA and OpenCL and is typically only used for GPU execution. In addition, there are several language extensions that aim at supporting heterogeneous resources. An OpenACC extension is proposed in [96], describing an single program multiple data (SPMD) programming model of OpenACC. The authors require a few extensions to an OpenACC code that extend the OpenACC memory model by logically distributed task address spaces and the use of a matching compiler that produces CUDA and OpenCL kernels. A backend compiler builds an executable using OpenMP and MPI in addition for later execution on multiple resources on a heterogeneous cluster with a provided runtime. StarSS [137] is a well-known pragma-based model and compiler for task-oriented programming on the Cell Broadband Engine Architecture. Two works have been provided that allow for execution on heterogeneous resources incorporating the StarSS approach. First, [21] provides an extension to StarSS to support multiple GPUs in addition to CPUs for an annotated sequential code. Task dependencies are denoted by directed acyclic graphs (DAGs) and resolved by a runtime. In a second work [20], StarSS ideas are used to extend OpenMP. StarSS extracts are added to OpenMP to aim at GPUs and the Cell BE Architecture. The approach thus can be seen as an alternative to OpenACC, but additionally provides a runtime. The focus of all approaches mentioned above is on single application execution on distributed systems or single-node heterogeneous systems. Stuart et al. [153] discuss a roadmap for an extension of MPI for the use with accelerators without providing an according implementation. In contrast to our programming pattern, all of these approaches require dedicated compilers or source-to-source translators to be used in addition. Moreover, these approaches help to provide task implementations for heterogeneous resources, but do not inherently allow to utilize these in an efficient way. Several frameworks aim at heterogeneous task execution and combine a dedicated programming model with an execution environment. The "Merge Framework" as introduced in [106] proposes an early general purpose programming model for heterogeneous multicore systems. It hides the hardware architecture details and offers a library-based methodology that can automatically distribute computation across these cores to achieve increased performance and energy efficiency. For its decisions, it needs additional information from the programmer and will map an application to a user-extensible set of primitives in the form of function-intrinsics. Luk et al. [111] provide a programming model that has similarities to ours. Applications provide multiple implementations for a kernel. As it aims at adaptive mapping of a task toward the available CPU and GPU architectures by a runtime, applications require using a specific API to define dedicated data structures used by the runtime, which requires additional effort during development. StarPU [17] allows to define "codelets", which comprise CPU and GPU implementations of a certain task. As within our approach, function pointers may be used to submit implementations. With StarPU, a focus is to enable single applications to be partitioned by data and to be run on multiple resources. A follow-up work [18] allows additional scheduling hints to be provided for the StarPU runtime, declaring a task priority and a performance model. Auerbach et al. [15] provide a new Java-compatible programming language called "Lime" and an according compiler and runtime system called "Liquid metal" for targeting heterogeneous computing platforms. While their work in contrast to most other works also targets FPGAs besides GPUs, a complete new programming language is required to be used. With the spread of OpenCL, we consider their approach non-competitive.

To conclude the above cited approaches, we consider our approach to be broader in scope. It is not limited to any specific programming language or type of accelerator. We allow C/C++ and Fortran applications and accelerator-specific languages that are based on C/C++ or provide an according interface for execution from a C/C++ wrapper. In addition, applications keep their general structure and use the same compilers. Despite delegate threads having been used as a concept before, our approach is lightweight but still extensive. It is applicable to many types of applications and heterogeneous systems, while keeping the application changes manageable. Moreover, our programming pattern aims at execution of tasks in a multitasking approach allowing tasks to preempt their execution through cooperatively releasing a resource. We additionally enable migration, which is not in the focus of other works. Instead shown approaches follow a run-to-completion paradigm and partly require extensive code modification.

4.5 Chapter Conclusion

This chapter introduced a novel approach for suspending task execution of tasks mapped to accelerators, yielding a resource, and migrating tasks between arbitrary resources. Our approach requires the developer to refactor an application to adhere to an intuitive programming pattern exhibiting basically distinct copy-in, execute, and copy-out phases. It, thus, requires a task to execute three phases that 1) init the task for execution on a computing resource, 2) perform the computations, and 3) store the results and releases the resource. Although an increasing spread of on-chip integrated accelerator solutions can be observed, most accelerators still require tasks to explicitly copy required input data to the dedicated resource memory and transfer results back to the host memory after task execution. This matches our approach. Preemption and migration are then realized by efficient and flexible checkpointing, which in the most simple case rests on preemption points introduced by a strip-mined outer loop of the kernel. Both dedicated source code regions for data transfers and kernels, as well as strip-mined kernel loops are typically found in applications for which accelerators are employed.

Based on this task structure, we introduced a programming pattern, which enables the depicted multitasking approach to work with any type of component that decides on the assignment of resources to tasks. Transforming an application to our programming pattern requires three intuitive steps. First, if required, a hardware kernel is strip-mined to introduce preemption points outside the kernel. Second, we encapsulate init, compute, and free kernel executions phases to functions. Lastly, a checkpoint data structure is added that is valid on all supported architectures and base the task execution on it by providing it the functions implementing the execution phases for each supported resource type. Otherwise, we rely on a standard operating system and on vendor-provided drivers and APIs, which makes our approach easily adoptable. A fourth step would be the cooperation and integration with a scheduler that executes tasks based on the provided pattern. An according interface is introduced in Chapter 6.

A scheduler requires executed tasks to be encapsulated in a schedulable entity. We, therefore, represent each task executed on a hardware accelerator as a thread to a scheduler that we call delegate thread. As such, it performs operating system interaction and management operations on behalf of the task to be executed on the accelerator. This includes data transfers to and from the computing resource and controlling its configuration and execution. We assume that the application developer provides delegate threads to be executed on heterogeneous resources. The structure of the delegate thread as well as providing relocatable system states is generic enough to be automatically generated by a compiler in the future. Moreover, to allow a mapping of tasks to different architectures, we allow the application programmer to provide distinct implementations for a task on a certain resource type to our scheduler. For execution, each task provides references to these implementations and a matching and resource-independent checkpoint data structure.

This novel approach provides preemption at defined preemption points through cooperative multitasking and heterogeneous migration of tasks, while continuing to use the accelerator vendor's drivers and APIs and, thus, does not require a complete rewrite of used applications. While scheduling for heterogeneous systems seems to be a natural application for checkpointing and migration in heterogeneous computing systems, our approach can have a much broader scope: Service-oriented cloud computing architectures can be improved through checkpointing and migration to better utilize cloud nodes based on current workloads and service level agreements. Applications are fully controlled by the service providers and may thus be subject to extensive analysis of checkpointing overheads. In a different scenario, restricted resources may be shared among applying users. Using a time-shared or prioritized accessing pattern to, e.g., a hardware-synthesis server may be beneficial, especially if the need of access-time varies a lot. Long-running tasks may delay short-running tasks enormously, which may be prohibited by interleaved execution.

Therefore, enabling preemption and migration for heterogeneous systems can be beneficial in different ways. Our programming pattern provides an intuitive way to empower applications to improve the efficiency of their own execution, but also of the complete system they are running on. In particular, it does not limit the used applications, the targeted accelerators and their usable APIs, which also distinguishes the approach from related work.

CHAPTER 5

Algorithms for a Heterogeneous Scheduler

The previous chapter introduced a programming pattern that allows for task preemption and migration between heterogeneous resources at application defined preemption points. It requires specific scheduling algorithms to make use of this pattern. This chapter first introduces metrics that are used to evaluate a scheduler and corresponding objectives for our scheduler. To improve on these objectives, we define scheduling parameters and derive scheduling policies that utilize preemption and migration subsequently.

5.1 Metrics For Evaluating Schedulers

Scheduling of heterogeneous resources can target at multiple objectives that are partly contradictory and, thus, may not be optimized at the same time. With restricting the general scenario to single-node heterogeneous systems, we define the following evaluation metrics to be relevant for the development of our scheduling approaches:

- **Performance:** As introduced in Section 3.3.2, we define a task's runtime affinity via speedup. In terms of scheduling a set of tasks on multiple resources, performance mostly is defined by the makespan of a schedule. We also define the minimization of makespan as a major target for our scheduling policies. In that case, we define speedup with the ratio of different schedule's makespan times for a certain set of tasks.

- **Energy consumption:** In Section 3.3.2, we define a single task's energy affinity toward a resource by the energy consumed by the task itself on that resource, i.e., without energy consumptions of idling resources. In a set of tasks, this is not meaningful, as idle resources also consume energy and, thus, are relevant for the total energy consumption. The target for a task schedule in terms of energy consumption may therefore be defined as minimizing the system-wide energy consumption of a task schedule instead.

- **Fairness:** Currently, no standard definition for fairness exists in the area of hetercgeneous computing. Generally, the idea of providing a fair share of computation time for all tasks running at a time seems meaningful in heterogeneous environments, too, and, therefore, defines a separate objective. Nevertheless, some questions arise quickly: Are tasks treated fair, if they are provided the same share of computation time, or rather if they make the same progress within a certain time span, e. g., compared to the potential progress on the best suited resource type? Moreover, assuming all tasks enqueued to a certain resource receive the same share of computation on that resource. How can imbalances in the number of tasks enqueued to different resources be considered? Both questions also require to consider other objectives. It is, e. g., contradicting the targets of increasing the performance or decreasing the energy consumption of a set of tasks, if a task that is not enqueued to its best suited resource type still gets the same share of computation time, although better suited tasks may be available for the same resource. Thus, fairness is more complex in the heterogeneous case. We combine possible interpretations of fair scheduling to a list of fairness objectives subsequently that we consider a valid mapping of the approach used by the Linux Completely Fair Scheduler (CFS) to the heterogeneous case.

These metrics are not generally independent from each other. While energy consumption inherently depends on the runtime, e. g., fairness, as introduced in Section 3.4, is supposedly contradictory to performance by introducing task switching overheads.

Utilization can additionally be an objective for scheduling, e. g., in datacenters, where a high utilization most likely goes along with a high throughput and less unused computing resources that otherwise still consume energy. As we motivated in Section 3.4.3, we only consider work conserving scheduling approaches. Thus, we generally aim at keeping the utilization high, but we do not evaluate it as a metric for the quality of scheduling. In addition, interactivity is defined an objective in several schedulers. While time-sharing will automatically increase the interactivity in a fairness approach, we will not evaluate it as a separate metric as it aims at a specialized application scenario only. Finally, we desist to use the energy-delay product (EDP), which is the product of runtime and energy consumption, as an additional metric. With evaluating the makespan and the total energy consumption of a task set, the EDP can easily be derived from the corresponding results.

5.2 Scheduling Parameters

We here define general parameters that characterize tasks and the system state. We first adopt basic definitions of the CFS and transfer these to the heterogeneous case. Then, we define additional parameters that are required to characterize the decision space of our heterogeneous scheduler.

5.2.1 CFS Characteristics

As already shortly introduced in Section 3.4.1 the CFS follows a fairness-based scheduling approach that relies on task priorities and virtual runtimes to define a scheduling granularity to be executed by a task. We reuse a selection of CFS parameters for our heterogeneous scheduling approach and adapt them to our needs.

Weight and Priority The *weight* of a task p is defined by its *priority* and is internally used by a scheduler to treat and represent a task with respect to its priority. To define a priority, Linux systems use *nice* levels that for non-real-time tasks are within the range of range $[-20; 19]$. A higher nice value represents a lower priority.

The CFS translates the given nice level to a weight, which is in a range of $[15; 88761]$ in decreasing order for increasing nice levels of range $[-20; 19]$. With given nice level $nice(p) \in \mathbb{N}$ of task p, the weight $wt(nice(p)) \in \mathbb{N}$ is defined recursively as:

$$wt(nice(p)) = \begin{cases} 15 & \text{, if } nice(p) = 19 \\ \lfloor wt(nice(p) + 1)) * 1.25 \rfloor & \text{, where } nice(p) \in [-20, 18] \end{cases} \quad (5.1)$$

We reuse the weight values in our heterogeneous environment as defined by the CFS to prioritize delegate threads. In the following, we use a simplified notation for $wt(nice(p))$:

$$weight(p) = wt(nice(p)) \quad (5.2)$$

Virtual Runtime The CFS defines a so called virtual runtime of a task that does not measure the actual execution time of a task, but a normalized time representing the used share of CPU-time for the available tasks. Above defined weights are used within the CFS to adjust the virtual runtime of a task toward its priority. The virtual runtime of a task increases slower, if the priority is higher. Therefore, the priority is not used directly within the scheduler, but as an attenuation factor which consumes the runtime of task with low priority quicker than the runtime of a task with higher priority. Using the reciprocal of the weight

$$iweight(p) = \frac{1}{weight(p)} \quad (5.3)$$

the CFS adapts the virtual runtime based on the real execution time $T(p)$ of a part of task p on a queue-wide clock as:

$$vruntime(p)+ = iweight(p) \cdot T(p) \quad (5.4)$$

This provides a priority-adjusted value that allows for runtime comparison of different tasks with respect to their priority and allows to provide fairness between the tasks: The virtual runtime of a task with higher priority increases slower and the task will be granted CPU time more frequently in a queue sorted by virtual runtimes.

Load Weight The CFS additionally defines a *load_weight* value for a certain run queue rq, which is the sum of the weights of the tasks on this rq and is used for load balancing:

$$load\_weight(rq) = \sum_{p \text{ queued in } rq} weight(p) \quad (5.5)$$

With this definition of *load_weight* and the definition of *sched_period* as introduced in Section 3.4.1, we can define a *time_slice* for a task p as provided by the CFS as

$$time\_slice(p, rq) = \frac{sched\_period * weight(p)}{load\_weight(rq)} \qquad (5.6)$$

with rq being the run queue p is enqueued to. Thus, tasks with higher weight will receive a larger part of the *sched_period*.

Based on that value, a scheduling policy balancing the load moves tasks from an overcrowded queue to a less full queue. Thus, if queues have equal values of *load_weight*, tasks are not only treated fair with respect to their priority on their current queue, but also treated fair in comparison to all tasks on the CPU. For simplicity, we will refer to *load_weight* as *load* only subsequently.

5.2.2 Heterogeneous Parameters

We inherit the definition of the virtual runtime of the CFS without adaptations, but to fully transfer the ideas of the CFS scheduling policies to the heterogeneous environment, we additionally define some basic values:

Heterogeneous Load Weight Given Equation 5.1, we can define the weight of p to be used in the heterogeneous case as being equivalent to its representation within the CFS. As all CPU tasks will eventually be handled by the CFS and each non-CPU task has a CPU representative executing its respective host code, every task handled in our heterogeneous scheduler will have a weight defined in the CFS.

Affinity Load Transferring the idea of a *load* definition to a heterogeneous environment we adapt the weight of a task to the resource it runs on. Similarly to including the priority, a task running very efficiently on a certain resource type should have a higher weight than on a resource type where its expected runtime is higher. We, therefore, define an affinity adapted load value *aload* for each combination of a task p with a resource type a using the affinity $Aff(p, a)$ as:

$$aload(p, a) = weight(p) \cdot Aff(p, a) \qquad (5.7)$$

The *aload*(p, a) therefore defines the affinity adapted load that task p adds to the queue of resource type a. This *aload* definition may be used with different types of affinity definitions, e. g., the energy affinity or the runtime affinity. The higher the affinity of the task toward the resource type, the higher is the load, as we want to reflect both affinity and priority when performing scheduling decisions.

We additionally define *aload*(p) as:

$$aload(p) = aload(p, a), \text{ a is the current resource type of p} \qquad (5.8)$$

It is important to notice that neither the sum of the *load* values nor the sum of the *aload* values of a queue are capable of predicting the runtime of the tasks currently enqueued to a queue. This reflects our general idea of performing scheduling decisions without knowing the runtimes of the tasks. Thus, these values may not be used for load balancing in terms of equalizing the estimated amount of work to be performed. Both values rather reflect the importance of a task's execution, with *aload* representing the importance of an execution on a certain resource type.

Despite that, the *aload* value could be used equally to the priority in fairness-based scheduling to balance loads. If tasks with high affinity add more load to a queue, less tasks add up to the same queue weight as many less suited tasks. Thus, the higher the affinity of the tasks to the resource is on average, the less competing tasks are available and the more CPU time will be provided to the enqueued tasks. Nevertheless, only equalizing the *aload* is not enough to achieve this. This approach only performs well, if the average affinity of tasks to their current resource is optimized over all resources and resource types. An equalized load can also be achieved in a queue state showing a low affinity of all tasks on all resources. In addition, the virtual runtime update shown in Equation 5.4 could use the reciprocal of the *aload* value instead of the reciprocal of the *weight*, to provide highly affine tasks with larger timeslices. However, tasks with a low affinity may experience long waiting times in that case, as these tasks are mostly competing with high-affine tasks. This might even lead to starvation of low affine tasks. Moreover, these low affinity tasks might be treated additionally unfair, if many tasks compete for their best suited resource type, forcing them to remain on the suboptimal resource. Thus, we do not use the *aload* in load balancing for fairness scheduling and rely on the queue *load* values instead.

Nonetheless, the *aload* may be used to sort tasks enqueued on a resource by their *aload*. The higher the *aload* value of a task p, the more important is its execution on the current resource, as it either has a high priority or a high affinity toward the current resource type, if not even both is given.

Potential Load   In addition to *aload*, we define the *pload* as the potential *aload* increase of a task, if it would be migrated to the best suited resource type in terms of its affinities. We use this value to determine a task for migration during load balancing:

$$pload(p) = max_a(aload(p,a)) - aload(p) \tag{5.9}$$

5.2.3 CPU Load

Besides scheduling parameters added by our scheduling framework and the tasks, operating system and hardware parameters need to be considered. This includes especially background load occurring on the CPU when cooperating with the CFS.

In case of a scheduler that is situated in user space, we do not have full control over the CPU, as we only cooperate with the CFS scheduler, which independently schedules CPU tasks. In that case, we only know about CPU tasks that are handled by our heterogeneous scheduler, but would additionally require to estimate the load of other CPU tasks. The CPU is not only used by tasks known to our scheduler, but also by the operating system, in particular the scheduler and accelerator drivers and other user-space CPU tasks. In addition, also the non-CPU tasks have a fraction of CPU-executed work that is required to run a task on an accelerator. Thus, controlling the CPU load becomes a critical issue. An overutilized CPU results in a potentially massive increase of response times, swapping of data or a decreasing cache hit rate. We especially observed a massive slowdown of non-CPU tasks on high CPU loads due to waiting and corresponding idle times, but also a major slowdown of CPU tasks themselves. Tasks executing on GPU or FPGA also require CPU time, both to initiate data transfers and partly also for intermediate computations. Thus, if these tasks are waiting on a CPU timeslice this might lead to idle times on the accelerator.

To avoid over- or underutilization of the CPU we provide two approaches that are used in combination. Both approaches make use of the *proc filesystem (procfs)*, which is an interface to access kernel memory provided by most Unix-like operating systems. *procfs* provides information on running processes and their statistics and other load information on the system. These statistics are updated at every scheduler tick within the CFS.

In a first approach, we access the */proc/stat* and */proc/loadavg* interfaces to read information about the CPU load in a regular fashion. This information may be used for load balancing and, thus, avoiding over- or underutilization of the CPU. The */proc/loadavg* interface provides rather long term information on the load of the CPU. The most regularly updated value of */proc/loadavg* provides the average CPU load value of the last elapsed minute. Thus, it is a useful information, but not very up-to-date. A scheduler can be expected to be much more reactive and base its decisions on more current values. Information from the */proc/stat* interface can, e. g., be used to compute the current utilization of each single CPU core, delivering an update with every scheduler tick.

A second approach tries to estimate the load of all CPU background tasks in an attempt to provide a *load* value for the CPU that is sufficiently correct to be used in a scheduling scenario that aims at load balancing between CPU and non-CPU resources for equal load values. To determine an exact value of the complete CPU load, every single CPU task weight would have to be read continuously from the *procfs*. This is complex and would produce high overhead due to a usually high number of background tasks on the CPU. In addition, the CFS makes use of task groups, which make it even harder to read the load values as they are structured hierarchically to a potentially large depth. To still enable load balancing on CPU load values, we estimate the load based on the assumption that we experience full load or close to full CPU load on most times during execution of tasks in an high performance computing environment.

We read the following values from the *procfs* using the *pid* of the tasks with t being the relative point in time when we update:

$weight(p)$: The weight of the CFS handled task p as provided in the

$se.load.weight$ field in the proc filesystem. $\qquad$ (5.10)

$sum\_exec\_runtime(p, t)$: Sum of CPU execution times provided to task

p by the CFS in nano-seconds (ns) until update time

t. Retrieved from the $se.sum\_exec\_runtime$ field. $\quad$ (5.11)

As we can also maintain these values for the heterogeneous tasks managed by the user-space scheduler, we can generally define

$$exec\_time(p, t) = sum\_exec\_runtime(p, t) - sum\_exec\_runtime(p, t - 1) \qquad (5.12)$$

to be the time task p was executing on one of the available resources in time period $[t-1, t]$. We call this time period $timespan(t)$:

$$timespan(t) = clock(t) - clock(t - 1) \qquad (5.13)$$

It determines the time units with respect to the used clock. The length of the $timespan(t)$ may be different depending on the context it is used in. Let $j(a)$ be the number of resources that are available of resource type a. Let additionally

$$arch\_comp\_time(t, a) = timespan(t) \cdot j(a) \qquad (5.14)$$

define the sum of available computation time on all resources (here: CPU cores) of the resource type in a $timespan(t)$. We assume a scheduler that perfectly distributes CPU time among tasks p_i enqueued on a. Then, if task p is executed on resource type a, the following relation of runtimes and weights is given, as a task's fraction of CPU times is depending on its weight:

$$\frac{weight(p)}{\sum_{p_i \ enqueued \ on \ a} weight(p_i)} = \frac{exec\_time(p, t)}{arch\_comp\_time(t, a)} \qquad (5.15)$$

Relating the weight of a single task p to the sum of the weights of all tasks running on the CPU expresses the "importance" of the task compared to others. With a perfect CPU scheduler, task p should then get the same fraction of the available computation time on the resource type, which is expressed by the right-hand side of the equation.

We thereby relate the tasks executed on the CPU by our heterogeneous scheduler to the CPU tasks executed by the CFS.

Equation 5.15 in that case is only true if CPU usage is 100%, i. e., each CPU core is running at least one task at every timestep in $[t - 1, t]$.

Assumption A *We assume all CPU cores of a multicore system to be utilized 100% or very close to it at any time a heterogeneous scheduler is used.*

We assume this to be the case at almost all times, as we are especially aiming at HPC environments. Figure 5.1 shows the utilization of the CPU during execution of an example schedule with our scheduler, both using a rather low utilization of 16 tasks and with a high utilization of 64 tasks. We can see that after a short phase of task initializations the utilization of the CPU is mostly close to 100%, which supports our assumption. Obviously, the utilization is reducing to the end, as we only regard the execution of a limited set of tasks.

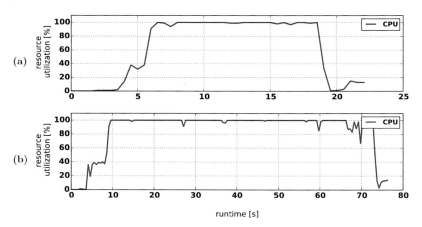

Figure 5.1: Example utilization on the CPU during execution of a set of 16 tasks (a) and 64 tasks (b).

We further define

$$hruntime(rq_{cpu_h}, t) = \sum_{p \in rq_{cpu_h}} exec\_time(p, t) \qquad (5.16)$$

as the execution time of all non-CFS CPU tasks managed by the heterogeneous scheduler within a $timespan(t)$. With rq_{cpu_h}, we denote the CPU run queue of the heterogeneous scheduler.

Based on our previous definition of a tasks *weight*, we furthermore define the *weight load* of our CPU run queue and the weight load of the CFS tasks in total as:

$$wload(rq_{cpu_h}) = \sum_{p \in rq_{cpu_h}} weight(p) \qquad (5.17)$$

$$wload(rq_{cfs}) = \sum_{p \in rq_{cfs}} weight(p) \qquad (5.18)$$

With rq denoting run queue for all CPU tasks only for the remainder of this section, we can derive the total CPU weight load of CPU tasks to be:

$$wload(rq) = wload(rq_{cpu_h}) + wload(rq_{cfs}) \qquad (5.19)$$

In the following we use Equation 5.15 under Assumption A. The sum of the CPU times assigned to tasks handled by our heterogeneous scheduler within a $timespan(t)$, i.e., $hruntime(rq_{cpu_h}, t)$, can be related to the total available CPU time $arch\_comp\_time(t, a)$, as depicted in Equation 5.20. As before, the resource type a here is restricted to the CPU.

We additionally can relate the load of the CPU tasks in our heterogeneous scheduler $wload(rq_{cpu_h})$ to the total weight of all CPU tasks $wload(rq)$. If assuming a perfect scheduler in terms of fairness, both fractions are equal, as assigned CPU computation times depend on the task weights. This allows us to estimate the load of CFS-handled tasks as:

$$\frac{wload(rq_{cpu_h})}{wload(rq)} = \frac{hruntime(rq_{cpu_h}, t)}{arch\_comp\_time(t, a)} \tag{5.20}$$

$$\Longleftrightarrow \quad wload(rq) = \frac{arch\_comp\_time(t, a)}{hruntime(rq_{cpu_h}, t)} \cdot wload(rq_{cpu_h}) \tag{5.21}$$

$$\Longleftrightarrow \quad wload(rq_{cfs}) = \frac{arch\_comp\_time(t, a)}{hruntime(rq_{cpu_h}, t)} \cdot wload(rq_{cpu_h}) - wload(rq_{cpu_h}) \tag{5.22}$$

$$\Longleftrightarrow \quad wload(rq_{cfs}) = (\frac{arch\_comp\_time(t, a)}{hruntime(rq_{cpu_h}, t)} - 1) \cdot wload(rq_{cpu_h}) \tag{5.23}$$

We thereby have derived a *load* estimation of the CPU tasks handled by the CFS only. This simplifies the scheduling model dramatically, as it prevents a scheduler implementation to gain all information from the rather complex structure of the CFS task groups.

To determine the average *wload* of the CFS tasks, i.e., the *wload* per CPU core created by CFS tasks, we have to divide the $wload(rq_{cfs})$ by the number of CPU cores. Using equations 5.14 and 5.22 we can then define the average *wload* of the CFS CPU run queues as follows:

$$avg\_wload(rq_{cfs}) = \frac{wload(rq_{cfs})}{j(a)}$$

$$\Longleftrightarrow avg\_wload(rq_{cfs}) = \frac{timespan(t) \cdot wload(rq_{cpu_h})}{hruntime(rq_{cpu_h}, t)} - \frac{wload(rq_{cpu_h})}{j(a)} \tag{5.24}$$

As denoted before, we assume the utilization of the CPU to be always 100% in the above definitions. We can assume this to be true in most cases, but we may also anticipate it is not always the case.

If less than num_cpu_cores tasks are active, i.e., less tasks than available CPU cores, then our assumption leads to a $wload(rq_{cfs})$ that is too high. In a load balancing approach that equalizes loads based on this value, this would result in a reduced probability that the load balancer will migrate tasks to the CPU, although it would make sense from the number of tasks in the queue. This will especially be true, if the load on all other resources is rather low. In that case, CPU affine tasks may run on other resource types although it was not needed. This effect is equalized as soon as the number of active tasks is as high as the number of CPU cores again ($num\_cpu\_tasks \geq num\_cpu\_cores$).

If in contrast our calculated $wload(rq_{cfs})$ would have been too low, the load balancer would migrate tasks to the CPU. Load balancing would equalize a corresponding imbalance as soon as the $wload(rq_{cfs})$ is correct again. We, therefore, redefine the $avg\_wload(rq_{cfs})$ to be:

$$avg\_wload(rq_{cfs}) = \begin{cases} \frac{timespan(t) \cdot wload(rq_{cpu_h})}{hruntime(rq_{cpu_h}, t)} - \frac{wload(rq_{cpu_h})}{j(a)}, \\ \quad \text{if } num\_cpu\_tasks \geq num\_cpu\_cores \\ 0, \text{ otherwise} \end{cases} \tag{5.25}$$

We make use of both approaches shown above to estimate the total CPU load in our user-space scheduler. While we use the first approach to determine the number of tasks that may actually be executed concurrently on the CPU without over- or underutilizing it, we use the second approach to estimate the load of the CPU and, thus, to determine the queue length of the CPU queue for equalizing load in a fairness-based approach. Our kernel-space scheduler has full access to CPU load information and, thus, is not required to use these values.

5.2.4 Fairness

Treating tasks fair in a system with homogeneous resources is simply achieved through providing each task the same amount of computation time on a resource with respect to defined priorities. This is also how fairness works in the CFS. In Section 5.1, we shortly discussed the fact that fairness in heterogeneous systems is not easy to define.

Each of the following ideas separately is possible requirements for heterogeneous fairness, but they can not be considered all at the same time: A task is treated fair, if

- it is provided the same amount of computation time within a *sched_period* according to all other tasks competing for its most affine resource type only,
- it gets the same amount of computation time within a *sched_period* as all other tasks on any resource type,
- it makes the same progress within a *sched_period* as all other tasks, independently from the used resource.

In contrast, a task is treated unfair, if

- it is executed on a suboptimal resource at all,
- it is provided less time on its best resource than competing tasks,
- it suffers starvation, e. g., by only running on suboptimal resources.

There are several tradeoffs when considering these conditions of fairness. Assuming several tasks are competing for the same resource and, thus, each task only is provided with a small fraction of a *sched_period*, while a suboptimal resource is available. Does a task that is moved to the idle resource benefit from it, because it does not have competitors, or is it penalized, because it is not provided a resource of best affinity? Likewise, it is hard to generally determine when the length of the run queue is dominating the affinity of the tasks toward the resource, especially if the queue holds differently well suited tasks.

No disadvantages are given through providing an arbitrary CPU core to a task in the CFS, as CPU cores are usually homogeneous. Thus, besides task switching overheads introduced through time-sharing, no performance decrease is expected. In a heterogeneous system, any decision has implications on the performance. Running a task on a suboptimal resource will only improve the system performance, if no other better suited tasks are competing for the same resource. If other tasks are available, a less suited task could either receive a larger part of a *sched_period* to be treated fair in terms of progress, the same amount of time to be treated fair in terms of computation time, or a smaller part of computation time when aiming at best possible system performance, which can lead to starvation of the task.

We draw the following conclusions from the discussion above: 1. Leaving a resource idle can not be considered useful in terms of performance and, thus, should also not be done in a fairness approach. 2. We consider it generally fair to run a task on its best resource and unfair to run on a suboptimal resource. Therefore, fairness approaches should also strive for best possible average affinity of all tasks. 3. We do not consider affinity to determine the timeslice of a task, to not decrease performance, but also to avoid starvation of tasks. Thus, all tasks on a resource get equally-sized timeslices. 4. We still consider priority. A high priority task should be run on its most affine resource and also receive a larger fraction of the *sched_period*. This is the case, if we consider the *aload* and *pload* values to find a task for task migration. 5. Striving for a completely fair approach with equally-sized timeslices for all tasks, i. e., with fully balanced queues is not meaningful in terms of performance. From these conclusions we derive different fairness-based scheduling policies in Section 5.3.

5.2.5 Hardware Parameters

Heterogeneous compute nodes may not only be heterogeneous in terms of resource types like GPUs and FPGAs, but also be heterogeneous by providing different characteristics in terms of memory sizes, number of compute cores, or data transfer bandwidths. We decided to not consider additional hardware-specific parameters in detail, as the level of complexity for scheduling decisions would increase significantly. It would especially require applications to define specific hardware requirements to be met by the scheduler. This again is against our general approaches of tasks being as independent as possible from scheduling and of lowering the requirements toward the task implementation. Instead we consider each available resource of the same resource type to be equal and, thus, exchangeable computing resources. Nevertheless, an extension of our approaches to increase the resource type diversity would be possible without major changes of neither the presented general approaches, nor of the implementations described in later chapters.

5.3 Scheduling Policies

A heterogeneous scheduler has to support the general tasks defined in Section 3.2.1. This Section defines scheduling policies for their fulfillment. All policies base their decisions on the current situation of the system, i. e., they do not plan ahead. Our schedulers thus are not planning systems, but rather dynamic runtime schedulers like they are commonly used in operating systems today.

We define the following policies:

PERF Policy: This policy optimizes the throughput of a task schedule, i. e., minimizing the makespan of a set of tasks. It enqueues tasks to the best fitting resource type that is denoted by their task affinities $Aff_{runtime}$ without balancing the load between resource types. However, to not waste computation time we run tasks that are waiting for the availability of a resource of their best resource type on suboptimal, but otherwise idle resources. If migration overheads are neglected, every progress in computation reduces the total makespan, as long as the running task does not block a better suited task at the same time. If a better suited task in terms of *aload* becomes available, the suboptimal task is requested to yield the resource and migrated back to its best suited resource. Besides that, a task is only preempted by a task with larger *aload*. On equal *aload* values we prefer the task with the lowest *pload* value for execution. This keeps tasks with higher *pload* values available for migration without migration overheads, as they are still waiting in the queue. The task execution granularity, i.e., the time a task may execute on a resource without being requested to yield only depends on the affinity and weight of the waiting tasks. Task execution granularities are further discussed in Section 5.3.1.

EGY Policy: This policy aims at minimizing the total energy consumption of the used set of tasks. The policy works exactly like the PERF policy, except that it uses energy related affinities Aff_{energy}. Therefore, it needs to be interpreted differently. While it may be mostly beneficial in terms of performance to run a task on an idle resource, this is not inherently true for energy-related scheduling. In contrast to that, it rather seems reasonable to run each task on the resource on which it consumes least energy. However, as motivated in Section 3.3.2 idle resources consume energy, too, so they produce costs that add to the total energy consumption of the set of tasks.

As discussed before, leaving a resource idle may extend the runtime of a schedule and, thus, may increase the total energy consumption. Therefore, a tradeoff between performance and energy consumption exists. As motivated by Figure 3.1 and already discussed in Section 3.4.3, we assume the correlation between runtime and energy on a certain resource to be significant in most applications. In addition, the energy consumption of idle resources is still relevant and can not be neglected. By enabling task migrations, suboptimal decisions for resources are not irreversible and may be revised in case a better suited resource becomes available. For these reasons and based on the fact that including idle power consumptions would require a planning system for well-founded decisions, we do not leave resources idle on purpose in this policy.

FAIR Policy: This policy aims at best possible fairness between tasks. It adopts the CFS idea to achieve fair execution of tasks for the heterogeneous case using a heuristic approach. As within the CFS, we define fairness based on the virtual runtime of a task. Tasks enqueued to the same resource are provided the same share of computation time with respect to their priority on the resource in a certain time interval, as likewise done in the CFS approach. However, as discussed before, this does not guarantee two tasks running on different resource types to be treated fair to each other and also does not consider the suitability of a task and, thus, its progress on a certain resource. Hence, we try to increase system wide fairness through balancing loads while increasing the average affinity of tasks to the resources they execute on. This is described in our load balancing approaches below.

PERF_FAIR Policy: This policy combines fairness with optimizing the throughput. It aims at computing tasks on their best architecture, but providing a fair amount of computation time for all tasks competing for the same resource. It, therefore, is based on the *PERF* policy, but requests tasks to yield on a regular timeslice basis instead.

PERF_FAIR CFS Policy: We use this policy in our kernel-space scheduling approach and integrate it with the scheduling policies of the CFS. It implements the same policy as the PERF_FAIR policy with two differences: We use *load* instead of *aload* and use a different approach to load balancing, as described in Section 5.3.3.

5.3.1 Task Granularity

In Section 3.4.3, we introduced the concept of task granularities. On resources other than the CPU we need to consider data transfer times to and from the resources for task execution. Thus, task execution granularities need to be significantly larger than on the CPU to guarantee a reasonable relation between data transfer overheads and the execution time on the resource.

We define a static and a dynamic part for the minimum granularity a task may execute on a non-CPU resource. We use a constant *min_granularity* that provides the minimum time a task may actually execute on a resource. After its consumption, it depends on the defined policy if another timeslice may be computed immediately. Assuming no knowledge about the data transfer times, the *min_granularity* is only consumed after completion of the data transfer to the resource, i.e., the *copy_in* time. The minimum timeslice granted to a task is then defined as:

$$time\_slice_{het}(p, a) = copy\_in(p, a) + min\_granularity \qquad (5.26)$$

In the fairness-based policies (*FAIR*, *PERF_FAIR*, and *PERF_FAIR CFS*), a task is allowed to compute at least the amount of time that is required to make up its current shortfall in virtual runtimes to the next waiting task. With $\Delta fairness$ being that time difference, we, therefore, increased the granularity depending on the amount of time spent in the *copy_in* to:

$$time\_slice_{het\_FAIR}(p, a) = copy\_in(p, a) + min\_granularity + \Delta fairness \qquad (5.27)$$

Hence, a task not only equalizes the unfairness delta $\Delta fairness$, but also is provided a certain "unfairness" compared to the next waiting task. The time needed for data transfers is also added to the virtual runtime of the tasks and thus is included in the fairness calculation. Additional knowledge about estimated *copy_out* times may improve the timeslice computation.

With the full consumption of the timeslice, the task will yield at the next preemption point, if required by the used policy. In most cases, reaching a preemption point will not match the end of a provided timeslice exactly as shown in Figure 5.2. This introduces an additional amount of unfairness that will be equalized through setting an according $\Delta fairness$ for other tasks later. The amount of unfairness depends on the distance between preemption points of the task. A larger preemption distance increases the probability for a large unfairness. On the other hand overheads for task switches are reduced in that case, so a tradeoff between overheads and fairness has to be considered. This is most relevant for the *FAIR*, *PERF_FAIR*, and *PERF_FAIR CFS* policies, in which additional overheads are introduced by more frequent yield requests. We, therefore, evaluate different *min_granularity*

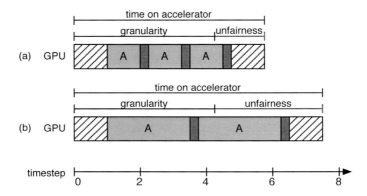

Figure 5.2: Scheduling granularity for a task A with a) a smaller preemption distance and b) larger preemption distance. Striped areas denote *copy_in* and *copy_out* phases. Grey columns denote preemption points at which tasks checks for the permission to continue execution. The larger the preemption distance, the larger is the expected unfairness, but the lower are scheduling overheads.

values with our scheduler implementations in Chapter 6. The consumption of the timeslice is detected before executing the *copy_out* phase, which additionally increases the unfairness toward the waiting tasks. Thus, without knowing the exact times a task requires for different execution phases and with yielding being restricted to cooperatively provided preemption points, fair scheduling is restricted. One can consider this approach completely fair for a subset of tasks, as it provides the same amount of computation time for all tasks competing for the same resource, even if the *sched_period*, in which every of the enqueued tasks should run once, is much longer than in CPU scheduling.

5.3.2 Task registration

During task registration, a scheduler checks if the submitted task p is valid for execution on at least one of the available resource types. If not, the task is rejected. We here do not care about the load of the resource type and resources yet and, therefore, simply select the resource type $a_{aff}(p)$ based on the affinity used by the scheduling policy to available resource types a and affinity $Aff(p, a)$ of task p in a:

$$a_{aff}(p) = \underset{a}{\mathrm{argmax}}(Aff(p, a)) \qquad (5.28)$$

If the enqueue decision leads to imbalances, we expect this imbalance to be equalized by load balancing as described below. Resource type-internally the queue of the resource with the smallest load is chosen. Task p is then inserted to that queue. We use this task registration policy for all described policies, based on the policy-specific affinity values.

5.3.3 Load Balancing Policies

The aims of load balancing according to our general scheduling objectives are threefold: First, we want to keep the average affinity of the enqueued tasks as high as possible for each resource type. Second, we want to avoid idle times on available resources, as they are most likely conflicting with our scheduling objectives, because they either waste computation times or consume energy on idle resources. Although the energy consumption on idle devices is significantly smaller than executing a suboptimal task in most cases, choosing the most affine suboptimal task to be executed will minimize the difference in energy consumption to executing the task on its best suited resource. Thus, it will in most cases be only slightly worse in energy consumption than being executed on its best suited resource, which, therefore, might even be less than the idle device's energy consumption on idle times. However, only a planning scheduler may determine this exactly, incorporating additional idle times that result from extending the makespan by leaving resources idle. And third, the *FAIR* scheduling approach additionally aims at balancing all available queues with respect to the *aload* to an extend defined by a threshold.

All load balancing approaches are 2-step algorithms. First, we migrate tasks between resource types, and secondly we equalize loads between all queues of the same resource type. Balancing loads between resources of the same resource type is simply based on the weight of the queues $wload(rq)$, which is used for all subsequently defined load balancing approaches. We, thereby, minimize the probability for idle resources. With the standard priority being represented through a weight of 1024, we define the maximum allowed difference between queues of the same resource type to be exactly 1024, striving for perfectly balanced loads. Allowed load differences between different resource types depend on the used load balancing policy.

We use the following load balancing policies:

Affinity Load Balancing (ALB)   Affinity-based load balancing provides a three-step algorithm that pursues the above described load balancing targets of low idle times and high average affinity of tasks toward their executing resources without aspiring equalized loads. To achieve this, we first push all waiting tasks to their optimal resource type. We, thereby, do not increase the number of idle resources, but do increase the migrated task's affinity toward their current resource type of the according tasks. In a second step, we check if we may migrate tasks to an idle resources, no matter if the resource is best suited for the task or not. We only do this, if we reduce the number of idle resources, i. e., the migration source resource type does not turn any resource idle by moving the task. If necessary, the second step makes migration offers to running tasks by setting a notification flag, which then may be migrated at their next preemption point.

CFS Load Balancing (CFLB)   This load balancing policy is used in the kernel-space implementation of our scheduler. A resource invokes the load balancer, if it runs idle. The load balancer traverses the run queues of all other resources and migrates the task with the maximum affinity to the idle resource. If several tasks are available with best affinity, the one of the queue with largest load in terms of *weight* is migrated. This also moves tasks to suboptimal resources, if no optimally suited non-running tasks are available. If the balancer is not able to find such a waiting task, it checks all tasks that are currently being executed. It makes a migration offer to any task where an improvement is assumed based on its affinities. After reaching a preemption point, tasks that have a pending migration offer may be migrated after reevaluation of the migration condition on a FCFS basis.

This approach additionally uses run queue limits that define the maximum length of a run queue for accelerators only. We, thereby, enable tasks running on accelerators to finish earlier, as they compete with less tasks. It implements a tradeoff between time-sharing and sequential execution. We provide two modes to refill that queue to the limit, if enough tasks are suited for an according migration. We either fill a queue once it runs idle, or refill it every time a task finishes computation.

Fair Load Balancing (FLB)   This approach aims at largely balanced queues, both among resources of the same and of different type. We follow this task with different strictness, depending on the system load. Through the use of a heuristic approach, this policy can only be considered fair, rather than completely fair. On high load, we are less strict in forcing tasks to a suboptimal resource than on low load. With high load, the risk of resources running idle is lower, so we reduce the fairness in favor of performance.

We perform a two-step algorithm to achieve balanced load between different resource types. In a first step, we try to avoid idle times. We first try to find tasks that are optimally suited to the idle resource, i. e., have maximum affinity to it. Then, we migrate these tasks in decreasing order of *pload* values, as a higher *pload* denotes a higher improvement for the system performance. If we do not find such a task, we force a suboptimal task to migrate to the idle device, if that does not force a different device to become idle. In a second step, we try to balance loads to a certain extend. We, again, first move tasks to their best resource type to fill up queues until they are balanced in terms of a load difference threshold, tasks with highest *pload* values first. If that does not fully equalize queues, we additionally search for tasks to be moved to a suboptimal resource. In this step, we consider queues of a resource type to be full, if there are twice as many tasks enqueued to the resource type as resources of that resource type are available. This avoids devices to run idle, before moving a task to the idle device and enforces time-sharing on all devices, as long as enough tasks are available. On the other hand this will reduce performance slightly in favor of time-sharing.

We reduce overheads to a minimum by only allowing running tasks to be migrated, if they are migrated to a otherwise idle resource and if no other task is available that can be migrated instead.

In both the CFLB and FLB approaches, fairness needs to be preserved, if a task is migrated. Thus, the difference in virtual runtimes of the task to be migrated and the task currently scheduled first in the source queue. i. e., the current "unfairness", needs to be computed in case of a migration. When being enqueued to the target queue, the migrated task receives the sum of the virtual runtime of the first task in the new queue and the computed difference. This ensures a task neither having an advantage, nor a disadvantage from migration in terms of fairness.

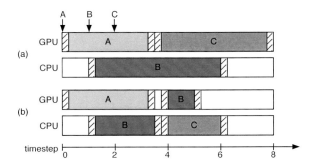

Figure 5.3: Affinity inversion problem using resource type affinities: (a) Both B and C compute on less affine computing resources. (b) Affinity inversion solved by our load balancer. Striped areas denote *copy_in* and *copy_out* phases.

Using affinities in our work-conserving scheduling environment results in a problem known from the use of priorities as *priority inversion*. Given the following scenario (Figure 5.3 (a)): task A is running on the GPU, the CPU is idle. Task B, with a higher affinity to the GPU arrives, but is scheduled to the idle CPU. After task A is finished, a task C arrives with higher affinity to the CPU that is blocked by task B. Hence, C is scheduled to the GPU and both B and C run on their less affine computing resource. We call this problem *affinity inversion*. This actually may happen in all defined scheduling policies, but especially is critical in the FAIR scheduling approach that focuses on balanced loads and allows tasks to be enqueued and executed on suboptimal resources. We perform two steps to solve this problem. First, we move a small random number of tasks to their optimal resource type, even in balanced situations, and expect originating imbalances to be equalized by later load balancing steps. In all of our load balancing approaches we, secondly, check this condition for all combinations of available resource types and their currently running tasks. If recognized, these tasks will be migrated at the next reached preemption point as depicted in Figure 5.3 (b).

Section 3.8 defined migration costs for task migration between resources. A migration of a waiting task to a different queue does not implicate migration costs, because no additional data transfers are required. In case of migrating a running task and estimated task runtimes are available, all policies additionally include migration overheads in their decision. We, therefore, compare the estimated remaining runtime or energy consumption respectively on the current resource with the estimated remaining runtime or energy consumption on the target architecture including migration overheads. Again, we perform decisions based on the current state. Thus, it may happen that a task has to be migrated back almost immediately after a migration if the system state changes, which introduces overheads that are unavoidable without planning ahead.

Scheduling Policy	User/ Kernel Space	Affinity Type	Queue Task Order	Yield frequency/ Task Granularity	Load Balancing Approach
PERF	US	$Aff_{runtime}$	1. highest aload 2. lowest pload	rarely/ varying length	ALB
EGY	US	Aff_{energy}	1. highest aload 2. lowest pload	rarely/ varying length	ALB
FAIR	US	$Aff_{runtime}$	lowest virtual runtime	often/ min_granularity	FLB
PERF_FAIR	US	$Aff_{runtime}$	lowest virtual runtime	often/ min_granularity	ALB
PERF_FAIR CFS	KS	$Aff_{runtime}$	lowest virtual runtime	often/ min_granularity	CFLB

Table 5.1: Comparison of scheduling policies. The *Queue Task Order* lists the task parameters by which the task queue is sorted, for instance, PERF policy executes the task with highest *aload* first. On equal *aload* values, the task with a lower *pload* value is executed first. *Yields* specifies the expected frequency of task yields for the policies, while *Task Granularity* depicts the expected length of a timeslice.

With all of these algorithms, we increase both utilization and the suitability of tasks to the queue they are on in terms of affinity. To conclude the above policy definitions, we summarize our policies simplified through their most important values in Table 5.1.

5.4 Related Work

The profitability of using a scheduler for heterogeneous accelerator-based systems has been shown in several works. For instance, Pellizzoni et al. [135] have shown the feasibility for both hardware and software scheduling of relocatable real-time tasks in CPU-FPGA systems providing reconfigurable computing resources. However, relocation is only considered to be possible at the beginning of tasks. Since the time, at which accelerator usage was beginning to spread fast, many approaches for heterogeneous scheduling have been discussed. We group related work to three groups that match our scheduling objectives: scheduling targeting performance improvements, energy-based scheduling, and approaches aiming at fairness.

Two general ways are used to gain runtimes for tasks when scheduling based on task execution times. Either scheduling decisions are based on task runtimes estimated from previously measured task executions, or they are estimated based on a performance model. EDF scheduling of periodic real-time tasks on FPGAs has been investigated by [54], who perform area optimization for a set of tasks, each requiring a certain amount of logic area on the FPGA. Two EDF-based scheduling algorithms have been presented that also make use of partial reconfiguration to preempt and relocate tasks for better resource utilization. HEFT [166] is a well known algorithm for heterogeneous task execution and has been applied in different work on heterogeneous scheduling [18, 93, 60, 115]. It originally aims on parallel real-time jobs with deadlines and uses an ordered DAG to resolve dependencies. While HEFT is a scheduling algorithm for real time systems, we focus on multitasking with cooperative task preemption without deadlines. A performance history is used in [40] to relate estimated CPU execution times to estimated GPU execution times. It includes both the previous runtimes of tasks and the estimated remaining runtimes of currently running tasks and chooses the target device based on speedup thresholds. Using that scheme, only the next tasks is scheduled best, possibly leading to low task affinity to chosen resources. Historical runtime data is also used in [71], who use the average measured runtime on a task-resource combination as a prediction. Wang et al. [173] use a set of training data and machine learning to build a machine-specific model that predicts whether it is worth running a data parallel program on the GPU. Comparable to our approach, [28] aim at reducing idle times for Cell BE scheduling. They use user-level work-stealing in case an SPE runs idle. Data transfers are considered in a cost estimation in [16], who use bandwidth and latency between each pair of accessed memories for estimating data transfer overheads. Other approaches use performance modeling. A static approach based on predictive modeling is presented in [73]. A static analysis is used to extract code features of OpenCL programs, which are fed to a model built from machine-learning to predict runtimes. Li et al. [105] extract timing and resource metrics for GPUs, for example the GPU initialization time and resource utilization, and use these to predict execution times of a group of tasks executed concurrently on a GPU.

Performing scheduling decisions that aim at reducing the energy consumption have also been investigated, but are mostly performed on distributed systems. Zhang et al. [180] assign as many tasks as possible to a cloud server with lowest energy while respecting given task deadlines. We do not consider task deadlines and additionally aim on a single-node scenario. In [78], the authors optimize overall energy consumption of cluster systems with modeling energy consumption for each used processor, including idle power consumption. They simulate the expected energy-delay product (EDP) values for several schedules and pick the schedule with lowest EDP value. Thus, they use an a-priori computation, which does not match our scenario. Liu et al. [107] propose power-aware, time-sensitive mapping techniques to utilize CPU/GPU systems using dynamic voltage/frequency scaling. GreenGPU [112] proposes a holistic energy management framework for CPU/GPU heterogeneous architectures. They avoid idle times on both CPU and GPU by distributing workload to finish on both architectures at the same time. In addition, they scale voltage based on the current workload. In [170], a power-efficient work distribution method for a single application on CPU-GPU heterogeneous systems is shown. We aim at multiapplication scenarios instead.

Third group of related work is on fairness in heterogeneous systems. Several projects have addressed the issue of fairness in GPU scheduling. Time-Graph [93] enables fairness by penalizing task that extend their resource reservation. Gdev [94] implement fairness through a non-preemptive version of the Xen Credit Scheduler. Xen credits are also considered in [76] to achieve fairness on GPUs through virtualization. Their work is extended in [77], where different fairness approaches for virtualized devices are discussed. However, we consider preemption based on writing checkpoints at defined preemption points rather than virtualization. Fairness for GPU spacial multitasking has been considered in [9]. Four policies are considered: equal compute resource usage for each application, equal throughput for each application, equal speedup for each application, and maximum system throughput, such that applications are not slowed relative to cooperative multitasking. All of these approaches seem valid to provide a fairness measure, but aim on GPU-internal fairness only. Tanasic et al. [160] define fairness as the measure of equal progress of applications in a multiprogrammed workload, relative to their isolated execution. They propose equal spatial sharing of GPU resources for a fair partition among all running GPU kernels. Two preemption methods used for that purpose are described in Section 3.5. PTask [139] defines fairness as priority-weighted access provided by the OS scheduler to processes contending for the GPU and balancing GPU utilization with other system tasks. Thus, their approach is similar to ours, but does not consider preemption. Instead, fairness is aspired between several independent task graphs that consist of OS-managed objects, switching to a different task graph after one or several node executions. We can see that fairness can be interpreted quite differently.

From the discussion of approaches above, it is evident that scheduling algorithms have already been widely examined. However, most of these approaches base on run-to-completion of tasks and thus can not be directly used for our scheduling objectives. If preemption is enforced by above described works, it is achieved by virtualization or through scheduling subtasks. This is restricting the granularity of fairness scheduling decisions and is less flexible than our approach. Instead, we base on the CFS idea of fairness scheduling, achieving fairness based on virtual runtimes. For performance scheduling, we do not primarily use runtime estimates or measurements directly, but base our decisions on affinities of tasks to resource types as a generalization. Energy consumption algorithms have also been investigated, but are mostly aimed at distributed systems.

5.5 Chapter Conclusion

In this chapter, we discussed scheduling objectives and metrics for their evaluation targeting the heterogeneous scheduling scenario introduced in Chapter 3. On this basis, we defined heterogeneous scheduling policies that aim at optimizing these objectives.

We defined three major metrics: increasing performance, decreasing energy consumption, and achieving fairness through the use of time-shared task execution on a set of heterogeneous devices. While the performance of an executed set of tasks can be measured through the makespan and the energy consumption may also be measured, no commonly used definition of fairness in a heterogeneous environment exists. We base our scheduling policies on several parameters. We use both, the affinity of a task and its priority translated to a task weight. They are the major parameters to be used for performance- and energy-related scheduling. Specifically, we introduce a combination of priority and affinity called *aload*, which is well suited to sort task queues and choose tasks to be migrated when aiming at best possible affinity, but also when preferring high priority tasks. We discussed different possible definitions of heterogeneous fairness for fair task execution. There is no obvious definition for fairness in a heterogeneous environment, because different possible objectives of fair scheduling are contradictory. They can not be put into relation easily. Therefore, we derived subtargets to achieve instead when aiming at fairness, while preserving the general performance goals: avoiding idle times, increasing average task affinities to their current resource, avoiding starvation and large execution times on suboptimal resources, and including task priority. Including these targets, we use time-sharing for all tasks enqueued to a certain resource with varying execution granularities. We measure fairness based on virtual runtimes that consider task priorities.

When using a user-space scheduler, exact CPU load information is not accessible but mandatory for load balancing. We, therefore, introduced two possibilities to estimate the CPU load through values provided by the *proc filesystem (procfs)* in Unix-baed systems. This estimation is essential for effective scheduling, because an overloaded CPU not only reduces the performance of CPU tasks, but also of non-CPU tasks that include portions of CPU computation and data transfers relying on the CPU. Moreover, the scheduler itself is executed on the CPU.

We aim at schedulers for a dynamic runtime system to perform decisions based on the current system state without planning ahead. We defined five scheduling policies with different optimization targets: maximizing performance or minimizing the makespan (*PERF* policy), minimizing energy consumption (*EGY*), improving the fairness among tasks (FAIR), and providing FAIR execution to a performance optimized scheduling approach (*PERF_ FAIR*). While all of these policies are aimed at a user-space scheduler, we provide the latter policy for both user-space and kernel-space scheduler. The kernel-space version (*CFS PERF_FAIR*) aims at the seamless integration with the current implementation of the Linux Completely Fair Scheduler and, therefore, adapts the fairness idea to the heterogeneous case.

Finally, we defined three load balancing approaches that are used in combination with the defined policies. Affinity-based load balancing (*ALB*) pursues the targets of low idle times and high average affinity of tasks toward their executing resources without aspiring equalized loads. With CFS Load Balancing (*CFLB*) that is in the kernel-space implementation of our scheduler, accelerator queues are filled with best suited tasks to a certain limit to avoid idle times. The choice of the limit defines the degree of time-sharing used on accelerator resources. Fair Load Balancing (*FLB*) is the user-space version of *CFLB* and thus also aims at largely balanced queues, both among resources of the same and of different type.

These scheduling algorithms in combination with matching load balancing approaches are used in our scheduler. Chapter 6 will present the user and kernel-space implementations.

CHAPTER 6

Thread Level Acceleration

We have developed two heterogeneous scheduling frameworks to demonstrate the benefit of thread level acceleration with the use of accelerator preemption and heterogeneous migration. In this chapter, we describe both a kernel-space and a user-space scheduler and show experimental results. We, therefore, first give a short introduction in common requirements and features of both schedulers before discussing their architectures and implementations separately. The presented frameworks not only consider the scheduler itself, but also integrate to the operating system (OS) and offer an interface to the applications. Experimental results show the benefits in performance, fairness, and interactivity of our approach.

6.1 Towards a Heterogeneous Task Scheduler

Independent from the concrete implementation of a heterogeneous scheduler, a heterogeneous scheduling framework has to perform tasks that are basic requirements for meaningful and efficient scheduling.

Figure 6.1 gives an overview of basic components a heterogeneous scheduler should provide in our point of view. First, a scheduler needs to base its decisions on a best possible knowledge base. This includes the mandatory knowledge about available computing resources and their parameters, which can be provided by a device detection component. In addition, a heterogeneous scheduler requires reliable information about the system state, i. e., the current set of executed or executable tasks and the load situation of all available resources. Devices and tasks need to be managed by the scheduling framework to perform scheduling decisions through using a scheduler. Moreover, the operating system's CPU scheduler, in our case the Linux Completely Fair Scheduler (CFS), needs to be taken into account and incorporated into the scheduling framework, if not being replaced by a substitute CPU scheduler. The CFS has been chosen, because it does not operate on traditional timeslices but on a notion of "unfairness" between the execution times of all ready-to-run tasks. This

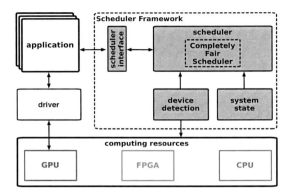

Figure 6.1: General architecture of a heterogeneous scheduling framework.

model is well suited for cooperative multitasking, which we have to use on the hardware accelerators since they do not (yet) support preemption, as cooperative multitasking does not guarantee that tasks return exactly at the end of a timeslice. Finally, a dedicated scheduler interface is required to allows tasks to be submitted for execution.

The scheduler itself provides run queues for each resource type and performs the following tasks according to the concepts described in Chapter 5: 1. assign tasks to matching run queues that are sorted according to different scheduling policies, 2. dispatch tasks for execution, and 3. balance load between resources.

To demonstrate the idea of accelerator preemption and heterogeneous migration, we have developed two heterogeneous scheduling frameworks. The first provides a direct extension of the CFS in kernel space. The second framework is located in user space and can be used detached from the underlying operating system scheduler in Unix-based Linux systems, but still incorporating the CFS for CPU scheduling.

Both frameworks are generally based on the concepts introduced in the previous chapters of this thesis. As such, they both rely on the cooperative multitasking approach that is based on cooperatively yielding resources at preemption points introducing migration support as presented in Chapter 3.

Applications matching the proposed programming pattern submit tasks for resource allocation to the scheduler via a scheduler interface. They provide the corresponding and necessary information as described in Chapter 4.

6.2 Kernel-Space Task-Scheduling Framework

As discussed, we consider the current state of the art of scheduling tasks to hardware accelerators as part of the application to be ineffective and to prohibit fair sharing of heterogeneous computing resources among several tasks. We argue that the operating system is predestined to also manage the scheduling of tasks to heterogeneous computing resources and to implement time-sharing of accelerators. The OS, as the central management component of a computer system, has a complete view on the available hardware resources, their utilization, and the tasks to be performed. It is thus optimally suited to perform scheduling decisions in order to optimize global objectives from a computer systems point of view, such as minimizing response time and turnaround time [149].

We now present an extension to the Linux Completely Fair Scheduler that

- provides awareness of installed accelerators,
- enables scheduling of specific tasks to accelerators, and
- allows time-sharing and task migration using a cooperative multitasking and check-pointing approach.

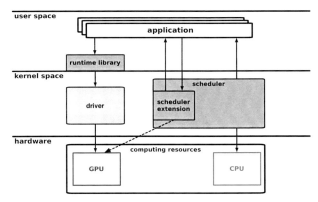

Figure 6.2: Scheduling framework for the kernel-space scheduler. Overview of the associated entities and their control hierarchy. Solid lines stand for direct control or communication, while the dashed line represents indirect management.

Figure 6.2 depicts an abstract overview of our framework concept. Our scheduler extension acts as centralized manager in the kernel space, indirectly controlling the execution flow on the accelerator by allowing or prohibiting the accelerated applications to use the available resources. The accelerator-specific interfaces provided by the hardware vendors consisting of a runtime library and a programming API that triggers the library are used by the applications in user space. The runtime library is still in direct control of the accelerator, by communicating with the driver in kernel space. The original CFS CPU scheduler controls the processors in the same way as in an unmodified Linux kernel, and thereby the assignment of applications to CPUs. The accelerated applications employ cooperative multitasking and hence collaborate with the scheduling extension allowing it to influence the task execution flow.

The scheduler hardware selection decision is based on meta-information (cf. Chapter 4), as provided by the applications. While we provide a basic scheduler mechanism and policy that schedules tasks based on static affinities to accelerators, our focus is to provide a complete framework for heterogeneous scheduling using a time-sharing approach. We evaluate our work with two applications that demonstrate the usability and benefits of the approach and supply data for an efficiency analysis.

In the following, we describe the data structures and APIs, which have been added to the Linux kernel to enable the scheduling of heterogeneous hardware accelerators.

6.2.1 Data Structures

Aiming at the extension of the current Linux scheduler to enable scheduling of heterogeneous resources, we have to make the kernel aware of existing heterogeneous hardware accelerators. We describe the additional information required by the CFS to enable scheduling on heterogeneous systems in the subsequent paragraphs. We extend the standard Linux Completely Fair Scheduler (CFS), which is implemented as a scheduling class inside the scheduler framework of the kernel. The CFS uses its own queues and statistics to ensure a fair treatment of all tasks with respect to their priorities. Our work reuses and extends these queues and mechanisms. The relation of the extended and new data structures to each other is depicted in Figure 6.3.

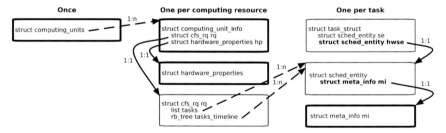

Figure 6.3: Extracts of extended and new data structures in the Linux kernel. Their descriptions are shortened to relevant aspects for our approach. Data structures with thick frame have been newly added to the kernel and bold texts show struct members that have been added to existing kernel data structures.

Computing Resources The modified kernel represents each hardware accelerator and CPU core by an instance of the `computing_unit_info` struct. The structs include an id, the type of the computing resource, and a run queue (`cfs_rq`) for the ready-to-run tasks. Additionally, an `api_resource_number` orders the instances of available computing resources of the same type. The struct also stores general hardware properties like the maximum number of kernels to be executed concurrently, the bandwidth, and the amount of memory. The number of concurrent kernels defines the size of the counting semaphore protecting a run queue. The computing resources are held in a mutex-protected array of lists, where each list holds the computing resources of the same type.

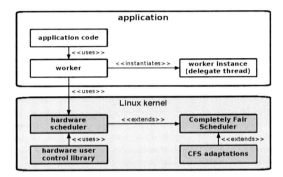

Figure 6.4: Extensions to the Linux kernel to support cooperative multitasking on heterogeneous systems.

Scheduling Entities and Queues   The task struct of the original CFS includes the `struct` `sched_entity se` representing one entity to be scheduled on the CPU. We define an additional scheduling entity `struct sched_entity hwse` as an extended copy of `struct` `sched_entity se` to represent a hardware task to be scheduled. We extend the original data structure by the meta-information, the minimum granularity ($min\_granularity$ in ns, cf. Chapter 5), and data structures needed for task migration.

The tasks to be scheduled and stored in the run queues are delegate threads representing CPU or accelerator tasks. Delegate threads that represent accelerator tasks wait in a blocked state for the completion of the task on the computing resource. The queue (`cfs_rq`) was extended to internally implement a counting semaphore and uses the CFS's red-black-tree as waiting queue. As described in Section 5.3, the queue is ordered by the amount of unfairness, i.e., by the time the task would have to execute undisturbed to be treated fair, as it is done in the original CFS. All tasks that wish to execute on a computing resource have to get the semaphore of the run queue before attempting to use it. The task chosen to run next from the queue is the one with the strongest need for computing time. We create one queue for each computing resource in addition to the CFS provided CPU queues and allow to restrict the size of each queue for load balancing purposes. Adapting existing data structures of the CFS implicated some adaptations to those functions within the kernel's fair scheduler (`sched_fair.c`) that handle these structures. We accumulated these functions in an additional file `sched_fair_hw.c` that provides adapted copies of the corresponding functions (*CFS adaptations* in Figure 6.4).

6.2.2 Scheduler API

With regard to the cooperative use of the scheduler aspired in our CFS extension, we provide an interface to the scheduler, which enables user-space applications to request and free computing resources. The scheduler API has been extended by three system calls to support cooperative multitasking: `computing_unit_alloc`, `computing_unit_rerequest` and `computing_unit_free` (represented as *hardware scheduler* in Figure 6.4).

Listing 6.1: System call used by application workers to allocate a computing resource.

```
SYSCALL_DEFINE(computing_unit_alloc, meta_info *mi,
                 computing_unit_shortinfo *cu){
  // current hardware scheduling entity
  sched_entity* hwse=current_task->hwse;
  hwse->mi=copy_meta_information(mi);

find_best_resource:
  computing_unit_info* cui=find_best_cu(mi, hwse, &affinity);
  inherit_priority_information(current_task);
  adapt_restore_unfairness_information(hwse, cui->cfs_rq);
  hwse->cfs_rq=cui->cfs_rq; //set run queue

  // blocking funtion to wait for a token to compute on cui
  // will return also, if hwse->need_migrate is set
  get_lock(cui);

  if(hwse->need_migrate || !cui->online){
    // existing offer from computing resource or requested
    //computing resource has been removed
    release_lock(cui);
    goto find_best_resource;
  }
  add_task_to_rq(cui);
  calculate_task_granularity(hwse, hwse->cfs_rq, mi);

  // make computing resource information available in user space
  copy_to_user(cu, cui);
}
```

Compute Unit Allocation The system call `computing_unit_alloc` (Listing 6.1) is a blocking call that acquires the semaphore of a computing resource for the calling task. It returns the type of the resource and, thus, defines the way to communicate with the resource via the corresponding resource API. The application can use this information to load and execute the corresponding implementation on the resource through calling the resource-specific init, compute, and free functions, as implemented in the programming pattern. This system call enables the scheduler to flexibly assign tasks to computing resources. When a task enters this system call, it enters the waiting queue of its assigned computing resource.

To determine the best possible computing resource, a matching of the meta-information of the task to the inherent hardware properties is performed (`find_best_cu` function), which in currently is a matching to the affinity. If no meta-information is available for a task, we have to assume that there is no specific accelerator implementation and we try to get any available CPU.

In case that a meta-information struct is available, we iterate through the array of computing resource lists and return the best possible computing resource, i.e., the one with the highest affinity. Less affine computing resources are only considered if they are idle and if the task would have to wait in the queue for the most affine unit.

If a task is waiting in the `get_lock()` function for the semaphore of a computing resource and another suitable unit is running idle in the meantime, then the load balancer wakes the task with a special migration flag (`need_migrate`), i.e., the task has an offer from a different computing resource. The scheduler then removes the task from the waiting queue and enqueues it on the offered computing resource. With the introduction of queue lengths, a computing resource may also remove as many tasks from the queue list of a different computing resource as its own queue allows to hold. If a computing resource is removed (`!cui→online`), the tasks also remove themselves from the queue and request the allocation of a different computing resource.

Using this mechanism the scheduler achieves a late binding of tasks to units, which ensures a better utilization of the resources, while still taking only a negligible amount of computation overhead in the scheduler, as most tasks are blocked and thus migrated while waiting on the semaphore.

Checkpointing If the program reaches a preemption point, it allows the system to perform a new scheduling decision by calling `computing_unit_rerequest` (Listing 6.2). The application requests to further use the computing resource, but offers to voluntarily release it. The scheduler decides if the task on the computing resource should be replaced by another, which depends on the type of computing resource and on the cost of switching the task. As mentioned above, the scheduler calculates an individual timeslice granularity with which the task should be scheduled. This roughly reflects the time it takes to upload the code to the resource and to up- and download the checkpoint data to it. We use a slight adaptation of Equation 5.27 reflecting the meta-information provided by the application developer:

$$time\_slice = min\_granularity[type] + 2 * (memory\_to\_copy/bandwidth) \qquad (6.1)$$

The *memory_to_copy* parameter is a user-provided value in this implementation and thus added to the meta-information (cf. Section 4.2). CPU granularities follow the original CFS mechanisms. Re-requests inside the time window of this granularity are always successful

Listing 6.2: System call used by a task to request further use of a resource.

```
SYSCALL_DEFINE( computing_unit_rerequest ){
   sched_entity* hwse=current_task ->hwse;
   granted=true;

   if (!next_entity_hw==NULL) // task is waiting
      unfairness = calculate_unfairness ();
      if (unfairness>hwse->granularity) {
         // voluntarily release computing resource
         granted = false;
      }

   if( offer_available && offer_valid ) {
      if( offering_cu_queue_not_full ) {
         accept_offer ();
         granted=false;
      }
   }

   return( granted );
}
```

and will be only denied after the granularity has expired, if other tasks are waiting for the resource, or if a migration offer is pending. The time a task may run then is the sum of the $\Delta fairness$, i.e., the time to compute until the (negative) unfairness is equalized, and the minimum granularity, i.e., the "positive unfairness" for this task (cf. Section 5.3.1).

If the application has either finished its work, unsuccessfully re-requested its computing resource or simply wants to yield, it calls `computing_unit_free`. This releases the semaphore and hands it to the next task or, in case no other tasks are waiting on this resource, invokes the load balancer.

6.2.3 Control API

Using most of todays hardware accelerators involves using their proprietary user-space APIs to communicate with them. Our extension leaves all interaction with the accelerators to the user space, since we are not aware of implementations to communicate efficiently with these resources from the kernel. The freshly booted scheduler has no inherent knowledge of accelerators available in the system. Instead, our kernel extension offers system calls to modify and examine its data structures from the user space in a controlled way (*hardware user control library* in Figure 6.4). We provide system calls to add a computing resource, to remove it afterwards, to iterate through all currently added resources and to alter a resource after it has been added. The system calls are used via a frontend in user space, which wraps the functionality of the computing resource API. As the system does not know about the available hardware architectures at startup, this frontend can be used to add and remove computing resources to and from the OS, e. g., by a startup script performing a device detection.

6.2.4 Scheduler Interface

We introduce a `worker` class that is the superclass of the delegate threads in an application (see Figure 6.4). Thereby, it acts as an application-sided interface to the scheduler. The worker class provides the pure virtual functions `getImplementationFor` and `taskMetaInfo`, which have to be implemented in the derived delegate threads. The `getImplementationFor` function returns the function pointers to the `init`, `compute`, and `free` functions of a certain resource type.

In addition to the code framework, the worker class provides system call wrappers to the Scheduler API, i. e., to `computing_unit_alloc`, `computing_unit_rerequest`, and `computing_unit_free`, such that derived delegate threads may communicate with the scheduler.

Through provided C++ templates the effort for adapting the application are further reduced and is easily legitimated by the benefits shown in Section 6.2.6. Applications that do not use the programming pattern, that was introduced in Chapter 4, are simply executed by the usual CFS scheduling mechanisms.

6.2.5 Experimental Setup

We have evaluated our kernel extension using the following system setup:

- SMP system with 2-way 4-Core Intel Xeon CPU E5620 @ 2.4GHz with hyperthreading enabled (appears to the OS like 16 cores), 12 GB main memory
- NVIDIA Geforce GTX 480, 480 CUDA cores, 1536 MB GDDR5 memory
- Ubuntu Linux 10.04.1 LTS, 2.6.32-24 kernel
- CUDA 3.1, GCC 4.4.3

Benchmark Applications   We used a brute-force MD5 hash cracker (MD5) and a prime number factorization (PF) as example applications to evaluate our scheduler extension. Both applications were implemented in C++ for the CPU and CUDA C to be run on NVIDIA GPUs. We examine the execution of several application instances concurrently.

MD5 Cracking   MD5 brute-force cracking (MD5) enumerates all possible strings of a fixed length with letters of a given alphabet and computes their MD5 hash value until a match with a target hash value is found. Each string is identified by an ascending unique number, which can be used as a checkpoint value specifying the progress of the search.

We choose the interval between two preemption points differently for the CPU (e. g., 500 search strings) and the GPU (e. g., 1 billion search strings) in order to consider the costs for retransferring the kernel to the computing resource and doing a re-request at a preemption point, which are much higher on the GPU.

The meta-information for this application is very simple, as practically no memory has to be copied. The parallel efficiency gain, as defined in Section 4.3, can be set depending on the size of the string length and the used alphabet, which defines the problem size. The performance differences between CPU and GPU are very high. Hence, the metadata is set up to express a clear affinity to the GPU.

As the runtime of this application largely depends on the target hash values in the search space, we fix these values for our experiments to obtain reproducible results.

Prime Factorization   Prime factorization (PF) algorithms decompose numbers into their prime factors. Our sample application searches through all possible divisors of the number up to its square root. Whenever a divisor is encountered, the number is divided by it as often as possible. Hence the application yields the divisor and its multiplicity. It then continues the search, now using the current remainder and its square root instead of the original number.

Checkpoints are defined by the pair of current remainder and potential divisor. Between two preemption points the algorithm advances the divisor to the value of the next preemption point, while keeping the remainder correct during the process. In our version the preemption points are typically 1, 000 divisors apart.

6.2.6 Experimental Results

We here evaluate our kernel-space framework with applications using the extended scheduler that dynamically switch between CPU cores and a GPU. We evaluate the overheads and show how adjusting the scheduler parameters affects the makespan of an executed set of task.

In addition, a scheduler can be evaluated by measuring the threads' response times and turnaround times compared to the traditional non-preemptive scheduling [19].

Fairness Evaluation   We discussed different load balancing migration modes for our kernel scheduling approach in Section 5.3.3. We either fill a queue once it runs idle, or refill it every time a task finishes computation to achieve time-sharing on accelerators. We show that cooperative multitasking is possible using the introduced checkpoints data structures and preemption points. All threads are treated fair and allocated the same amount of computation time until they have completed.

The vertical axis in Figure 6.5 represents the search space that has been searched for the MD5 cracking application, while the horizontal axis denotes the runtime in seconds. We run 15 GPU affine threads, with a limited queue length of 5 for the GPU. As we spawn 15 threads, 9 threads initially run on CPU cores, 6 (1 running, 5 queued) on the GPU. Each thread is displayed by a different color. The GPU threads can be identified by the fast progress in the search space. The ascent of the curves representing CPU threads can hardly be seen, only a minor progress can be noticed in region e). The ability of the tasks to be stopped and replaced for later continuation on the GPU can, e. g., be seen in region a). In that region, we see that the 6 GPU threads share the computation time based on

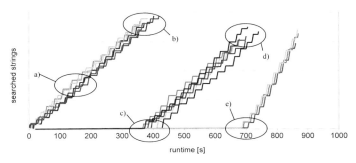

Figure 6.5: Migration of GPU affine tasks from CPU to GPU with a queue limit of 5 using a fixed queue length.

their fairness, the granularity, and the time needed to reach the next preemption point. In this example, the load balancer refills the GPUs queue as soon as a thread finishes its computation (regions b) and d)). Regions c) and e) show how CPU enqueued threads are migrated to the GPU and afterwards compute much faster.

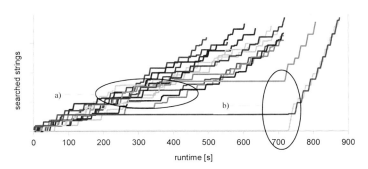

Figure 6.6: Migration of GPU affine tasks from CPU to GPU with a queue limit of 5 using a variable batch of tasks and random choice of tasks to be run on the GPU.

In Figure 6.6, the GPU queue is filled up with a CPU task as soon as a task finishes. In addition, it enqueues tasks to the CPU after GPU execution. A replacing task to fill the GPU is migrated from a CPU randomly to increase the fair use of the GPU. Region a) shows that most tasks get a portion of execution time on the GPU. Region b) shows the drawback of the random approach by migrating certain tasks only very rarely to the GPU, which decreases fairness.

Performance Evaluation   The turnaround time is the interval between the submission of a process and its completion [149]. The effect of scheduling with time-sharing on turnaround times can be seen in Figure 6.7. Subfigure a) shows the turnaround times of 25 MD5 and 50 PF instances on a single GPU. One thread is spawned by each instance and time-sharing is not used. As tasks are scheduled one after another, long running tasks (e. g., task 5 or 20) block all other tasks, such that the average turnaround time is increased. Using time-sharing instead, short tasks are not blocked any more, such that the average turnaround time is lower. Subfigure b) shows that the tasks are not finished in the same order as they are started. Longer jobs (e. g., tasks 1, 2, 5, 20) do not block the shorter, as their timeslice is of the same length as that of a short job. This increases interactivity, as response times are decreased. After 150 seconds only long running threads remain in the system. The average turnaround time was reduced from approximately 123s to 97s.

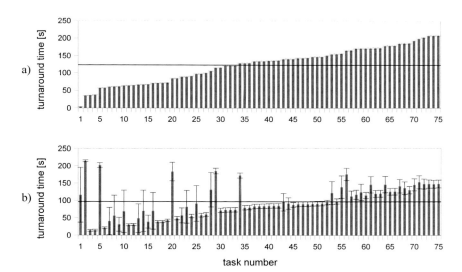

Figure 6.7: Turnaround times for all threads on a single GPU using a) no time-sharing and b) time-sharing with 4s granularity using 25 MD5 threads (word length 6) and 50 PF threads. The respective average values are denoted by a horizontal line. We can see that time-sharing achieved a major reduction of the average turnaround time.

In addition to the reduced average turnaround times, the overall performance of several running applications may be increased, if more than one computing resource can be used. This is shown in Figure 6.8, which depicts the total runtime of a varying number of PF

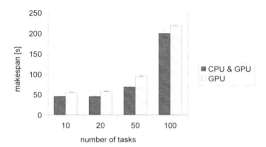

Figure 6.8: Average runtimes of different counts of PF instances on a GPU and on a combination of GPU and CPU cores.

applications on the GPU alone and on both the GPU and the available CPU cores. As can be seen, the average runtime of all instances can be reduced by using the scheduler extension. All instances compete for the use of the GPU, but profit from the fallback computation on the CPU.

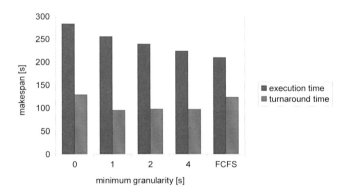

Figure 6.9: Mean of total runtimes for 30 runs with 25 MD5 threads (string length 6) and 50 PF threads on the GPU with different minimum granularity values. FCFS performs scheduling without preemption.

Overheads Figure 6.9 shows the influence of the granularity of timeslices on the runtime and the average turnaround time of the example applications. All tasks in this test were run on the GPU only. Decreasing the granularity raises the total runtime, as task switching overheads are introduced. This is expected, as we only use a single GPU resource. We can see that introducing time-sharing is a tradeoff between overheads and interactivity, as a higher granularity decreases the response times of the threads and first-come first-served (FCFS) scheduling, i. e., scheduling without preemptions, obviously has the smallest overhead. Regarding the average turnaround time, using a granularity of 0 leads to fast-paced task switching and a very high interactivity and thus introduces huge overheads. On the other hand, submitting all tasks at the same time to the GPU queue and using FCFS for the tasks on the GPU results in higher average turnaround times due to the fact that long running tasks are blocking short tasks.

In Figure 6.10, we evaluate the efficiency of the scheduler under high loads. The figure shows how the ratio between computation times and load balancing times changes depending on the amount of concurrently queued threads. We compare the times spent in the computation of the threads to the time spent in the `compute_unit_free` function that performs the load balancing if a computing resource runs idle. The more threads are started the higher is the overhead for the load balancing. The reason is that the load balancer has to traverse all 16 CPU queues and calculate the affinity for each task to find the best suited tasks to be migrated to the GPU and therefore is of $O(n)$ complexity, with n denoting all tasks in the system.

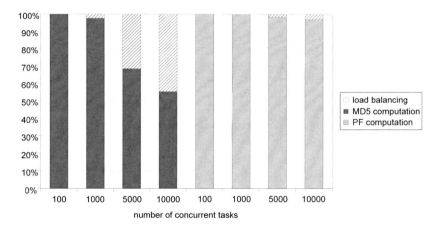

Figure 6.10: Ratio between load balancing and computation with high loads of MD5 cracking or prime factorization tasks. Prime factorization has a higher computation time than MD5 cracking, so that load balancing has less impact on the total runtime through resources running idle less often.

The problem can be solved by avoiding to search for the most affine threads in all queues, but to stop as soon as enough threads being more affine to the computing resource that has run idle have been found. We removed this limitation in our user-space scheduler with a new load balancing approach as described in Section 5.3.3. Our user-space scheduler is introduced next.

6.3 User-Space Task-Scheduling Framework

Instead of extending the Linux kernel directly, we present *HetSched*, a scheduling framework that is closely connected to the operating system but located in user space to refrain from kernel modifications and allow easy extensions, e. g., new scheduling policies. A user-space solution enables every user to use the scheduler and, e. g., add new scheduling policies even without superuser rights and in-depth knowledge of the Linux kernel. Moreover, we have to rely on the accelerator APIs that have to be executed from user space anyway. Our kernel-space scheduler thus requires to incorporate the user space and offer system calls to access the kernel-space scheduler. A user-space scheduler faces the opposite problem when accessing kernel-space information like CPU loads. We use available Linux user-space interfaces to read kernel information for cooperation with the Linux scheduler, as described below. Our user-space framework for heterogeneous task scheduling generally follows the same approach as our user-space scheduling framework, but improves on various points, as described in the following. After a comparison on conceptual level, we introduce details of our user-space framework and evaluate it with respect to several scheduling goals.

6.3.1 Differences to the Kernel-Space Task-Scheduling Framework

The user-space task-scheduling framework follows the idea of task scheduling with task migration on heterogeneous resources as used in the CFS extension presented above. We reuse the approach of cooperative multitasking through a dedicated programming pattern and also consider fair scheduling. However, major conceptual improvements have been achieved in comparison to the kernel extension. These can be summarized as follows:

- We add new and improved scheduling algorithms to the scheduler, as described in Section 5.3, which not only consider fair scheduling, but also energy and performance scheduling approaches that desist from incorporating the fairness idea.
- We remedy inefficiencies of load balancing by providing improved load balancing algorithms and techniques that also speed up load balancing decisions.
- We remove the direct dependency to the Linux kernel implementation, which increases portability to different systems, makes the framework independent from kernel changes and updates, allows automatic device detection, and retrieves kernel-space information only through available kernel interfaces.
- We vastly simplify the programming pattern for used applications through providing a reduced interface to a scheduler library. Automatic affinity determination based on benchmarks and a measurement framework for energy measurements have been added. Therefore, meta-information on parallel efficiency gain, transfer size, memory consumption, and affinity are not part of the programming pattern any more.

Certainly, scheduling in user space comes with some drawbacks in comparison to a kernel extension, which resulted in the following requirements:

- The state of the system as a basis for scheduling is not inherently available in user space and thus needs to be read from kernel interfaces. This especially includes the CPU load information. The available and used information is less up-to-date and precise, as discussed before.
- If not replacing the CPU scheduler of the operating system, a user-space scheduler has to cooperate with it. Thus, it does not have full control over the CPUs. In addition, the scheduler itself is a user-space task that is scheduled by the operating system's CPU scheduler. Thus, this cooperation has to be well defined and possible latencies have to be considered.
- The user-space scheduler is a stand alone scheduler that does not integrate to already given data structures and scheduling policies, as, e. g., given by the CFS. Thus, an initial implementation overhead is inevitable that requires more time to meet the quality of the long lasting CFS implementation in terms of software engineering standards.

We present our user-space scheduler framework next to approach these requirements.

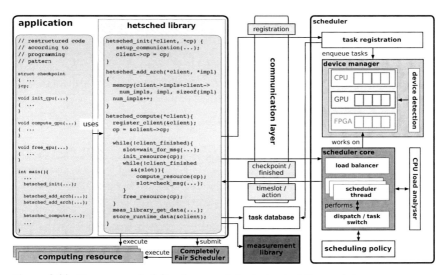

Figure 6.11: User-space scheduling framework for task scheduling on heterogeneous computing resources.

6.3.2 Scheduler Framework Architecture

We here present the general framework architecture of our user-space scheduling approach and how it integrates with the concepts presented in previous chapters. The framework is depicted in Figure 6.11 and consists of three major parts: 1. a scheduler library as interface between applications and the scheduler (cf. Section 6.3.3), 2. a Linux user-space scheduler component that manages the tasks and their execution (cf. Section 6.3.4), and 3. a measurement library allowing us to determine energy consumption values for tasks running on the available resources (cf. Section 6.3.5).

Applications that adhere to the programming pattern, as introduced in Chapter 4, register with the scheduler library (`hetsched` library), which again registers tasks to the scheduler via a dedicated communication interface. The library handles the complete task execution and the interaction with the scheduler. Communication is performed via an exchangeable asynchronous communication module using Unix sockets and message queues at both ends. Computing resources are automatically detected by using the *lspci* tool and the *cpuinfo* interface of the *proc filesystem*, both provided by Unix-like operating systems. Each computing resource is represented as a resource queue in the scheduler that holds tasks enqueued for execution on the resource. We avoid a global run queue to avoid congestion during task enqueue and dequeue operations and use fast O(1) access to the first waiting task when dequeuing a task from a presorted queue (cf. Chapter 5) instead of searching the next matching task in the queue. Providing a queue for each resource type instead of each resource is a valid alternative that avoids resource internal load balancing, but is more expensive by waiting on resource type locks and enqueueing tasks to the red-black trees. A dedicated device detection thread updates the available resources and, thus, the run queues frequently.

As soon as a resource runs idle due to a finished or yielding task, the first queued task is notified and assigned to a certain resource for an execution granularity, i. e., the computation timeslice. The task then transfers all needed data to the resource by itself and starts the computation. CPU tasks are executed via the CFS, only keeping a handle to the task to enable migration through *HetSched*. Scheduling and load balancing policies are used to determine the resource and the granularity the tasks are allowed to execute. The policies use task-specific affinity information measured offline and stored in a task database to base their resource selection on. If required by the policy, tasks are requested to perform a state transition at a preemption point according to the task state model introduced in Figure 3.12. This includes running a new time slot, reporting to the scheduler at a preemption point, or clean up and leave the resource. Each performed state transition is decided by the scheduler.

A CPU load analyzer is part of the scheduler and consists of two components. First, CPU load information is monitored from the *proc filesystem*, as described in Section 5.2.3, and reported to the scheduler. Second, this information is used to increase or decrease the number of tasks that are allowed to be executed concurrently on the CPU. Thereby, our scheduler is able to avoid over- or underutilization of the CPU. This also influences load balancing as explained in Section 6.3.4.

All parts of the framework are modularized and use well defined interfaces. Therefore, they are exchangeable. For instance, the energy measurement library or the device detection may be exchanged or extended depending on the used hardware components without changes within the scheduler or the scheduler library, as long as the resource types are generally supported by the scheduler. The communication module is exchangeable while keeping the interfaces to the scheduler library and the scheduler, e. g., allowing to use a distributed communication model using message passing. In addition, scheduler logic is easily exchangeable. Policies for task scheduling, load balancing, or task registration are modularized and, thus, exchangeable without major effort.

Our user-space scheduler uses data structures from the CFS. For instance, we use the *task_struct* and *sched_entity* data structures corresponding to their definitions in the CFS and use red-black-trees to represent queues. That way we ensure to be closely related to the CFS and even allow for a later integration of our concepts to the kernel space.

6.3.3 Scheduler Library

Our programming pattern requires that tasks follow a cooperative multitasking approach and return control to the scheduler when reaching a preemption point. To this end, our scheduler provides a library (`hetsched` library, see Figure 6.11) that encapsulates the complete execution of submitted tasks until they finish their computation and handles the communication with the scheduler. Applications submit a task for resource allocation to the scheduler using the scheduler library as depicted in Figure 6.12.

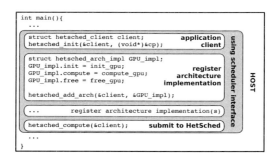

Figure 6.12: Registering different resource implementations with the scheduler and starting the computation handled by the scheduler library.

The main function, as shown in Figure 4.4, is extended for the use of the `hetsched` library. Each task defines a `client` data structure comprising pointers to the checkpoint data and function pointers to the init, compute, and free functions for each target resource. With submission of the data structure to the scheduler library, the task hands control over execution times and used resources to the scheduler.

As depicted in Figure 6.11, executing a corresponding function is triggered by the scheduler library, if a time slot is provided by the scheduler or the task needs to leave its current resource. The scheduler library calls the `compute_resource()` function in a loop according to the lifecycle of a task, as introduced in Figure 4.2, or `init_resource()` and `free_resource()` functions executing scheduler provided decisions. If a time slot has been fully consumed, the scheduler library checks if a message needs to be consumed, or otherwise computes the next time slot. The library additionally is responsible for collecting affinity data in a JSON task database that is read by the scheduler during task registration. According runtime information is collected through the scheduler library itself and energy consumption information is provided by the measurement library described in Section 6.3.5.

While the scheduler library executes corresponding measurements, the scheduler reads the data and uses both runtime and energy values of tasks for certain task instances, i. e., task implementations and their input sizes. This information is used to determine affinities of tasks to resource types according to the used scheduling policy.

6.3.4 Scheduler Implementation

Listing 6.3 shows how a scheduler thread manages a resource run queue. The shown loop performs all operations on a certain run queue, except task registration and load balancing, which both are handled by dedicated threads. Thus, independent run queue scheduler threads assure that queues only interfere with each other during load balancing. For each resource, we run an infinite loop that performs actions on the run queue in a certain scheduling interval (`timeout`, *200ms*) or if a currently running task returns control to the scheduler. In case nothing happens within the timeout while a task is running, we perform an update of the run queue internal clock and the execution times of the current task and update its virtual runtime, in the `task_tick` function. These values are needed to check if the task needs to be requested to yield in case a new task arrives. If `preempt_runqueue_current` has been set for a task that needs to yield, the task receives a cleanup message, which requires it, after a reevaluation of the necessity at a preemption point, to free the according resource. As tasks are dequeued from the red-black-tree holding the ready tasks of the run queue, tasks are reenqueued after cleaning the resource they have been running on. If no task is currently running, the schedule function checks if a task is waiting and, if given, provides a time slot to the first task in the resource-specific queue. By using such an event triggered implementation of the main scheduler functionality, communication and CPU load of the scheduler itself is minimized. A separate load balancing thread works accordingly, i. e., it also implements a message queue to which tasks report after having received a migration offer by the load balancer. Load balancing checks for necessary task migrations under the terms of the used scheduling policy on a regular basis (every *500ms*), but is also triggered if a resource runs idle.

Most of the functionality that requires decisions on how to handle a task or system state are modularized in a scheduling policy, which is replaceable according to the scheduling objectives. This includes task registration, enqueue and dequeue functions, the `task_tick`

Listing 6.3: Scheduler thread for a single computing resource.

```
scheduler_thread(){
  while(!runqueue_shutdown){
    if(runqueue_has_tasks){
      state=wait_for_client_message(runqueue_msg_queue,timeout);
      //update execution times and clock
      runqueue_update_current(runqueue);
      switch(state){
        case TIMEOUT:
          break; //no task returned}
        case TASK_HET_PREEMPTIBLE:
          //update virtual runtimes
          task_tick(runqueue, runqueue_current_task);
          if{preempt_runqueue_current}
            //initiate yield request
            request_cleanup(runqueue_current_task);
          else
            //no yield requested, continue
            grant_time_slot(runqueue_current_task);
          break; //no task returned}
        case TASK_HET_CLEANED:
          preempt_runqueue_current = False;
          //reenqueue tasks after yielding
          put(runqueue_current_task);
          break; //no task returned}
        case TASK_HET_FINISHED:
          //task freed resources
          runqueue_current_task = NULL;
          break; //no task returned}
    }
    else
    {
        //no tasks in queue, cleanup queue is performed
        sleep(timeout);
    }
    if(runqueue_current_task){
      //update runtime statistics
      task_tick(runqueue, runqueue_current_task);
      if(preempt_runqueue_current && s == TIMEOUT)
        //task switch (yield)
        request_task_switch(runqueue_current_task);
      else
        //no task running: task switch (dispatch)
        schedule(runqueue);
    }
  }
}
```

function, the check for setting `preempt_runqueue_current`, the sorting of the queues, and load balancing.

State Machines   Our scheduler provides independent threads for both queue management and load balancing for each resource. Both communicate directly with the applications and receive state updates from the application threads by the application's delegate threads using a message queueing system. Both the `hetsched` library and the delegate thread use state machines to keep track of the current state. The delegate thread knows about the state on client and server side and, thus, coordinates state transitions triggered by messages to be delegated to the correct scheduler or load balancing thread. The task states that are used in Listing 6.3 have been introduced in Section 3.4, and state transitions are depicted in Figure 3.12. Scheduler or load balancer operations (i. e., task switch or migration) on the task are communicated by an according offer to the task. As soon as the task reaches a preemption point, it checks its message queue and returns with a state update, so that the operation may be initiated. If still intended by the scheduler, the task gets informed to leave its current resource (call `free_resource()`) and give a status update again. The scheduler then may run the next task or migrate the task to a different queue.

Load Balancing   To avoid overheads and improve the $O(n)$ load balancing of the kernel-space scheduler, we hold a list of migratable tasks for each resource type. To achieve fast filling of idle resources, each resource type provides a `pull-list` that keeps handles of suitable tasks currently not enqueued on any of the queues of the resource type. With this list being sorted by *aload* values, it is easy to pull the best suited and available task to an idle resource. In addition, we manage a `push-list` for each queue that holds the tasks of a queue sorted by their *pload*. During load balancing based on queue loads, we push tasks from *overfull* queues to less full queues based on the defined load balancing policy. While these lists introduce enqueue and dequeue overheads for each new or migrated task, finding suitable tasks for migration is performed much more often and is very fast.

If running tasks are selected for migration, we make offers to all running tasks, as we do not know which task reaches a preemption point next. It should be noted that the number of currently running tasks is limited by our scheduling system, even on the CPU. Therefore, these migration offers are of low overhead and make sure that an idle device is filled as soon as possible. The necessity of a migration is rechecked as soon as the task reaches a preemption point with a pending migration offer.

Balancing CPU Load   Besides the threads described above, a CPU load analyzer thread is run that keeps track of both the CPU utilization and the CPU load. To prevent over- or underutilization of the CPU, we extract utilization and load average values from the Linux *proc filesystem* at intervals of $500ms$. We implement different strategies to increase or decrease the number of tasks that are allowed to run concurrently on the CPU based on these values. We use an exponential moving average to avoid too fast changes that might lead to switching between over- and underutilization of the CPU.

Our definition of the *load* of a run queue (see Equation 5.2) does not include the parallelism of the running tasks. The load of the CPU can be considered much higher for a number of OpenMP parallelized tasks, than for the same number of sequential tasks. The higher the parallelism, the less tasks are needed to fully utilize the CPU. By changing the number of concurrently running tasks with respect to the utilization, this number gives an estimate about how parallel the current tasks on the CPU are. Let $j(CPU)$ be this number. We redefine the average weight load (*wload*) for the CPU run queue according to Equation 5.19 to:

$$avg\_wload(rq_{CPU}) = \frac{wload(rq_{CPU})}{j(CPU)} \tag{6.2}$$

Thus, the average load of a single task is considered higher, the higher the parallelism of the tasks is. We thereby can use the average task load of tasks enqueued to a resource instead of the total *load* of the resource when performing load balancing based on load values. This makes the load of the CPU dependent on the current number of CPU tasks allowed and, thus, reflects the current parallelism. The number of tasks waiting on the queue of the CPU therefore is dependent on the parallelism of currently running tasks.

6.3.5 Experimental Setup

We have evaluated our user-space scheduler using the following heterogeneous system setup:
- SMP system with two 4-Core Intel Xeon E5-2609 v2 CPUs @ 2.50GHz, 32 GB main memory
- Nvidia Tesla K20c GPU, 2496 CUDA cores, 5 GB GDDR5 memory
- Maxeler Vectis card based on Xilinx Virtex 6 FPGAs (xc6vsx475t)
- CentOS 6.6 (Linux kernel 2.6.32), gcc 4.6.3, CUDA 5.5, PGI OpenACC compiler 14.9, Maxeler toolchain 2013.3.

We have carefully selected these components to support precise energy measurements for all computing resources without need for dedicated measurement equipment such as digital multimeters. All resources feature on-die respectively on-card power sensors, which are readable via system interfaces and libraries provided by the Linux kernel or the device manufacturers. The following paragraphs describe details on our energy measurement library.

Benchmark Applications Since available benchmark suites currently do not natively support FPGAs besides CPUs and GPUs, we could not rely on a given evaluation framework for our scheduler. Instead, to evaluate the scheduler we chose four benchmark applications ported to the target architectures ourselves: a Markov Chain computation, a heat distribution simulation, a Gaussian blur image processing algorithm, and correlation matrix calculations, which represent different application classes. All of these applications provide loop-based kernels that are accelerated on the three resource types. Figure 3.1 shows runtimes and energy consumptions of these applications. The correlation matrix application is the only application that not inherently provides an outer loop, so strip-mining was applied. The other three applications could be used with loop index-based preemption points directly. All benchmarks have been implemented following the proposed programming pattern using OpenMP parallelization for CPUs, CUDA or OpenACC for GPUs, and MaxJ for Maxeler FPGAs. The Markov Chain example could not be ported to FPGAs for all input matrix dimension, because routing problems occurred during synthesis for the largest examined problem size.

Energy Measurement In order to obtain the energy affinities of each task as well as the energy consumption of all running tasks scheduled by our scheduler, we must be able to retrieve energy measurements of all utilized processing resources at runtime. For this, we use a measurement library encapsulating the energy measurement procedures to read CPU, GPU, and FPGA energy-related sensors. Moreover, we also need to measure the energy consumption of each task stage (init, compute, and free) in order to calculate the energy affinity of an entire task. Therefore, our scheduler handles the measurement framework in such a way that it records the energy consumption of each task stage separately.

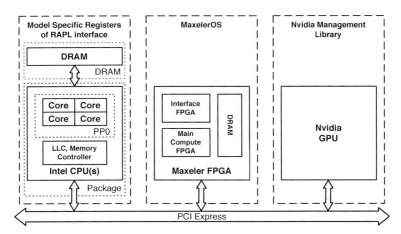

Figure 6.13: Heterogeneous computing node. The dashed shapes denote libraries and system interfaces for energy measurement. In addition, the dotted shapes symbolize the RAPL (Running Average Power Limit) power domains.

All used resources periodically update registers memorizing energy, power, current, or voltage measurement values. Our scheduler can read these registers via particular libraries, drivers, and system interfaces provided by the Linux kernel and hardware manufacturers. Figure 6.13 presents an overview of our heterogeneous testbed with its hardware components and the utilized interfaces and libraries. A major advantage of our measurement framework is that we do not need any dedicated measurement equipment such as digital multimeters, current clamps, or bus extenders to obtain energy measurements from processors or accelerators. Since the measurement process is realized as a CPU task that periodically samples the interfaces and libraries, it has influence to the performance of our scheduler and the tasks, which are simultaneously executed on the CPU.

Resource type	Parameter	Accuracy	Sampling rate
CPU	Energy	$\pm 10\%$	30ms
GPU	Power	$\pm 5\%$	40ms
FPGA	Voltage	$\pm 1\%$	60ms
	Current	$\pm 20\%$	60ms

Table 6.1: Accuracy of energy-related measurements.

To achieve an acceptable CPU load of 2% in maximum through energy sampling, while receiving an appropriate high precision of the energy-related measurements, we have to set the sampling rates to the values shown in Table 6.1. Below we detail the measurement infrastructure of the chosen resources.

CPU Modern Intel processors include the RAPL (Running Average Power Limit) interface. This interface provides mechanisms to enforce CPU power consumption limits. Therefore, it implies a couple of non-architectural MSRs (Model-Specific Registers), which we use to obtain the CPU's energy consumption. Each of these MSRs is related to one specific RAPL power domain. The following three power domains are available on Intel server processors: 1. The PP0 (Power Plane 0) power domain encapsulated the cores and their first and second level caches. 2. The package power domain supplements PP0 by the last level cache and the DDR3 memory controller. 3. The third complementary domain is the DRAM power domain, which is related to the memory modules. To obtain the total energy consumption, we accumulate the package and DRAM power domain MSR register contents of all CPUs. Table 6.1 gives an overview of the resources, their measurable quantities, and the quality of the sensor readings.

GPU All Nvidia Tesla GPUs based on the Kepler microarchitecture have an integrated on-card power sensor. This sensor can be monitored via the NVML (Nvidia Management Library). Our measurement library samples the power output to provide energy information to the scheduler.

FPGA The Maxeler Vectis device features multiple voltage and current sensors. Their measurement results can be received from the MaxelerOS daemon, which is the software component that is responsible for bitstream uploading and the communication between the host and the FPGA. The measurements delivered by MaxelerOS give a fine-grained overview of the latest voltage and current measurements, such as the main compute FPGA, the interface FPGA, and the on-card memory.

6.3.6 Experimental Results

This section provides an applicability analysis of our concepts in user space. We present a performance and overhead evaluation of our programming pattern approach and its implementation in our heterogeneous user-space scheduler.

HetSched aims at achieving the following goals when scheduling a set of tasks to CPUs and heterogeneous computing resources: 1. reduce the makespan for executing the whole sets of tasks (maximize throughput), or 2. reduce the overall energy consumption (minimize energy costs), or 3. provide a fair share of computation times to available tasks.

We evaluate overheads that occur through yielding resources and task migration below and subsequently analyze performance benefits of our scheduler when using the policies introduced in Section 5.3. We precede the introduced algorithm names with "HETSCHED", to denote the implementation in our framework. E. g., *HETSCHED EGY* defines the EGY policy, defined in Section 5.3, as implemented in *HetSched*. For easier interpretation of variability in the results, we generally use min/max error bars in our evaluation and show mean values on measurement results.

Migration Overheads   Generally, the overheads introduced for checkpointing and migration are highly dependent on the application, i. e., the checkpoint data size, the resource type, and especially for GPUs and FPGAs on the system's PCI Express bus throughput. The overheads might become a practical limitation of our approach. For example, in a fair time-sharing scenario the overheads will have a large impact and demand a minimum timeslice size. In the following overhead analysis, a preemption shall describe the process of writing a checkpoint at a preemption point, freeing the resource memory, and copying the checkpoint data to the same resource again before continuing the computation.

Figure 6.14 quantifies the preemption overhead on the example of our Gaussian blur application on a GPU. Refactoring the code according to our programming pattern but actually not yielding at given preemption points comes with negligible overhead. The overhead is also hardly measurable for one preemption where checkpoint data has to be transferred to and from the CPU, but grows linearly with the number of preemptions for both runtime and energy consumption. Overheads for counts of 64 or more preemptions are estimated on measured overheads for a single preemption. Intermediate migrations are not included. Using fairness-based scheduling with small timeslices, a reasonable tradeoff between preemptability and overheads has to be found through defining reasonable task execution granularities. Apart from fairness scheduling, heterogeneous scheduling of larger sets of tasks typically requires few migrations, as depicted in Figure 6.17.

Figure 6.15 shows the overhead introduced by the adaptation of our correlation matrix application to the programming pattern, the overhead occurred by the scheduler while handling the application, and the influence of 1, 2 and 3 preemptions to runtime and en-

application: Gaussian blur, resource type: GPU, data input size: 2048

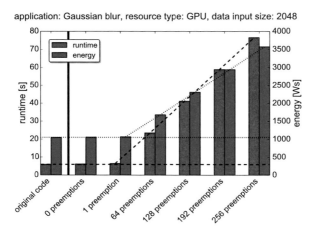

Figure 6.14: Preemption overheads for the Gaussian blur application on a GPU. The original code can not be preempted. For the preemptive versions, the code has been restructured according to our programming pattern. Horizontal dashed and dotted lines illustrate that runtime and energy overheads are negligible for zero and one preemptions. Diagonal dashed and dotted lines demonstrate the linear correlation between the number of preemptions and the resultant overhead.

ergy consumption. The task is computed on GPU with matrix dimensions $n \times n$, with n being 4096 and 16384. We compare the measured runtimes and energy consumption values of our approach with runtime and energy of the original GPU implementation. The patterned variant consists of the three application phases as described in Chapter 4. These phases are usually triggered by our scheduler. Since the patterned version must work as a scheduler-independent standalone application, the invocation of the phases is embedded in the application's main function. We discovered, which restructuring the original code to match the programming pattern produces a negligible overhead even exceeded by the average measurement error. The overhead of the scheduler is induced by scheduler routines and inter-process communication with the application or rather the `hetsched` library included in the application. The preemption overhead of GPU as well as FPGA tasks is dominated by data transfers via the system's PCI Express bus. Therefore, the linear increase in runtime and energy is due to the number of preemptions and the number of bytes transferred in each init and free phase. Moreover, a comparison of our correlation example for data input sizes 4096 and 16384 in Figure 6.15 indicates that the introduced scheduling and preemption overheads are more expensive in relation to the application runtime on short running tasks. While this is intuitive, a scheduler in best case handles this by including remaining runtimes into migration decisions. Consequentially, tasks with

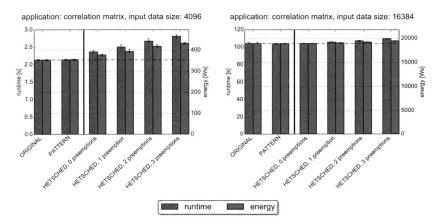

Figure 6.15: Comparison of runtime and energy consumption between the original implementation of the correlation matrix application, a patterned variant of the
original version and the application handled by our scheduler. All variants
are computed on the GPU.

small problem sizes trend to be hardly migrated since a migration of these tasks does not
gain appreciable speedups or energy reductions.

Finally, we take up our motivational example from Figure 3.10 that describes the expected
migration benefit or loss. Figure 6.16 shows the results for the Gaussian blur. It studies the
speedup (a) and energy reduction (b) we can gain if we perform only a single migration at
a specific point in task execution. For instance, if the task is entirely executed on an FPGA
(CPU to FPGA migration at 0% of task execution in Figure 6.16 (a)), we gain a speedup
of almost 30 over the CPU. It is important to note that we can still gain performance,
even if 95% of the task has already been executed, which indicates that the overheads for
a single migration are insignificant in this exemplary study.

Reference Scheduling Algorithms   For comparison, we have implemented a set of reference scheduling approaches that mimic how a user would execute a set of jobs on a heterogeneous system today using a queuing system, like HTCondor[162] (supporting CPU
and GPU tasks only), or with batch scripts. We present three approaches to compare our
results to, which implement algorithms for scheduling heterogeneous resources.

1. *GREEDY ALL and GREEDY BEST* strive for task execution on its best or best
   available resource type. While GREEDY BEST exclusively uses the most affine
   resource type, GREEDY ALL also runs tasks on suboptimal resource types if no
   better suited tasks are left for the corresponding resource type. With a preordered
   list of remaining tasks for each resource type, we dynamically choose the next task for

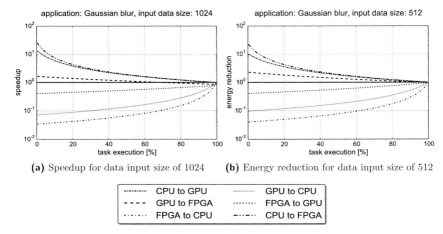

(a) Speedup for data input size of 1024   **(b)** Energy reduction for data input size of 512

------	CPU to GPU	··········	GPU to CPU
- - -	GPU to FPGA	········	FPGA to GPU
·······	FPGA to CPU	-··-··	CPU to FPGA

Figure 6.16: Speedup and energy reduction for one task migration of the Gaussian blur depending on the progress of the task. The different curves are for different migration directions.

a resource that has the best affinity for it. While GREEDY ALL is work-conserving and, thus, reduces idle times, it may happen toward the end of the execution of the set of tasks that long-running tasks are assigned to suboptimal resources. This may increase the makespan over a non-work-conserving approach that waits for a better suited resource type.

2. *Heterogeneous Earliest Finish Time First (HetEFT)*: HEFT [166] is a well known algorithm for heterogeneous task execution and has been applied in different work on heterogeneous scheduling [18, 93, 60, 115]. It originally aims at parallel real-time jobs with deadlines and uses an ordered DAG to resolve dependencies. We use a special case of HEFT and adapted it to only work as an EFT algorithm for the heterogeneous case, desisting from deadlines and dependencies. As HEFT, we assume all runtimes to be known and provide a global random order of tasks. Tasks are queued to resources in order of appearance and get enqueued on the resource where it will finish earliest at current state, independent of affinities. This schedule is computed statically with having additional task runtime information that our scheduler does not require mandatorily. HetEFT only optimizes runtimes, but, due to a usually large correlation between runtime and energy affinity, we compare it to our energy results too.

3. *Heuristic Optimization (OPT-HEURISTIC)*: We use a heuristic optimization method to compute an upper bound for our comparison and as a basis to compute an optimal schedule using a branch and bound approach in future work. We use 5 heuristic starting solutions for both energy and runtime optimization that provide simple, but

meaningful schedules, e. g., by sorting tasks by decreasing runtimes and queueing a task at the resource with minimum finish time. We then use 2 improvement heuristics that: a) try to improve schedules by moving tasks from the worst queue to the best queue in terms of our optimization metric, and b) exchange tasks between best and worst queue to check for possible improvements. An improvement replaces a starting solution. This is repeated until no further improvements are found. The best of the 5 solutions is then used as our schedule.

Both static solutions (*HetEFT, OPT-HEURISTIC*) are run in our benchmarking and energy measurement frameworks to deliver real world results. These measurements include all side-effects that *HetSched* has to face as well.

While *HetSched* is able to balance CPU load dynamically at runtime, simple batch solutions can not do this easily. As almost all of the tasks are parallelized, best results are achieved with only 1 CPU task at a time and, thus, used in our comparison. However, all of our example tasks have a CPU-only and non-parallel part at the beginning of computation, which wastes CPU time in a 1 CPU configuration. While compared approaches can also limit the number of tasks assigned to the CPU, they can, however, not react dynamically lacking the feature of heterogeneous migration. They are thus vulnerable to both CPU overutilization, which also impairs tasks running on accelerators, and CPU underutilization, which leads to poor resource usage.

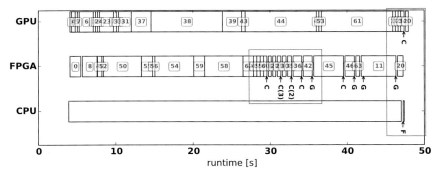

Figure 6.17: 64 mostly CPU or GPU-affine tasks executed on our test environment with HETSCHED PERF scheduling. Labels define task numbers. CPU task numbers are omitted, as several tasks are running concurrently. Migrations are denoted below each bar showing the resource type tasks have been migrated from (C:CPU, N:Nvidia: M:Maxeler) and the number of migrated tasks.

Schedule Analysis   Figure 6.17 shows a typical schedule that depicts the execution of a set of tasks using *HetSched* with the HETSCHED EGY policy. All applications are started at once, approximately after three seconds into the schedule. The time before is used to initialize the benchmark framework and the scheduler. The schedule clearly shows that all resources are well utilized over the runtime of the set of tasks due to migrating tasks to idle resources. We can observe several things in this schedule: There are very few migrations at the beginning of the schedule, because there are enough tasks available with highest affinity to each resource. This changes from around second 30, when tasks optimally suited to the FPGA have been completely computed. Moreover, Figure 6.23 shows the number of enqueued and running tasks for the same schedule. It denotes that from approx. that time only 1 task is executed on the FPGA due to the policy migrating tasks only in case a resource runs idle. In Figure 6.17, tasks are migrated from both CPU or GPU, depending on the suitability of the available tasks. At the end of the schedule, task 20 is first migrated from GPU to FPGA, due to the FPGA being idle and the task has been waiting for execution in the GPU queue. It is then migrated to the idle CPU shortly afterwards, which has higher affinity compared to the FPGA. The CPU runs idle just a short time before the GPU. The task then is again migrated to the most affine resource, i. e., the GPU. Timeslot lengths depend on the task runtime, as yielding is not requested for tasks running on their optimal resource and tasks all have the same priority.

Figure 6.18 shows the scheduler's capability to run tasks in a fair way by interleaving their executions through time-sharing using the HETSCHED PERF_FAIR scheduling policy. We can see that the size of timeslices is highly varying on the accelerator resources. First, this is due to the fact that we are using a cooperative approach and tasks are not forced to match the provided execution granularity with their preemption distance. Less suited tasks or tasks with a large preemption distance may, therefore, use large portions of computation time at once. Second, the average unfairness of tasks on a resource might be differently large, depending on the preemption distance and the suitability of the tasks on the used architecture. After a migration this unfairness is possibly resolved through a larger timeslice. And third, if only one task is left (e. g., task 48 on the FPGA), it will be granted computation time until it finishes or another task arrives.

Through the use of time-sharing with a very small task granularity, we introduce overheads that extend the makespan in favor of responsiveness and fairness for a set of tasks.

Average Turnaround Times   The turnaround time is the interval between the submission of a process and its completion. Figure 6.19 shows that the average turnaround time (ATT) can be decreased by using fairness-based approaches. Because of the fairness provided by time-sharing, long running tasks will also get their share of execution time from the beginning, so that our fairness approaches will never reach a minimal ATT. Despite that and the fact that fairness increases overheads (see Figure 6.22), we still are able to decrease the ATT in relation to compared algorithms and, thus, also increase interactivity of the used system. Generally, the better a scheduling algorithm reduces the makespan, the more likely is a lower ATT. Therefore our HETSCHED PERF and HETSCHED EGY approaches show lower ATT values compared to the simple and yet quite fast GREEDY approaches. Moreover, this leads to the HETSCHED PERF_FAIR algorithm showing better results compared to HETSCHED FAIR algorithm, as HETSCHED PERF_FAIR prefers performance over system-wide fairness.

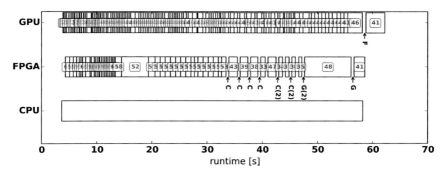

Figure 6.18: Execution of the equivalent sets of tasks as shown in Figure 6.17 with HETSCHED PERF_FAIR scheduling. timeslices were provided with a minimum granularity of 250ms.

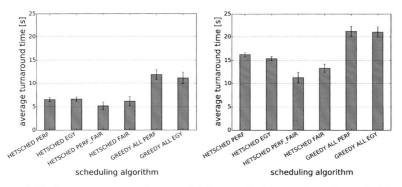

Figure 6.19: Average turnaround times of different scheduling policies for 32 (left-hand graph) and 64 tasks (right-hand graph). Both HETSCHED PERF_FAIR and HETSCHED FAIR algorithms use timeslices of 250ms.

Makespan and Energy Consumption Figure 6.20 depicts the total runtime and energy consumption for a set of 32 tasks, comprising the four different applications, as introduced in Figure 3.1, with varying data sizes. The results clearly show that our schedulers, which utilize heterogeneous migration, outperform all GREEDY approaches in both makespan and total energy consumed.

Measurements showed that subtracting the energy consumption of the idle resources for the computation of affinities, as described in Section 3.4.3, results in an average reduction of energy consumption values for evaluated sets of tasks of 4.8% for the used energy scheduling algorithm. All presented results, therefore, use the definition of Equation 3.10, which computes the affinity by first subtracting the energy consumption of idle resources.

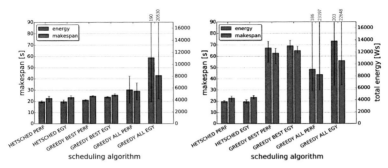

Figure 6.20: Mean makespan and energy consumption of 32 tasks running on CPU, GPU
and FPGA. PERF scheduling algorithms aim at optimizing the makespan,
while EGY algorithms reduce the total energy consumption. In the left-hand
graph, all GREEDY-based algorithms always run only one task on the CPU;
in the right-hand graph the number of tasks assigned to the CPU is limited
to two.

While tasks mapped to GPU and FPGA benefit from the parallelism offered by these
technologies, CPU-mapped tasks utilize the available CPU cores through OpenMP multithreading. Since the CPU does not only execute application tasks but also the operating
system, in particular the scheduler and accelerator drivers, controlling the CPU load becomes a critical issue. In the *HetSched* framework, we maintain a certain CPU load by
limiting the number of tasks running on the CPU in dependence of the current load. While
all GREEDY approaches can also limit the number of tasks assigned to the CPU, they
can, however, not react dynamically lacking the feature of heterogeneous migration. The
GREEDY ALL and GREEDY BEST approaches are thus vulnerable to both CPU overutilization, which also impairs tasks running on accelerators, and CPU underutilization, which
leads to poor resource usage. The results shown in the left-hand side of Figure 6.20 compare *HetSched* with GREEDY algorithms, when only one task is assigned to the CPU. The
OpenMP parallelization of the CPU tasks make this a rather ideal case for the GREEDY
scheduler, which is only slightly worse than HETSCHED. There are two drawbacks the
GREEDY ALL and GREEDY BEST approaches suffer from in this scenario. First, all
tasks have a certain non-parallel initialization phase that is executed on CPU before they
benefit from OpenMP parallelization. Because of that, assigning only a single task to the
CPU in this phase leads to underutilization of the CPU. The second drawback is that in
case of tasks being used on a suboptimal resource, this decision is not reversible, so that
such tasks may extend the schedule at the end of executing the set of tasks.

The right-hand side of Figure 6.20 presents the results when the GREEDY approaches
allow for two tasks on the CPU. While this reduces underutilization in the initialization
phase of the tasks, it leads to overutilization otherwise. Two tasks with an OpenMP
parallelization, each already utilizing all CPU cores by itself, leads to overutilization of

the CPU, which harms the performance on non-CPU tasks significantly. Moreover, once assigned tasks may not be migrated any more, which extends the length of the schedule with only CPU tasks remaining in the system at the end of executing the set of tasks. This underlines the benefit of heterogeneous migration and the need for load restrictions on the CPU. Increasing the number of tasks on the CPU even further strongly hurts the GREEDY approaches in utilization while it does not harm the *HetSched* scheduler much.

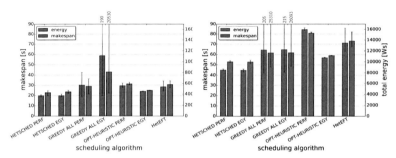

Figure 6.21: Mean makespan and energy consumption over 32 (left-hand graph) and 64 tasks (right-hand graph) running on CPU, GPU and FPGA. PERF scheduling algorithms aim at optimizing the makespan, while EGY algorithms reduce the total energy consumption.

Figure 6.21 depicts the total runtime and energy consumption of 32 and 64 tasks comprising the four different example applications with varying data sizes and being executed with our four evaluated scheduling policies. Through dynamic and affinity-based decisions and the flexibility to migrate running tasks between resources, the scheduler is able to reach a high performance and utilization that outperforms the comparison algorithms. These results are achieved by taking scheduling decisions based on affinities only, i.e., using less information than *HetEFT* and *OPT-HEURISTIC* comparison algorithms. While *OPT-HEURISTIC EGY* achieves quite good results, the effort to achieve this results requires not only knowing energy consumptions, but precomputing a complete schedule beforehand. Dynamic reactions on newly arriving task are limited, as already running tasks may not be rescheduled, and also require to recompute the complete remaining schedule. With *GREEDY ALL*, the problems mentioned above remain. Using a static set of tasks for evaluation, best suited tasks are computed first, i.e., the longer a sets of tasks runs, the worse the tasks fit a certain resource. Thus, it may happen, which the very last tasks have a very low affinity, sometimes leading to very long running schedules, as denoted by the min/max error bars. The same is true for our scheduler, but through checkpointing and task migration we are able to react as soon as a better suited resource gets idle again. *HetSched*, therefore, is a very dynamic and flexible approach that performs decisions including the current state of all involved system components and, thus, is able to not only use a very broad decision base, but is especially able to revert previous decisions based on changing system states. Both policies may be improved by including additional information that our scheduler is already able to acquire. Using collected data on task runtimes and energy consumptions, we may consider remaining runtimes for scheduling or migration decisions and also include energy consumptions of idling resources. However, while our implementation allows to exploit these runtime values, it is not within the main scope of this evaluation.

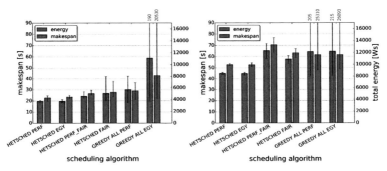

Figure 6.22: Mean makespan and energy consumption over 32 tasks (left-hand graph) and 64 tasks (right-hand graph) running on CPU, GPU and FPGA using four different *HetSched* scheduling policies.

Figure 6.22 additionally compared the makespan and total energy consumption of our fairness-based scheduling policies. As discussed before, fairness is a tradeoff between introduced overheads and increasing the interactivity while decreasing the average turnaround time. Therefore, our fairness-based approaches increase the runtime compared to the HETSCHED PERF algorithm, but still outperform the GREEDY approaches in both makespan and energy consumption.

Utilization and Load Balancing Figure 6.23 shows how load balancing keeps utilization of resources high and CPU load in an acceptable range. Initially, all resources are provided with tasks according to the task affinities. As computation proceeds, tasks are moved between run queues to balance loads (Figure 6.23 (c)). If a resource runs idle, the scheduler, if possible, immediately migrates a suitable task to the idle resource. Waiting tasks can be migrated immediately, while running tasks are migrated after a preemption point is reached. All applications are started at once, approximately after three seconds. Therefore, the CPU starts with a high number of tasks due to some sequential CPU-only parts of the applications at the beginning of their execution. The utilization of the CPU is rather low at this stage of the execution ((e)), so that the scheduler allows a larger

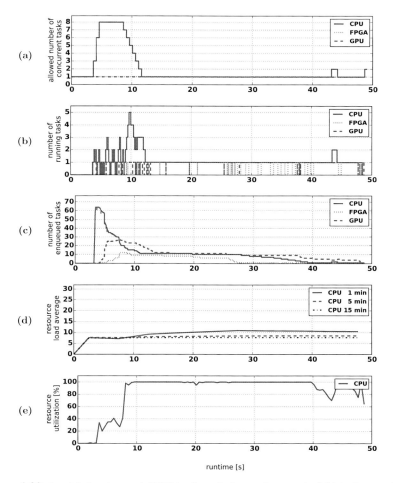

Figure 6.23: Load balancing and CPU load analysis running a set of 64 tasks running with HETSCHED PERF scheduling. The number of concurrently running tasks (b) adapts to the number of allowed concurrent tasks (a) based on CPU load and utilization, independent from the number of enqueued tasks (c). The utilization is kept high (e), while the average load is kept in a reasonable range ((d), roughly 1.5 times the number of CPU cores (here: 8) in maximum).

number of tasks to run concurrently ((a)). While up to five tasks are actually executed concurrently on the CPU at the beginning ((b)), their OpenMP parallelized parts of the execution allow only one CPU task to be executed after about 12 seconds. This is regulated automatically by the load monitoring and load balancing components of *HetSched*. As soon as tasks are available for the GPU and the FPGA, too, they are enqueued or migrated accordingly. The effectivity of load balancing between CPU and accelerators can be seen in Figure 6.23 (d). It shows the load average of the CPU to not exceed roughly a factor 1.5 of the number of available cores. Therefore, it avoids overutilization of the CPU, while keeping the general utilization of the CPU high (Figure 6.23 (e)).

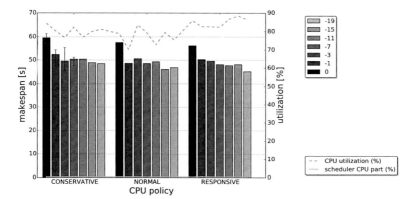

Figure 6.24: Makespan of 64 tasks using the PERF policy under the use of different CPU load restriction metrics and a variety of priorities (-19 to 0) used for the delegate threads of GPU and FPGA tasks. Modifying these parameters leads to significant differences in makespans. The scheduler fraction of the CPU utilization is insignificantly low ($< 0.5\%$).

We additionally implemented different strategies to define the number of tasks that are allowed to run on the CPU concurrently. Figure 6.24 shows three strategies (CONSERVATIVE, NORMAL, RESPONSIVE) to adjust this number based on the utilization and the load average of the CPU for 64 tasks. Moreover, we tested different priority boosts for the delegate threads of non-CPU tasks to avoid waiting times that lead to idle times on accelerators. We set priorities to different levels, from very high priority (nice level -19) to standard priority (nice level 0). We can see a slight trend to lower makespan times if adapting the number of concurrently run CPU tasks more frequently (RESPONSIVE) rather than less frequently (CONSERVATIVE) by blocking and unblocking tasks in the CPU queue. Furthermore, adapting the priorities as described leads to large performance improvements of more than 20%, which underlines the importance of considering the load of the CPU in heterogeneous scheduling. The larger the CPU load, the less time is provided to non-CPU tasks to perform data transfers, which decreases overall performance. For our scheduler analysis shown above we set the priority of non-CPU delegate threads to -15 to avoid bottlenecks. In addition, we set the scheduler threads itself, which are also user-space threads, to -20, i. e., the highest priority available to user-space programs.

In addition, the graph shows the fraction of the total CPU utilization that is added by the scheduler itself, i. e., the percentage of the CPU time used in by all CPU tasks in the system. Values stay constantly below 0.5% and are, therefore, negligible.

6.4 Comparison of Presented Scheduling Frameworks

Section 6.3.1 discusses major differences between the kernel-space and user-space versions of our scheduling framework. We point out, which the user-space approach provides significant improvements both conceptually and in the actual implementation of the framework and its scheduling algorithms. Table 6.2 provides a summary of major differences between the two scheduler implementations.

6.5 Related Work

Many related works have already been discussed in previous chapters. Runtime systems for scheduling tasks to heterogeneous resources, without preemption and migration, have been studied in many efforts. StarPU [18] and DAGuE [32] are well-known frameworks relying on Directed Acyclic Graphs (DAGs) to compute a schedule and dynamically execute tasks on CPU and GPU resources for real-time environments. Their major aim is to resolve task-dependencies at runtime, which defines a different problem. In our approach, tasks can only be scheduled, when all dependencies have already been resolved. StarPU[18] is based on an extension of the GPU driver to automatically request application codelets, fetch the needed data and execute the codelet on a hardware selected by different scheduling policies. Driver extensions have to be provided for each supported resource type in StarPU, while our approaches exclusively rely on available vendor-provided drivers and APIs, so that arbitrary architectures can be used. DAGuE[32] implements a runtime system that schedules tasks to compute nodes and enables work-steeling between cores of the same node at runtime. To avoid data transfer overheads the application developer has to specify which architecture (GPU or CPU) shall be used for certain task classes. Dependencies are denoted by data flows between kernels and are resolved by the runtime. Both approaches have in common, which substantial code changes may be necessary to exploit their full potential. While our programming pattern also requires changes to the applications, we restructure the code toward our scheduler interface instead of using an extensive programming model. We consider our approach to be less invasive compared to these approaches.

The Elastic Computing Framework [175] defines so-called elastic functions that are provided as a library of implementations for specific computations. These functions provide an abstract work metric to determine the expected runtime on a resource for a set of input

Property	Kernel-space Scheduler	User-space Scheduler
operating system integration	integrated with the Linux kernel, stand-alone scheduler	not integrated, requires user-space scheduler/CFS cooperation
dependency on Linux kernel	high	low
CPU load determination	exact, up-to-date	estimated based on values from kernel interface (proc filesystem): CPU utilization, load average
portability	medium	high
extendability	costly	simple
scheduling policies	increase performance while aiming at fairness	reduce energy consumption, increase performance, fair scheduling, increase performance while aiming at fairness
load balancing	basic	differentiated
complexity (n tasks in queue)	enqueue: $O(log\ n)$ dequeue: $O(1)$ choose task to migrate: $O(n)$ task dispatch: $O(1)$	enqueue: $O(log\ n)$ dequeue: $O(1)$ choose task to migrate: $O(1)$ task dispatch: $O(1)$
scheduler interface	simple	very simple
interface implementation	C++	C
task-scheduler communication	tasks use system calls to communicate with scheduler	direct communication over exchangeable channels
affinity measurements	runtimes, offline, by hand	runtimes and energy consumptions, offline, automated

Table 6.2: Comparison of user-space and kernel-space schedulers.

parameters and are fed to an offline planning tool determining an optimized execution order for a specific target system.

Recent publications show a trend to move from custom task models to standard OpenCL concepts. Several works have, for example, extended OpenCL with a task scheduler that dynamically dispatches OpenCL tasks to available CPU and GPU resources to increase system performance [174, 155, 161]. Wang et al. [173] use a set of training data and machine learning (ML) to build a machine-specific model that predicts whether it is worth running a data parallel program on the GPU by using a generated OpenCL version of the program, or running an OpenMP version on the CPU. Executed kernels require an extraction of code features at compile time and runtime parameters that are fed to the ML-model to decide on the used resource. Their ML-model is independent of the used applications, but requires an evaluation of runtime parameters with used features at runtime and limits the approach to OpenCL. While the limitation of above approaches to CPUs and GPUs might be removed with FPGAs supporting OpenCL in the near future, a run-to-completion model is followed, which limits leveraging the full power of the targeted systems.

Some work has been provided on operating system (OS) integration of GPUs [94, 156, 139] and FPGAs [8]. Further approaches for scheduling in heterogeneous systems have been discussed, e. g., [57, 22, 155, 136].

In comparison to the approaches discussed above, we can summarize differences in three major points: 1. Our approach can be used with arbitrary resource types, as long as corresponding resources may be used from C/C++/Fortran applications. 2. None of the approaches allows for heterogeneous task migration between arbitrary architectures, which is possible in our approach, as long as a hardware-independent checkpoint data may be defined in host memory. 3. By reacting dynamically to changing situations like newly arriving tasks and the possibility to migrate tasks between resources, we provide a higher flexibility compared to approaches that compute schedules ahead. We, therefore, consider our approach to be unique in its kind and to provide a new way of utilizing heterogeneous resources efficiently.

6.6 Chapter Conclusion

This thesis discusses concepts for task scheduling on heterogeneous systems. We presented two scheduling frameworks in this chapter that make use of the ideas introduced in previous chapters. To this end, we provide an extension of the Linux Completely Fair Scheduler (CFS) in kernel space and *HetSched*, a user-space scheduling framework. Both approaches enable task migration between heterogeneous resources through tasks cooperatively yielding resources at preemption points that are provided by the applications.

We first presented an extendable approach to integrate the scheduling of heterogeneous accelerators into the Linux kernel. Along with the way CPU scheduling is performed, we consider the operating system as inherently suited for the management of computing resources and scheduling tasks for execution on these. We provide awareness of installed accelerators, task scheduling with time-sharing, and load balancing for fair task execution as an extension to the CFS. Thus, our approach is in line with the goal of the CFS to provide a fair treatment of available tasks and to increase system interactivity. Applications submit delegate threads that are derived from a superclass, which offers the interface for an execution with the scheduler. The superclass provides wrapper functions to system calls enabling a task to *allocate* a computing resource and to *re-request* further use of a resource from user space. In addition, a *free* system call allows the task to yield a resource at a preemption point or finish execution on the resource. Results show that our approach effectively uses the heterogeneity of a CPU/GPU system by decreasing the makespan as well as the average turnaround time of an executed set of tasks.

Besides the CFS extension, we presented a user-space scheduler that is a completely new framework and enhances the kernel-space scheduler in several points. The user-space scheduler is vastly independent from the kernel space. It, therefore, improves its portability among different Unix derivates and makes is mostly independent from Linux kernel updates. Currently dependencies are only given through the use of the *proc filesystem*, which provides a very stable interface and is replaceable on other Unix derivates without major effort, e.g., by using the *sysctl* utility in Unix derivates based on the BSD (Berkeley Software Distribution). We enable energy-related scheduling through the use of a energy measurement library and add several new scheduling policies for throughput, energy efficiency, and fair scheduling. Furthermore, we show that our framework is feasible for the use of CPUs, GPUs, and additionally, FPGAs. While the general concepts of task management are similar to the CFS extension, our user-space implementation narrows the application interface. For that purpose, we use scheduling policy-dependent affinities of tasks to resource types that are based on offline benchmarks and calculated by the scheduler at runtime. We were not only able to validate the results shown by our CSF extension in user space, but additionally point out that our solution has more comprehensive benefits. Our approach allows to reduce the energy consumption of an executed set of tasks through the effective use of available resources. Moreover, we showed the usability of task migration through an overhead analysis and highlighted the importance of restricting the CPU load within heterogeneous scheduling to avoid idle times on accelerators. Our scheduler includes these results in scheduling and load balancing decisions to improve on scheduling objectives.

Our discussed scheduling approaches are the only available solutions that provide complete scheduling frameworks for heterogeneous task execution with migration support. Related work instead focuses on scheduling for real-time tasks and resolving task dependencies at runtime. These approaches are restricted to run-to-completion, i.e., providing a resource to a task until the task completed its execution on the resource. We were able to show that our approaches are beneficial in different aspects, especially in reducing the makespan and energy consumption of an executed set of tasks, but also in increasing fairness and interactivity. These improvement are reached through automatic scheduling and load balancing that provides a holistic view on the system, its resources, and the executed tasks.

Nevertheless, our approaches leave some room for further improvements. We have seen that energy-based scheduling is excelled by performance-oriented scheduling in terms of energy consumption. While there is a strong correlation between energy and performance, we believe that energy consumption may be additionally reduced by further examining the fraction of idle power consumptions in the different scheduling approaches or using a planning system. Furthermore, automation may be improved by performing online affinity measurements while executing a set of tasks and adding corresponding affinity models. In the long run, a reembedding of the user-space approaches on energy and performance scheduling into the kernel space are of interest, as we consider the operating system generally to be the most valid and best suited location to perform scheduling.

CHAPTER 7

Function Level Acceleration

To be able to apply the programming pattern presented in Chapter 4 for acceleration of an application, two preconditions need to be met. First, we need to have access to the source code of the application, and second, accelerated implementations of a part of the application need to be available. However, using third-party or legacy applications for a certain purpose is a common scenario. To achieve an acceleration of such an application to harness it for heterogeneous scheduling, one has to provide additional task implementations. In case only a binary application is available, using binary translation methods is a theoretically available possibility to adapt an application for accelerator usage. However, this is very complex, if possible in the first place.

In this chapter we present a novel approach to make the performance of heterogeneous computing resources transparently available without requiring any programming from the user's side. The approach uses a technique called *shared library interposing*. Shared library interposing provides a mechanism that allows to modify existing applications without requiring access to the original source code, by intercepting and replacing calls to shared library functions with alternative functions. We first introduce the general idea of function level acceleration and motivate the use of shared library interposing for application acceleration in a heterogeneous execution environment. We then discuss different approaches to shared library interposing before introducing a framework for transparent acceleration that makes use of accelerator-specific library implementations. We discuss a case study, which allows us to evaluate the benefits and the overheads of our approach with the BLAS library for linear algebra. Finally, a comparison of our work to other approaches for transparent acceleration and recent related work in the field is provided.

7.1 Function Execution Model

In our task model defined in Section 3.3, we specify tasks to be executed in our heterogeneous scenario to be threads. Therein, a schedulable thread is an arbitrary sequence of commands with a fixed entry and exit point to be executed by the operating system sched-uler. In this chapter, we consider function level acceleration on heterogeneous resources based on the use of shared libraries. A library function has a well defined interface as an entry point and is exited after its execution is completed. A library user at most times does not know the source code behind a provided function implementation, but expects a cer-tain functionality. Therefore, we may not have the possibility to preempt library functions with respect to our programming pattern and face a run-to-completion paradigm.

To achieve acceleration, we may leverage the fact of libraries using a known interface to accelerate applications. By manipulating application binaries, we may redirect library function calls to accelerator-specific versions without actually knowing the source code implementation of the functions. This even enables us to accelerate proprietary applications we otherwise have no access to. In addition, accelerated functions may generally be used according to our task model defined in Section 3.3 by being wrapped in a schedulable thread, even if preemption is not possible. However, we need to make sure that exchanging a library call does not have unintended side-effects on the original application, if the provided functionality is not equivalent.

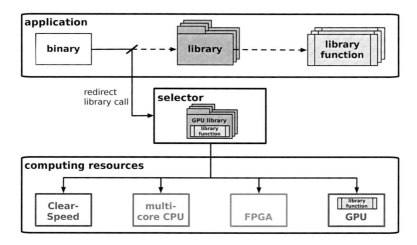

Figure 7.1: General scenario: library functions are transparently mapped to different re-source types in a heterogeneous system.

Figure 7.1 shows the general scenario of a heterogeneous system that we are targeting in our approach. Applications provided as executable binaries internally use one or several shared libraries that provide a set of functions used by the application. We aim at redirecting these library calls to available hardware accelerators by replacing the executed function by an accelerator-specific version. A selector component chooses suitable replacing library functions based on given inputs, available libraries, and resource types, and dynamically replaces the original library call by them.

For leveraging transparent acceleration through accelerator libraries, we exploit the fact that many scientific codes make extensive use of highly optimized libraries for computationally intensive operations. Examples of frequently used libraries are the BLAS library for linear algebra [103], the GNU scientific library GSL for numerical calculations [70], or the Vector Signal Processing Library VSIPL for embedded signal processing platforms [90]. These numeric libraries are typically installed as shared libraries, which are dynamically loaded by the applications at runtime. Therefore, one approach for using a particular hardware accelerator without the need to recompile the application is to replace the shared library with a compatible library, which implements the same interface, but executes the code on the hardware accelerator.

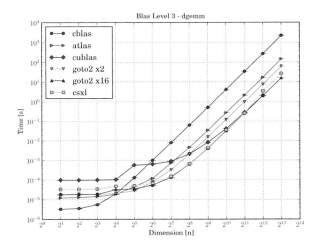

Figure 7.2: Runtimes of the DGEMM function using different BLAS implementations and resource types on input matrices of dimension n.

To justify the approach, we have measured the runtimes of commonly used BLAS functions on different resource types of our benchmark system (cf. Section 7.4). DGEMM is one of the most frequently used BLAS functions. DGEMM performs one of the matrix-matrix operations $C := \alpha A \times B + \beta C$. An unoptimized version of DGEMM has a computational complexity of $O(n^3)$ for multiplying two $n \times n$ matrices, but only requires data transfers of communication complexity $O(n^2)$. Therefore, it can be considered one of the promising applications to be executed on accelerators. Figure 7.2 shows the results as a function of the matrix dimension n (problem size) for different library implementations. The runtime measurements include the overhead of copying data to the accelerator and back. We can observe that the runtimes differ significantly between different implementations and resource types. The problem sizes are crucial for the decision on which BLAS library is most efficient for a library call. For very small n, the unaccelerated single-core CBLAS CPU BLAS library [27] is fastest. From input size 2^4 it is the goto2 library (using 2 CPU cores) and with increasing n, the CSXL library [41] for the ClearSpeed architecture and the goto2 CPU library [69] (running on 16 cores) are the fastest implementations. The CUBLAS library [131] for NVIDIA GPUs is inefficient for a small value of n, performs better on a larger n, and is best, along with the goto2 library, at $n = 2^{12}$. This is the largest input size fitting into the GPU's device memory. The Automatically Tuned Linear Algebra Software (ATLAS) [176] is a self-optimizing CPU BLAS library. Its DGEMM implementation is only competitive to the fastest alternatives at a size of $n = 2^4$.

These observations motivate our approach: Depending on function and input data sizes we may choose to delegate the call to the optimal resource type.

7.2 Approaches to Shared Library Interposing

Applications used for scientific computing are often third-party and are therefore usually not utilizing multi-accelerator systems. Accelerator libraries for specific computationally intensive operations may be used to alter the applications functionality and to make use of available computing resources. This is only unproblematic as long as access to the original source code is available. In many situations, this is not the case, i. e., only the binaries are accessible. Dynamically linking libraries to an application is an alternative that allows to replace existing libraries with newer or altered libraries.

Dynamic linking allows to postpone most of the linking process to the runtime of an application. This has several benefits for software development: dynamically linked shared libraries are easier to be created and updated than static libraries. Moreover, dynamic linking allows code sharing among different programs, which saves disk space. One disadvantage of dynamic linking is that the executables depend on the separately stored libraries in order to work properly. If the library is moved, renamed or deleted, or if an incompatible version of the library is copied to a place searched first, the executable would fail to run.

While dynamic linking only allows to replace existing libraries, shared library interposing does not need to replace the library system-wide and, thus, only effects the interposed application. It simply redirects the calls to a standard library to calls to a customized library. This technique allows easy and transparent parallelization by replacing known libraries by substitute libraries that are optimized for certain accelerators. That way the domain-specific developer is kept from the need of deep accelerator knowledge.

A precondition for this technique is the use of a standardized library, which implements functions worth parallelizing. The library has to have a specific and well known interface to allow a replacement for certain functions. Providing a library for accelerating applications on multiple resource types, provides the possibility, but also the need, to dynamically choose the best possible accelerator for a certain function call depending on known runtime behavior and accelerator utilization. The BLAS library can be named as an example, which fulfills these requirements and is available for several different resource types. We use the BLAS library for evaluating our approaches shown in this chapter. BLAS functions are widely used in complex mathematical applications and the interface is widely standardized. In Linux systems, the *dlopen()* system call [58] implements the interface to the dynamic linking loader. By either getting passed a library name or a path to a library, *dlopen()* loads a shared library and returns a handle to it. There are two general ways of how the filename is handled. If an absolute path is given (begins with "/"), *dlopen()* refers to exactly that path and returns an error, if the shared library is not found. If no absolute path to a library name is given, the requested library is searched at the search path specified in the LD_LIBRARY_PATH environment variable. If the library cannot be found there, the system's default library folders are searched (/lib, /lib64, etc.). The handle returned by *dlopen()* can subsequently be used to load a symbol from the library into memory. This is done by *dlsym()*, which uses the handle and a symbol name to return the address of the memory location to which the symbol is loaded. A counter is maintained, counting the library handles to unload the library only if the last handle was closed.

Generally these methods offer two ways of modifying executables with the intended purpose of exchanging a shared library call: Either we modify the binaries of the application directly or we intercept and redirect the calls to shared libraries by manipulating the dynamic linker. Replacing a library call of a compiled and linked executable is only possible if the call refers to a shared library. If libraries are statically linked, the complete external functions are copied from the library into the final executable and, thus, are not easily replaceable.

In the remainder of this section, we introduce and evaluate the following approaches that allow to substitute specific shared library calls within binaries:

1. customizing the behavior of the default dynamic linker with environment variables,
2. using a different, customized dynamic linker,
3. statically patching application binaries to use different library calls, and
4. dynamically modifying the code of applications after they have been loaded to memory.

7.2.1 Dynamic Linker Configuration

The simplest method to intercept library calls in GNU/Linux systems is to point the LD_PRELOAD environment variable to a list of shared libraries substituting libraries used as standard shared libraries. LD_PRELOAD affects the runtime linker and defines one or several shared libraries that are loaded and searched for matching symbols first and, thus, overload the original functions. This capability allows for selectively replacing symbols to be favored over the regular symbols resolved with *dlsym()*.

This method can be used to exchange a standard library with an accelerator-specific parallel library. The parameters, passed to the called shared library function, have to be adapted to the interface of the replacing library, as discussed later. To avoid the interception of library calls in every application the LD_PRELOAD environment variable is typically not defined globally, but is selectively set in the environment of the target application only, e. g., using a wrapper shell-script.

The main advantage of the LD_PRELOAD method is that it is very convenient to use, as it is supported by the standard dynamic linker of the operating system and no dependencies to other tools are introduced. However, problems may arise when the process environment is not completely controlled by the user, for example, if the application itself configures environment variables affecting the linker.

7.2.2 Exchanging the Dynamic Linker

Another approach to intercept the library calls is to redirect them using a different dynamic linker. The ELF binary format, which today is used on most Unix-derived systems, explicitly supports to specify, which dynamic linker is to be used to resolve dynamic linking requests. To this end, the PT_INTERP ELF header entry points to the executable of the dynamic linker. On Linux systems this field generally points to the default dynamic loader (/lib/ld-linux.so.2).

We can use this custom dynamic linker mechanism for our purpose of shared library interposing by modifying this header to point to our own, custom dynamic linker. If the source code of the program is available, we can pass the option *–Wl –dynamic-linker=/path/to/our/linker* to the GNU linker *ld* when linking the final executable. Without access to the source code, we can use the *readelf* tool to locate the PT_INTERP header and replace the linker name in the application's binary. The drawback of this method is that it requires to patch the application's binary, which is not always desirable. Moreover, implementing a custom dynamic linker that can act as a full replacement for the standard dynamic linker is a non-trivial endeavor, requiring substantial knowledge about binary formats and linking.

An application of this technique is described in the work of Reiser [138] on *rtldi*, which is an alternative dynamic loader that enables each application to use its own runtime environment with different library search paths.

7.2.3 Static Binary Infection

The previously introduced methods use different ways of intercepting and subsequently delegating library calls of existing applications. An alternative approach is to modify the binary itself, thus, not only replacing the dynamic loader, but replacing the library call itself within the binary.

The techniques required for this binary modification strongly depend on the used operating system and binary format. One particular approach that can be used for this purpose is named *ELF PLT infection* and is applicable to binaries and shared libraries in the ELF object format, which is used, for example, by Linux. ELF shared libraries use position independent code and can thus be loaded at runtime to any address without modification. Dynamic linking is done by the ELF linker using essentially two process-specific tables, the Procedure Link Table (PLT) and the Global Offset Table (GOT). The GOT stores the static absolute offsets of the position independent symbols, such as functions and global variables, in the position independent shared library. When calling a function in the shared library, the program is not calling the addresses specified in the GOT directly, but calls a matching symbol in the PLT, providing the address of the corresponding GOT entry. This level of indirection allows to postpone linking to runtime and to use the same memory image for a shared library from several applications.

To delegate a call to a different shared library function, the PLT entry of a called symbol can be modified to point to the address of the replacing shared library function directly. By modifying the program entry point in the application binary, it is possible to wrap the actual application execution with code, which loads the needed library and maps it to the address space of the application. Cesare [36] presents a detailed discussion of how PLT infection can be used to redirect library calls.

ELF PLT infection is a powerful method of implementing library interposing. As no environment variable is used, the interposing process is completely hidden from the application and does not influence other processes. However, controlling static instrumentation of ELF binaries at this low level is error prone and requires in-depth knowledge about the binary format and the interceptable calls to avoid possible damage. This makes ELF infection hard to use for software engineers. An alternative to this static binary modification approach is to alter the loaded binary image of the application at runtime. This can be achieved, for example, with the powerful *Pin* tool for binary analysis and binary instrumentation, which will be discussed in the next subsection.

7.2.4 Binary Instrumentation with Pin

Pin [110] is a binary instrumentation tool. It provides a framework for writing customized program analysis tools (*Pintools*). Pin can be thought of as a compiler that recompiles executables with new code segments inserted to the binaries to do fine-grained analysis. Pintools are plugins modifying the code generation within Pin. Instrumentation within Pin is composed of a mechanism to decide, which code to insert at which point (*instrumentation*) and the *analysis* code itself.

Dynamic instrumentation in Pin can be done in two ways: using the Just-In-Time (JIT)- or the Probe-Mode. The Probe-Mode replaces instructions in the original program with so called trampolines, which branch to instrumentation code. Thus, the application can be executed natively and no slow down arises. This method can be used to exchange methods or calls to shared libraries. The signature of the replacing function must match the original function. JIT uses a Just-in-Time compiler to dynamically insert instrumentation code into the application binary at compile time. JIT provides access to low-level functions and enables modifications at the assembler level, however, executing applications in JIT mode is about one order of magnitude slower as in probe mode. While this execution overhead excludes JIT mode from being used for library interposing, JIT mode has still proven to be very useful for analyzing applications.

The advantage of using Pin for the purpose of library interposing is its modular design and the availability of high-level functions for binary analysis and modifications. This allows to conveniently perform binary instrumentation at runtime without requiring low-level knowledge on dynamic linking, binary formats, or calling conventions. A major drawback in the Pin implementation at the time of publicizing our work on this topic [2] was that Pintools were not allowed to link against libpthread or use pthread functions, limiting the code inserted to the binary to single-threaded code.

7.2.5 Summary

Summarizing the approaches, all methods come with certain drawbacks of different importance. With the goal of making library interposing available to many developers, complexity has to be kept low and the approach has to work for most possible use cases. This is currently only given using LD_PRELOAD. Pin would be a reasonable alternative, but suffered from the incompatibility with libpthread. Table 7.1 gives an overview of the different approaches and their characteristics.

	Using dynamic linker	Exchanging the linker	ELF infection	Pin
Static/dynamic	dynamic	dynamic	static	dynamic
Environment variable	yes	no	no	no
Binary modified	no	yes	yes	yes
Complexity	low	medium	high	medium

Table 7.1: Library-interposing approaches

7.3 Library-Interposing Framework for Transparent Application Acceleration

In this section, we describe our *Library Interposing Framework for Transparent Application Acceleration* (*liftracc*), which is based on shared library interposing. We introduce a plugin-based library approach that separates the concerns of implementing accelerator-specific functions from the mechanism of library interposing and from the policy for selecting a particular function implementation at runtime. As a case study, we have chosen the widely used BLAS library for linear algebra, for which optimized implementations for CPUs and hardware accelerators exist.

7.3.1 Accelerating BLAS Libraries

The original specification of the BLAS library was published in 1979 [103] and was made available as an open-source Fortran implementation through the Netlib software bibliography for scientific computations [128]. The BLAS library specification has been extended several times and is still being maintained nowadays. A number of versions of the BLAS library have been released. The most well-known ones are CBLAS (Appendix B of [27]), Intel Math Kernel Library (MKL) [47], AMD Core Math Library (ACML) [83], Automatically Tuned Linear Algebra Software (ATLAS) [176], and GotoBlas [69]. Additionally, there exist implementations for specific hardware accelerators, such as CUBLAS [131] for GPUs. All of these implementations date back to the original Netlib BLAS implementation. While the function names and their functionality of the library implementations are basically the same, there exist certain variations between different implementations. Variations are, e. g., in parameter types or argument order for specific functions that lead to incompatibilities when simply exchanging the library. In addition, some BLAS libraries only offer a subset of the original BLAS interface, which is particularly the case for accelerator-specific BLAS libraries.

By tracing the calls to BLAS functions of an application at runtime, we can understand acceleration potentials by redirecting BLAS calls to optimized libraries. Functions that might be accelerated by specific BLAS libraries can be searched by their names. The parameters of these functions are not easily readable from the binary, hence, we need additional information about the interfaces expected by the application. We choose CBLAS as the fallback implementation for all BLAS functions that are not implemented in the library for a particular hardware accelerator. CBLAS is the the most widely used complete reference implementation of the original Netlib specification and is freely available. As many BLAS libraries (e. g., MATLAB, CSXL, CUBLAS) use the MKL BLAS library as reference implementation, we also support the MKL BLAS interface in addition to the CBLAS interface to be intercepted in our framework.

7.3.2 Plugins for Shared Library Interposing

Using one of the shared-library-interposing approaches for transparent acceleration requires to adapt the technique to the needs of a heterogeneous system. A corresponding shared-library-interposing solution needs to satisfy the following requirements: It

- initializes each accelerator automatically,
- performs automatic name translation to matching functions,
- adjusts the original call to the library-specific demands, and
- chooses the best possible hardware accelerator for a specific call.

Figure 7.3 gives an overview of our framework implementing these requirements. To support a broad range of available accelerators, we have implemented a plugin-based wrapper library, which allows us to insert additional support for supplemental hardware easily. It delegates the applications library calls to the hardware accelerators. In the current implementation, we deploy the method introduced in section 7.2.1 for library interposing, which uses the LD_PRELOAD mechanism to inject shared libraries. This method provides suf-

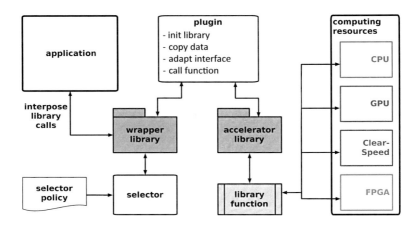

Figure 7.3: Overview of our library-interposing framework called *liftracc* that uses a wrapper library to redirect intercepted library calls to performance efficient accelerator libraries.

ficient performance and flexibility for our current use case. The plugins implement the gateway from the wrapper library to the accelerator-specific libraries. As each supported accelerator needs to be initialized in a different way, this is done by the specific plugin.

Listing 7.1: Example plugin for DGEMM CUBLAS function call (pseudocode).

```
void dynblas_plugin_dgemm(order,transa,transb,alpha,*a,*b,beta,*c)
{
    //match matrix transpose requirements of CUBLAS function
    ta = check_transpose(transa);
    tb = check_transpose(transb);

    //create data pointers and transfer data
    create_device_pointers(dev_a, dev_b, dev_c);
    cublasAlloc(dev_a, dev_b, dev_c);
    cublasSetMatrix(dev_a, dev_b, dev_c);

    //call DGEMM of CUBLAS library
    cublasDgemm(ta,tb,alpha,dev_a,dev_b,beta,dev_c);

    //copy back results
    cublasGetMatrix(dev_c, c); //results are in c
    cublasFree(dev_a, dev_b, dev_c);
}
```

Listing 7.1 shows an example plugin for the DGEMM function that calls the DGEMM version of the CUBLAS library. The original library function call does not include any data transfer, as it computes on data located in main memory. Because of that, the plugin also needs to perform additionally required data transfers, depending on the used library. Listing 7.1 shows according CUDA calls surrounding the actual DGEMM function call. Furthermore, the calls to the library are adjusted to the accelerator-specific library call by modifying the function name and the parameters. In the example plugin, the CUBLAS library expects additional parameters ta and tb that denote whether the provided matrices are transposed or not. Thus, the plugin needs to set these values before calling the library. The plugin finally performs the actual library call and returns the results calculated by the accelerator libraries. The wrapper library as well as the plugin stubs are generated automatically, as described in subsequent sections. We provide plugins for CUBLAS and ClearSpeeds CSXL, which both are based on MKL. Plugins for the ATLAS library as well as a GotoBlas2 (GotoBlas version 2, short goto2) library are additionally implemented, which spreads the BLAS computation to several CPU cores in an SMP machine using OpenMP.

Additionally, the wrapper library may use different selector policies to decide, which plugin is best used for a specific call as described next.

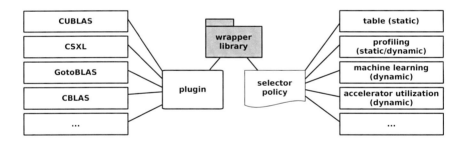

Figure 7.4: Library-interposing framework using a wrapper library for intelligent dynamic linking of accelerator libraries. Each accelerator library is connected via a plugin. A selector policy uses different decision mechanisms to map an intercepted library call to a certain resource type.

7.3.3 Selector Policy

The selector policy is the component deciding which plugin an incoming library call is delegated to. We call it selector policy rather than scheduling policy, as is only decides where to execute an interposed function. It neither defines an order of execution nor a

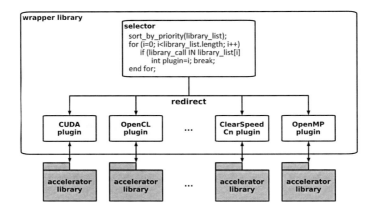

Figure 7.5: Each accelerator-specific library replacement of the original library needs to be provided a plugin that matches intercepted library calls to the according accelerator library. The selector searches for the best suited and available library and redirects the function call to the according plugin. Here, the selector policy uses library-specific priorities and matches the calling function to the highest prioritized library with an available function implementation.

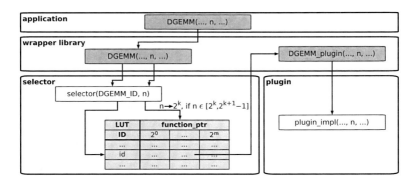

Figure 7.6: Execution flow of an intercepted library call to the DGEMM BLAS library function. The wrapper library extracts required input information from the original library call and feeds it to the selector policy. The policy here is represented by a preconfigured look-up-table (LUT) containing function pointers to accelerator functions based on a mapping of data input sizes to a matching table entry.

duration of how long a task may use a resource. Thus, it also does not perform preemption or migration on the task. These policies rely on different function- and system-specific information as depicted in Figure 7.4. Static information, like performance data, collected during profiling of BLAS functions or dynamic information, such as the utilization of accelerators or machine learned performance affinities could be used. Currently, we have implemented two policies *Library priority* and *Lookup table*, both relying on static offline-measured information.

The *Library priority* approach as shown in Figure 7.5 assigns each plugin a priority value. For each intercepted library call, a priority-sorted list of available plugins is searched for the availability of a function matching the request. The library call is delegated to the first plugin providing a matching implementation. The lowest priority is assigned to the non-accelerated CBLAS library, which is used as the fallback library, if no other library offers a matching function. While different libraries might be chosen depending on the availability of the intercepted function, priorities are given per library, such that no function-specific affinity for a target library is defined.

The *Lookup table* policy depicted in Figure 7.6 improves on this drawback. It not only considers the requested function but also a problem size metric for selecting the plugin to which a call is delegated. Furthermore, caching in the form of a precomputed lookup table (LUT) is used to perform this lookup quickly. The LUT contains $s \times f$ library function pointers, where each entry represents the best possible accelerator library function based on the problem size s and the used BLAS function f represented by an id. A mapping function is used to translate the input dimension n to a value s, defining regions of input data sizes, e. g., matching size n to a region $[2^k, 2^{k+1} - 1]$. During the initialization phase the LUT is populated with the optimal mapping from functions and problem sizes to a particular plugin, which can be determined experimentally using profiling. Once initialized, this method is significantly faster than the library priority strategy since only a single table lookup is required, while the library priorities approach in the worst case requires the selector component to send a request to all available libraries to find out whether the function is supported. The lookup table implementation also allows for dynamically configuring and adapting the preferred library mapping by modifying the LUT contents, e. g., based on measured execution times of the plugin functions.

7.3.4 Profiling Support

To compute and estimate the amount of acceleration that can be obtained when accelerating library calls of a specific application, we have to know, how frequently any BLAS function is called by the application and how fast each library call executes on a particular accelerator. This information can be used as a decision criteria for the wrapper library. Currently, this information has to be determined manually by using profilers, as stated on the left hand side of Figure 7.7.

We use Pin (cf. Section 7.2.4) for this profiling task. Pin provides a tool to trace function calls of binaries. With the knowledge about how BLAS function calls are named, we can use a substring search to identify the library calls. We can extract this information

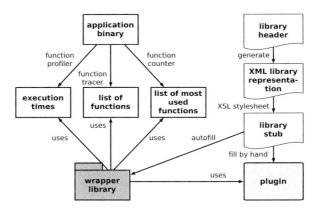

Figure 7.7: Workflow and toolchain to construct a plugin for the interposing wrapper library and to provide profiling data to base selector decisions on.

from the library header files. Using CBLAS as an example, every call to a routine begins with the pattern *"cblas_"*. This procedure is transferable to other BLAS libraries. The signatures of the BLAS functions are known and recognizable by an unambiguous substring. In addition, we are using the instruction counter tool of *Pin* to evaluate how often the functions are called. Unfortunately, Pin does not allow to get accurate function timings, as Pin introduces measurement overheads that may not be excluded. Hence, we use custom micro-benchmarks for accurately determining the execution time for each function for varying problem sizes. Some results from these benchmarks are shown in Section 7.4.1.

7.3.5 Automatic Plugin Generation Using XSLT

For automating the process of generating the plugins, we have developed a toolchain, which is shown on the right hand side in Figure 7.7. We use an XML specification of the CBLAS library as an input specification for the toolchain, which describes all available functions with the respective parameter names and types. This XML specification is generated directly from the CBLAS header by a script.

For generating the wrapper library, we automatically derive an interface supporting the most commonly used CBLAS and MKL library functions using an XSL stylesheet and a standard XSLT processor. The CBLAS interface is generated directly from the XML description. Function stubs for all BLAS functions are generated and automatically filled with the corresponding call to the selector component and the subsequent call to the plugin. The MKL interface is known as well and can be mapped from the CBLAS interface by a set of custom rules, such as mapping *call-by-reference* to *call-by-value* or changing the order of parameters. The plugin interfaces are also generated from the CBLAS XML description. Within the generated function bodies, the CBLAS interface has to be mapped to the specific library interface.

Currently, filling the plugins stubs has to be performed manually, based on the known interface of the specific accelerated BLAS library. Generally this requires simple conversion of data types, such as converting enumeration values to a set of single parameters. Moreover, usually only a few library function calls are candidates for being interposed. This is owed to the fact that mostly few functions are frequently used and additionally provide a significant acceleration compared to the original implementation. For CUBLAS function calls, the function arguments have to be marshaled with Set/GetMatrix or Set/GetVector operations to copy the needed data to the GPU, as the library functions expect device memory pointers as parameters. CSXL by contrast automatically transfers the data to the ClearSpeed board when a library function is called. As not all CBLAS functions are supported by the accelerator libraries, the corresponding function bodies have to be deleted from the plugin interface to avoid calls to not implemented functions. The CBLAS library is used as the fallback solution in that case. All of these adjustments have to be done only once for every accelerator and may be used without any changes for different target systems afterwards. In addition, the specific accelerator initialization code has to be implemented for each plugin.

7.4 Liftracc Experimental Results

We have evaluated the framework using the following system setup:
- SMP system with 2-way 4-Core Intel Xeon CPU E5520 @ 2.27GHz with hyperthreading enabled (looks to the operating system like 16 cores), 12 GB main memory
- NVIDIA Geforce GTX 295, 2*240 thread-processors, 2*896 MB GDDR3
- ClearSpeed Advance e710 accelerator, 2 GB DDR2-533 SDRAM, ECC support
- CentOS 5.4, 2.6.18-164.11.1.el5 kernel version
- CUDA 3.0, OpenMP 3.0, GCC 4.4.0

7.4.1 Runtimes

In Section 7.1, we already showed the DGEMM BLAS function to provide significantly varying runtimes between different implementations, resource types and input sizes. Other frequently used BLAS functions that are sufficiently complex to achieve an acceleration not only show a different, but also a more constant order of the library runtimes. In contrast to DGEMM, for instance with *DDOT*, the dot product of two vectors or *DAXPY*, which computes a constant alpha times a vector x plus a vector y (see Figure 7.8), a static decision table saving only the library priority is sufficient to decide which library to choose, as the order of libraries does only vary for very small input sizes. This validates the idea of using different selection policies as described in Section 7.3.3 and implemented in the framework. Including the DGEMM function runtimes shown in Figure 7.2 into the analysis, we can see that there are runtime differences by orders of magnitude between different library implementations. While runtimes of the DDOT and DAXPY functions have comparably small runtimes, the DGEMM function partly has runtimes of several seconds. Therefore, the overall speedup that an application may achieve largely depends on the used functions

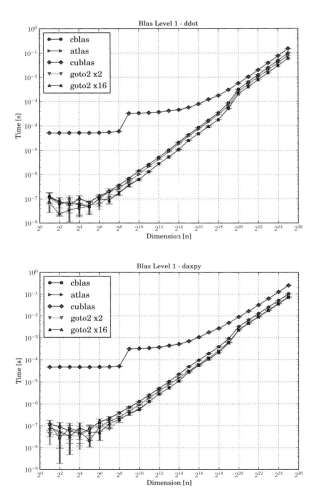

Figure 7.8: Runtimes of DDOT and DAXPY functions using different BLAS implementations and resource types with varying input matrix dimension n.

and the number of calls to these. A single DGEMM library call to, e.g., the CBLAS library with an input size of 2^{10}, may achieve a runtime reduction of more than 4 seconds if replaced by a call to CUBLAS. However, for most BLAS functions the possible speedup is much lower, e.g., with DDOT and DAXPY, so that a large number of library calls is required to achieve a significant speedup for an application.

7.4.2 Overheads

To verify whether the necessary overheads arising from the framework use are worth the effort, we have to contrast it with the gained speedups. We distinguish between necessary overheads of the framework setup (creation of selection policies), framework initialization (library and LUT initialization) and runtime (library interposing and selection policy).

When implementing and studying new delegation policies for the selector component, basic overheads are inevitable. Profiling the performance of library functions has to be performed to measure runtimes for different input data sizes. These are used as basis for decision making in the selector component. These overheads are one-time overheads and do not affect the runtime of the application. More important are the overheads that occur at runtime, as listed in Table 7.2.

Step	Count	Library priority	Lookup table
Wrapper library init	1	9.68 s	9.71 s
- Cublas plugin init	1	2.01 s	2.01 s
- Goto2 plugin init	1	7.64 s	7.64 s
LUT init	1	–	586.49 ms
Normal call	n	2.93 ns	4.73 ns
Call through lib	n	7079.66 ns	37.43 ns
- Select used library	n	4148.72 ns	9.96 ns

Table 7.2: Library interposing overheads

The one-time initialization overhead for the wrapper library includes the times for initializing all plugins and for the wrapper library itself. As can be seen from the measurements, the library initialization cost is dominated by the times for initializing the goto2 and the CUBLAS library, which we cannot avoid. Nevertheless, these overheads have to be be taken into account by the selector component. If only few library calls are made, the overhead might not be worth it. On the other hand, overheads for starting up the library can be neglected in the long run, as the library may remain initialized after being started with, e.g., system startup.

Using the much faster lookup tables for the library selection instead of static library priorities results in an initial overhead of roughly 0.58 seconds for a tested LUT configuration of

13×143 (problem size regions $\times$ number of BLAS functions). Depending on the count of calls to a library, this overhead will be amortized by the much faster library calls (roughly 7000ns faster per call) and the function-based selection of the accelerator. Interposing and delegating a shared library call involves additional overheads that arise for every call. Selecting the used library makes up the major part of a dynamic library call through the wrapper library. As denoted before, data transfers are performed by the plugin of the library.

Each intercepted library is treated individually and we have no knowledge about whether a different task has used a certain resource between two calls to a library function. Therefore, we can not assume data transfers to the resource to be reusable for additional library calls by the same task. We, therefore, currently transfer required input data to the resource for each library call and copy back data afterwards. However, caching effects and data reuse are achieved, if checking for memory modifications on used memory regions of both host and target resource that have occurred since the last library call. This would allow to avoid data transfers and further speed up a library call.

7.5 Related Work

Using libraries as a collection of optimized functions also used for accelerators has been applied for a long time. For example, [154] uses an OpenGL-based API for automatic acceleration of graphics applications on FPGAs as a static replacement for the original OpenGL. However, this approach is purely static and may even affect applications that expect a specific version of that library. In contrast, our approach leverages shared library interposing, which does not require replacing libraries at the file system level and allows for a fully flexible and even dynamic mapping of library functions to hardware accelerators. The flexibility allows us to exploit the fact that the optimal accelerator for a particular library function depends not only on the function, but also on other factors, such as the size of the input data.

Using library interposing to map shared library functions to heterogeneous accelerators is a new approach and has hardly been investigated. However, intercepting library calls has been done in several previous works. Curry [52] proposed an approach of profiling and tracing dynamic library usage using library interposing based on LD_PRELOAD. Library functions are resolved to special wrapper functions at run-time that collect statistics before and after calling the real library. The application and library remain unaltered. This allows to trace multiple processes and analyze applications to get useful performance data. The authors of [100] present a library-interposing approach to generate audit data without recompiling the application. The ability to detect and prevent unsafe programming practices, race conditions and buffer overflow attacks was shown by surrounding original function with analysis code using LD_PRELOAD. González et al. [68] present a tracing mechanism based on dynamic code interposition. They add monitoring code to unmodified parallel binaries and shared libraries at run-time to produce input traces to feed an analysis tool. Interposing is performed by changing the linker tables using Dynamic Interposition Tools (DITools).

To the best of our knowledge only ClearSpeed has shown a library-interposing mechanism to intercept standard BLAS library calls in favor of an accelerated one. LD_PRELOAD is used to preload the CSXL library [41], which uses CSX BLAS code replacements to accelerate specific BLAS functions with the ClearSpeed floating-point accelerator card. The host BLAS library is used as a fallback for unsupported function calls. We use the same mechanism, but present a more general infrastructure offering several accelerator technologies and arbitrary policies to select an adequate accelerator.

An approach for seamlessly using heterogeneous hardware systems through utilizing a library is presented by Moore et. al. [124]. The VSIPL++ for Reconfigurable Computing (VForce) library allows VSIPL++ applications to use FPGAs and GPUs as coprocessors by defining an interface that decouples the software from the hardware development. The approach mainly differs from our approach in the need to modify the existing code by including a VForce header and, thus, being able to access the original code and the lack of a runtime selection support for the best performing function implementation. A different approach is shown in [167] that targets transparent acceleration without modifications to the application. Instead of library calls the authors accelerate selected loops on FPGAs. For the loop acceleration, they generate code for both the CPU and an FPGA that is wrapped in functions and perform run time decisions whether to use the CPU or FPGA implementation. LLVM is used in an automatic toolchain to insert decision blocks into the application code providing a runtime check that evaluates the loop trip count and decides whether it is beneficial to run the code on the FPGA coprocessor.

Summarizing the approaches above, we can conclude a large interest in transparently modifying applications for either adding runtime analysis of performed executions or replacing parts of the application with improved alternative implementation. We also aim on the latter case, but use a novel approach that utilizes shared library interposing to redirect library calls for acceleration on heterogeneous resources. Combining this approach with a hardware selection method has not been considered before and allows for transparent acceleration.

Recently, using library interposing for utilizing heterogeneous systems has been regarded by other workstoo. Matoga et al. [117] use library interposing for transparent acceleration of kernels implemented as library functions. The authors present a framework that transparently collects profile information on library functions including processor performance counters and data transfer sizes. They generate a tracing library for that purpose, which collects data for a target set of functions and estimates speedups that can be obtained by kernels replaced through library interposing. A wrapper library preloaded with LD_PRELOAD is fully generated from the library binaries and header files by using micro-generators, i.e., classes that generate pieces of code related to a specific feature. The estimated global speedup of applications achievable through replacing library showed a maximum relative error of 10% for tested DGEMM BLAS functions, data encryption using OpenSSL, and a Discrete Cosine Transform from libjpeg.

Colaço et al. [43] extend this approach by additionally using a scheduler for intercepted library calls. Their proposed framework is very similar to ours. It provides a wrapper library that has resource-type-specific plugins, which are filled manually and a scheduling component. Their work builds on our general approach and integrates additional scheduling algorithms. A "partitioning policy" finds a balanced distribution of the given loads to available devices. A second algorithm chooses the best suited device for indivisible loads comparable to our LUT approach, but uses dynamic performance models built at runtime. Evaluations use DGEMM BLAS function and a Fast Fourier Transformation (FFT).

7.6 Chapter Conclusion

Programming applications to utilize heterogeneous systems is a complex process and requires good knowledge about the hardware architecture. Automatic and transparent use of these resources is a major concern of domain-specific software developers and users. This chapter introduced our novel approach of using shared library interposing for transparently replacing libraries in binary applications with highly optimized accelerated versions. We have introduced different methods for interposing library calls and have discussed their suitability for our purpose. We identified LD_PRELOAD as an easy to use solution with low overheads for our transparent acceleration use case. LD_PRELOAD allows us to dynamically preload a wrapper library that intercepts library calls.

We have developed a plugin-based framework, which allows to interpose shared library calls and delegate them to an accelerator-specific library plugin. Each such plugin adapts the library call to the library-specific interface of the replacing target resource library. Accelerator-specific library plugins can be added with a high degree of automatism. We have developed an exploratory but fast and extendable selection component that chooses the best possible accelerator for a shared library call based on offline profiling data. Once implemented for a set of libraries, the developed wrapper library can be used consistently to accelerate applications with just a small effort. Preparing the wrapper library for that purpose is widely automated, although the mapping of the source library interface to the accelerator-specific library interfaces is still done manually in this stage of the prototype. Our implementation is portable to other libraries with a small initial adaptation overhead.

We have shown that the approach is practicable by a proof of concept implementation targeting the BLAS library for linear algebra. We demonstrated that our framework may be efficiently used to transparently speedup existing applications. Runtimes of BLAS functions were measured on different resource types and expose significant differences depending on the used implementation and hardware, showing the potentially high speedups of the approach. The runtimes of cost-intensive BLAS functions have shown, which the one-time overhead of the accelerator initialization and the recurring library call overhead pay off when using sufficiently large input data and using the framework in long running processes that make extensive use of BLAS functions. We expect the benefit of delegating functions to accelerated versions to increase with the use of on-chip integrated heterogeneous chips, as data transfer times to accelerators are minimized. We defined mappings of the CBLAS and Intel MKL BLAS library interfaces to optimized version like ATLAS or CUBLAS.

With the presented approach, we have shown the possible benefit of using accelerator libraries and identify an efficient way to transparently use them. For that purpose, library calls that are issued by binary applications are delegated to optimized libraries by a proof of concept framework. We see two possible improvements of our current implementation. First, more sophisticated algorithms to select an appropriate accelerator for each library may be used. Machine learning approaches might be applicable as well as monitoring functions on the accelerators to take the current utilization into account. Second, the initial mapping of the standard BLAS interface to the accelerator-specific library interfaces is partly done manually when used for the first time. To achieve fully automated plugin generation, rules have to be identified and formalized to automatically map the calls to different libraries. Both limitations were approached in related work, as discussed in Section 7.5. Two works [43] [117] are based on our research and extended our general approach accordingly.

Recalling that a function can be wrapped by a thread, our approach may be integrated with our thread scheduling approaches. The selector component may be replaced by one of the schedulers presented in the Chapter 6 to allow a multi-application library-interposing approach that integrates with our thread acceleration approaches. The chosen target library in that case additionally depends on the availability of the system resources.

CHAPTER 8

Summary and Outlook

This chapter summarizes the contributions of this thesis and draws conclusions. It further discusses future research directions.

8.1 Contributions

Heterogeneous computing has received great attention in recent years and is still in the focus of both research and industry. Heterogeneous computing resources nowadays are used within a broad scope of computing devices including embedded systems, mobile devices, datacenters, and high-performance computing (HPC) supercomputers. The use of heterogeneity allows for customized systems that offer high performance and low energy solutions for a broad spectrum of application areas. This thesis discusses a number of challenges raised by providing and exploiting heterogeneous resources that affect the complete hardware/software stack reaching from the chip design, to compilers and drivers, to programming models and execution environments. Great efforts are carried out to simplify heterogeneous computing and make it available to a larger group of people. These include the increasing interest in on-chip heterogeneous computing resources and standardization approaches in programming models and compilation toolchains like OpenCL and OpenACC.

In this thesis, I focus on the field of execution environments, which lags behind other fields of heterogeneous computing, namely heterogeneous architectures and programming frameworks. While CPUs are transparently managed and utilized by the operating system, even the widely used general purpose graphics processing units (GPUs) are not automatically and transparently controlled by it yet. Batch computing approaches, like HTCondor [162], support heterogeneous resources nowadays but do not follow the operating system point of view that is provided for traditional CPU scheduling. In this thesis, I discuss approaches to make heterogeneous devices known to the operating system and provide methods that enable automatic scheduling of tasks that support multiple target devices.

The approaches shown in this thesis allow heterogeneous task execution environments to improve in performance, energy consumption, and fairness when executing a set of tasks. Specifically, I make the following contributions to the field of heterogeneous computing:

- I present a concept that allows tasks to yield their execution at user-defined preemption points for later continuation or migration to a different resource type. To this end, I provide a programming pattern, which can be applied to applications that support multiple target implementations for the same task. If a task yield is aspired, a checkpoint data structure is used to store the current state of the execution, which is defined by resource independent data structures. The programming pattern allows for a later continuation on any supported resource type by wrapping resource-specific execution functions that work on the defined checkpoint data. These functions are optionally executed by a scheduler and therefore allow to apply this programming pattern for heterogeneous scheduling. This thesis showed that the changes to typical applications targeting heterogeneous executions are small.

- I provide algorithms for heterogeneous scheduling of tasks enabled for migration by, e. g., the presented programming pattern. With enabling task migration, scheduling decisions are not final and therefore are different to most heterogeneous scheduling approaches presented by related work. I discuss the advantages and disadvantages of tasks yielding at preemption points and their subsequent migration. I define scheduling parameters and decision policies to assign tasks to resources, perform task switches, and migrate tasks based on the task's suitability, its priority, and expected overheads. For task scheduling, I define several policies that aim at the optimization of different scheduling objectives: increasing the throughput, i. e., reducing the makespan of a set of tasks, reducing the total energy consumption, and striving for fairness among tasks. Separate load balancing policies are combined with the scheduling policies to support the followed scheduling objectives. These scheduling policies are used in two scheduling frameworks and showed good results according to their targets.

- I provide an extension of the Linux Completely Fair Scheduler (CFS) for scheduling tasks on heterogeneous devices in kernel space. The kernel extension makes heterogeneous devices known to the CFS and automatically executes tasks that apply the defined programming pattern. Applications use a scheduler interface that provides wrappers to system calls, which allow the applications to request the assignment of any of the supported resources from the CFS or to release a resource. Due to preemption not being supported by current accelerator resources, my approach makes use of cooperative multitasking. This requests tasks to voluntarily release resources at preemption points that may be used to write a checkpoint according to the programming pattern. Loads among available resources are balanced by a load balancer to avoid idle times on resources and make sure tasks are executed on the best available resource. In addition, the approach adopts the fair scheduling of the CFS aiming at a fair distribution of execution times among available tasks while respecting their priorities. Results show that this approach improves on the makespan compared to non-heterogeneous execution and reduces the average turnaround time of the tasks.

- I provide a user-space scheduling framework that is an extension of the kernel-space approach both conceptually and in terms of functional range. It additionally provides support for FPGAs, includes automatic device detection, reduces the interface to the scheduler to a minimum, and includes measurement frameworks for both runtime and energy measurements of tasks. Besides a fairness scheduling approach, the framework provides further scheduling policies for reducing the energy consumption and the total runtime of a set of tasks. My scheduler relies on scheduling policy-dependent affinities of tasks to resource types that are based on offline benchmarks. The user-space scheduler relies on the original CFS for CPU scheduling without requiring a specific interface. However, it uses the proc filesystem provided by many Unix derivates to access information on the CPU load. This keeps the interface minimal and vastly independent from Linux kernel updates. In addition, this improves the portability between different Unix derivates, as the underlying CPU scheduler is exchangeable. The approach validates the results shown by the CFS extension in user space and additionally points out that the migration mechanism succeeds on performance- and energy-related scheduling objectives. Moreover, an overhead analysis underlines the usability of task migration in the heterogeneous case and highlighs the importance of restricting the CPU load in heterogeneous scheduling to avoid idle times on accelerators.

- Finally, I provide a novel approach for transparent acceleration using shared library interposing. A library-interposing framework is introduced, which allows to intercept calls of binary applications addressing shared libraries and to redirect them to a wrapper library. The wrapper library serves as a gateway to different accelerator-specific library versions of the same library and translates the call to match the corresponding interfaces. To this end, it provides plugins to each supported library, which adapt the provided inputs to match the interface of the target library and representatively executes the function on it. The target library is selected based on provided input data sizes and expected runtimes that are determined beforehand. Using the BLAS library, I could show that this framework comes with overheads of a few nanoseconds in comparison to the expected speedups for a single library call. Speedups are depending on the used BLAS function and the input sizes. With only $38ns$ of average overhead for a library call, runtime reductions are in the seconds for, e. g., calls to the DGEMM function and still in milliseconds for many other functions. Thus, it allows to transparently accelerate binary applications that otherwise can not be directly adapted for acceleration. My methodology is already used in other research projects. Colaço et al. [43] extend my framework with performance models that are constructed at runtime.

Parts of the presented results have been published on international conferences:

Programming Model and kernel-space scheduler:

Tobias Beisel, Tobias Wiersema, Christian Plessl, and André Brinkmann. Programming and scheduling model for supporting heterogeneous accelerators in Linux. *In Proc. 3rd Workshop on Computer Architecture and Operating System Co-design (CAOS)*, pages 28–36, January 2012.

Tobias Beisel, Tobias Wiersema, Christian Plessl, and André Brinkmann. Cooperative multitasking for heterogeneous accelerators in the Linux completely fair scheduler. *In Proc. IEEE Int. Conf. on Application-Specific Systems, Architectures, and Processors (ASAP)*. pages 223–226, Piscataway, NJ, USA, September 2011. IEEE Computer Society.

Shared-library-interposing framework:

Tobias Beisel, Manuel Niekamp, and Christian Plessl. Using shared library interposing for transparent application acceleration in systems with heterogeneous hardware accelerators. In *Application-specific Systems Architectures and Processors (ASAP), 2010 21st IEEE International Conference on*, pages 65–72, July 2010.

These and other author publications are listed in the *Author's Publications* section in the appendix.

8.2 Conclusions and Lessons Learned

From the work presented in this thesis, I draw the following conclusions:

While searching a solution for heterogeneous task scheduling, I was mostly driven by the idea to bring traditional CPU scheduling to the heterogeneous world. That is, integrating accelerator usage to the operating system or closely relating a scheduling framework to it. However, heterogeneous scheduling is more complex and faces different challenges that prevents instant adaptation of CPU scheduling methods for the heterogeneous case. I introduced cooperative multitasking, which is a substitute for the missing preemption on accelerator resources. Cooperative multitasking, as introduced by my programming pattern, requires to adapt the applications and therefore can not finally replace task preemption. I interpret the shown results on cooperative heterogeneous scheduling to show the potential benefits to be achieved if preemption was available. With integrated on-chip heterogeneous systems and corresponding memory models, preemption is likely to be available at some point in the future and will refrain from the need to use a programming pattern.

I was able to show that tasks yielding at preemption points and their subsequent migration can be beneficial for several objectives. But, results also show that overheads need to be considered for each scheduling decision. This is especially true for time-sharing, where task switches are performed frequently. Time-sharing can improve on certain scheduling metrics, but overheads can be significant. Overheads are dependent on the application. Thus, task yielding requests and migration decisions should be task-specific. Therefore, preemption based on preemption points and checkpoint data structures is beneficial, if used with caution, i.e., with respecting overheads.

By providing both a user-space and a kernel-space scheduler, I was able to better understand their differences. The major drawback of scheduling in user space is that is has to rely on kernel interfaces to have full access to the system state including the CPUs. Nevertheless, I showed that knowing the CPU load is mandatory for comprehensive scheduling decisions. On the other hand, a user-space scheduler has major advantages from a developer's point of view, as kernel-space development requires larger effort and possible adaptations with each kernel update. In addition, drivers and runtime environments of accelerators are currently triggered from user space, while according kernel-space libraries are not yet available. However, scheduling eventually should be performed in kernel space to have complete access to the system state. This is supported by the observation that the CPU utilization has major impact on heterogeneous scheduling, even of accelerators.

For energy-based scheduling, I discussed the possibility to exclude the energy consumption of idling resources from a task's measured energy consumption to provide a more task-specific energy consumption. However, the energy that idle resources consume is still relevant and should not be neglected. Therefore, energy related scheduling can hardly be optimal without a planning system, as leaving resources idle most likely extends the schedule's runtime, which again adds to the total energy consumption of a certain task set. Moreover, a strong correlation between energy consumption and performance was recognizable. This is based on the fact that the self-induced energy consumption of a task, i.e., without considering idle devices, can roughly be computed by its runtime times the resource's power drain on full load. Therefore, its energy consumption is depending on its runtime. Thus, striving for high throughput also is beneficial energy-wise.

For both energy consumption and runtime measurements it is hardly possible to measure precise values while executing a set of tasks. True time-sharing on CPUs prevents to assign measured energy consumptions to individual tasks. Additionally, it introduces task switching overheads or waiting times to runtime measurements. Both limitations affect tasks executed on accelerators, too, as these also use the CPU for a certain part of their execution.

The library-interposing approach showed the ability to perform a library redirection including a selection mechanism with reasonable overhead. Thus, it is applicable as a novel approach to transparently accelerate binary applications. A drawback that can be concluded is that it is difficult to find applications that make use of shared libraries and spend a major fraction of the runtime in a few single invocations of library functions, which is the scenario, for which our approach is most suitable. Another restriction is that library providers unfortunately do not hold to a library's standard interface, which makes providing additional libraries, like, e. g., the Fast Fourier Transform (FFT), difficult to be fully automated. A larger effort to adhere to these interfaces would be helpful for library-based acceleration approaches.

I faced a comparable problem for benchmarking the thread scheduling approach. An evaluation of the presented approaches with a standardized benchmark suite would have been beneficial. Unfortunately, no benchmark suite exists that support a variety of resources types, i. e., (multicore) CPUs, GPUs, and especially also FPGAs.

8.3 Future Directions

I see the following major directions of future research, which are related to the proposed heterogeneous-scheduling and library-interposing approaches:

- **Programming Pattern:** Although automatic preemption using checkpoints that are inherently supported by multiple architectures might be enabled sometime in the future, I believe this is not a near future. Therefore, I consider the programming pattern presented in this thesis well suited for its purpose. However, some improvements can be considered. First, the definition of checkpoint data and preemption points can be automated and combined with an optimization approach to find minimum-sized checkpoints. The goal is to reduce data transfers while keeping possible migration points frequent. This has partly been done in this thesis by applying a compiler-driven automatic kernel context definition method for heterogeneous task migration as presented in [67]. Second, the programming pattern may be integrated with a given heterogeneous programming model like OpenCL. This would not only increase acceptance, but simplify the identification of resource-independent checkpoint data and avoid multiple implementations for targeted resource types. However, supported architectures of current candidate programming models are limited.

- **Memory Management:** The memory management of the presented scheduling approaches can be improved. Transparent on-demand data fetching and using mapped-memory could be considered, as well as overlapping execution with data transfers to reduce overheads introduced through data transfers. OpenCL nowadays supports shared virtual memory, which allows host and OpenCL resources to share the same virtual address range and prevents explicit data transfers. Moreover, allowing a task to continue computation on the data of a previous tasks that remains in resource memory can safe data transfers. However, this introduces data dependencies between tasks, which requires an extension of the general task model presented in this thesis. Submitting a list of tasks including their dependencies would give a scheduler further knowledge to profit from data locality.

- **Performance Prediction:** Affinity determination is currently based on offline measured runtimes and energy values. In the long run, this should be replaced by more portable approaches with a higher automation. Prediction models may be used to determine estimations of performance or energy consumption based on measurements of historic performance and energy metrics using machine learning techniques. As discussed earlier, runtime measurements limit the accuracy of CPU measured values and require more sophisticated approaches, e. g., relating a task's runtime to the fraction of CPU time consumed by it during its execution. Alternatively, offline models may be used to estimate runtimes based on instruction counts or used code features and combine the models with estimated input data sizes at runtime. However, this kind of performance prediction is a different field, which has not been in the focus of this thesis.

- **Planning System:** As discussed before, energy-related scheduling might be enhanced. Replacing the provided dynamic scheduling approach through a planning system would be a radical approach. Nevertheless, improvements on the current approach seem possible, so a deeper analysis of the effects of the used energy affinity definition is required.

- **Task Scheduling Models:** This thesis defines a system model, a task model, and an execution model for heterogeneous task scheduling. While these models are based on the objectives of this thesis, they might be revised in certain ways. I here state some possibilities that are valid options, but would partly require extensive changes to the current system. First, considering a resource as a single computing device is a restriction that might be hindering to leverage the full potential of the system. Spatial multitasking may be used on GPUs and FPGAs, which breaks the one-to-one relation of a task and a resource. In addition, this relation may be broken up in the other direction, too, by allowing a task to be assigned two or more devices at the same time. This, e. g., allows device-to-device communication to be used for task threads that interact with each other. Second, resources may be equipped with further information, like memory sizes, to better match the requirements of tasks. Nevertheless, this would also require to gain more information about the task, i. e., an adapted task model. And third, reserving CPU cores for accelerators is a valid alternative or extension to the CPU load restriction provided in this thesis. While reserved CPU cores might partly be underutilized, waiting times for accelerators are possibly reduced.

- **Library Interposing:** Regarding the presented library-interposing approach, some interesting extensions have already been provided by related work [43, 117] that is based on the concepts presented in this thesis. However, their work is further extendible. A more precise estimation of the possible acceleration through using library interposing is desirable. Modeling different aspects, like bandwidth, data sizes, or even the runtime of library function, would allow to estimate the influence of each parameter on the possible acceleration. This would, e. g., allow to estimate the performance differences between on-chip and off-chip GPUs for an application. In addition, data reuse for several library calls by the same application may be considered to reduce data transfer overheads. Finally, a combination of the library-interposing approach with the presented thread scheduler would integrate library acceleration to the multitasking approach.

Acronyms

ABI	Application Binary Interface
AMD	Advanced Micro Devices
API	Application Programming Interface
ASIC	Application-specific Integrated Circuit
ATI	ATI Technologies Inc.
ATT	Average Turnaround Time
BLAS	Basic Linear Algebra Subprograms
CBEA	Cell Broadband Engine Architecture
Cell BEA	Cell Broadband Engine Architecture
CPU	Central Processing Unit
CUDA	Compute Unified Device Architecture
CFS	Completely Fair Scheduler
DAG	Directed Acyclic Graph
DFG	Data Flow Graph
EDP	Energy-Delay Product
EGY	Energy, Energy scheduling policy
FAIR	Fairness, Fairness scheduling policy
FCFS	First Come First Served
FFT	Fast Fourier Transform
FPGA	Field Programmable Gate Array
GPU	Graphics Processing Unit
HDL	Hardware Description Language
HPC	High Performance Computing
HSA	Heterogeneous System Architecture
IPC	Inter-Process Communication
ISA	Instruction Set Architecture
JSON	JavaScript Object Notation
LUT	Lookup Table
MIC	Intel Many Integrated Core Architecture
MIMD	Multiple Instruction Multiple Data
OS	Operating System
PERF	Performance, Performance scheduling policy
PERF_FAIR	Performance/Fairness, Performance with fairness scheduling policy

PCI	Peripheral Component Interconnect
PCIe	Peripheral Component Interconnect Express
rSoC	Reconfigurable System-on-Chip
SIMD	Single Instruction Multiple Data
SM	Streaming Multiprocessor
SoC	System-on-Chip
SPMD	Single Program Multiple Data
TDP	Thermal Design Power

List of Figures

List of Tables

Listings

Author's Publications

[1] Tobias Beisel, Stefan Lietsch, and Kris Thielemans. A method for OSEM PET reconstruction on parallel architectures using STIR. In *Nuclear Science Symposium Conference Record, 2008. NSS '08. IEEE*, pages 4161–4168. IEEE, 2008.

[2] Tobias Beisel, Manuel Niekamp, and Christian Plessl. Using shared library interposing for transparent application acceleration in systems with heterogeneous hardware accelerators. In *Application-specific Systems Architectures and Processors (ASAP), 2010 21st IEEE International Conference on*, pages 65 –72, July 2010.

[3] Tobias Beisel, Tobias Wiersema, Christian Plessl, and André Brinkmann. Cooperative multitasking for heterogeneous accelerators in the linux completely fair scheduler. In *Application-Specific Systems, Architectures and Processors (ASAP), 2011 IEEE International Conference on*, pages 223 –226, Sept. 2011.

[4] Tobias Beisel, Tobias Wiersema, Christian Plessl, and André Brinkmann. Programming and scheduling model for supporting heterogeneous accelerators in Linux. In *Proc. 3rd Workshop on Computer Architecture and Operating System Co-design (CAOS)*, pages 28–36, Jan. 2012.

[5] Christian Plessl and Tobias Beisel. An overview of GPU architectures and programming and their application in high-performance computing. Technical report, Paderborn Center for Parallel Computing, University of Paderborn, July 2012.

[6] Kris Thielemans, Charalampos Tsoumpas, Sanida Mustafovic, Tobias Beisel, Pablo Aguiar, Nikolaos Dikaios, and Matthew W Jacobson. STIR: software for tomographic image reconstruction release 2. *Physics in Medicine and Biology*, 57(4):867, 2012.

Bibliography

[7] J.T. Adriaens, K. Compton, Nam Sung Kim, and M.J. Schulte. The case for GPGPU spatial multitasking. In *High Performance Computer Architecture (HPCA), 2012 IEEE 18th International Symposium on*, pages 1–12, Feb 2012.

[8] A. Agne, M. Happe, A. Keller, E. Lübbers, B. Plattner, M. Platzner, and C. Plessl. ReconOS: An operating system approach for reconfigurable computing. *Micro, IEEE*, 34(1):60–71, Jan 2014.

[9] P. Aguilera, K. Morrow, and Nam Sung Kim. Fair share: Allocation of GPU resources for both performance and fairness. In *Computer Design (ICCD), 2014 32nd IEEE International Conference on*, pages 440–447, Oct 2014.

[10] Gene M. Amdahl. Validity of the single processor approach to achieving large scale computing capabilities. In *Proceedings of the April 18-20, 1967, Spring Joint Computer Conference*, AFIPS '67 (Spring), pages 483–485, New York, NY, USA, 1967. ACM.

[11] Mehdi Amini, Béatrice Creusillet, Stéphanie Even, Ronan Keryell, Onig Goubier, Serge Guelton, Janice Onanian Mcmahon, François-Xavier Pasquier, Grégoire Péan, and Pierre Villalon. Par4All: From convex array regions to heterogeneous computing. In *IMPACT 2012 : Second International Workshop on Polyhedral Compilation Techniques HiPEAC 2012*, Paris, France, January 2012. 2 pages.

[12] Joshua A. Anderson, Eric Jankowski, Thomas L. Grubb, Michael Engel, and Sharon C. Glotzer. Massively parallel monte carlo for many-particle simulations on GPUs. *Journal of Computational Physics*, 254(0):27 – 38, 2013.

[13] Krste Asanovic, Ras Bodik, Bryan Christopher Catanzaro, Joseph James Gebis, Parry Husbands, Kurt Keutzer, David A Patterson, William Lester Plishker, John Shalf, Samuel Webb Williams, et al. The landscape of parallel computing research: A view from Berkeley. Technical Report UCB/EECS-2006-183, EECS Department, University of California, Berkeley, 2006.

[14] Krste Asanovic, Rastislav Bodik, James Demmel, Tony Keaveny, Kurt Keutzer, John Kubiatowicz, Nelson Morgan, David Patterson, Koushik Sen, John Wawrzynek, et al.

A view of the parallel computing landscape. *Communications of the ACM*, 52(10):56–67, 2009.

[15] Joshua Auerbach, David F. Bacon, Ioana Burcea, Perry Cheng, Stephen J. Fink, Rodric Rabbah, and Sunil Shukla. A compiler and runtime for heterogeneous computing. In *Proceedings of the 49th Annual Design Automation Conference*, DAC '12, pages 271–276, New York, NY, USA, 2012. ACM.

[16] Cedric Augonnet, Jerome Clet-Ortega, Samuel Thibault, and Raymond Namyst. Data-aware task scheduling on multi-accelerator based platforms. In *Parallel and Distributed Systems (ICPADS), 2010 IEEE 16th International Conference on*, pages 291–298. IEEE, 2010.

[17] Cédric Augonnet, Samuel Thibault, and Raymond Namyst. StarPU: a runtime system for scheduling tasks over accelerator-based multicore machines. Rapport de recherche RR-7240, INRIA, March 2010.

[18] Cédric Augonnet, Samuel Thibault, Raymond Namyst, and Pierre-André Wacrenier. StarPU: a unified platform for task scheduling on heterogeneous multicore architectures. *Concurrency and Computation: Practice and Experience*, 23(2):187–198, 2011.

[19] J. Axboe. latt – Linux scheduler benchmarking tool. http://git.kernel.dk/, 2009.

[20] Eduard Ayguadé, Rosa M. Badia, Pieter Bellens, Daniel Cabrera, Alejandro Duran, Roger Ferrer, Marc Gonzàlez, Francisco Igual, Daniel Jiménez-González, Jesús Labarta, Luis Martinell, Xavier Martorell, Rafael Mayo, Josep M. Pérez, Judit Planas, and Enrique S. Quintana-Ortí. Extending OpenMP to survive the heterogeneous multi-core era. *International Journal of Parallel Programming*, 38(5-6):440–459, 2010.

[21] Eduard Ayguadé, Rosa M. Badia, Francisco D. Igual, Jesús Labarta, Rafael Mayo, and Enrique S. Quintana-Ortí. An extension of the StarSs programming model for platforms with multiple GPUs. In *Euro-Par 2009 Parallel Processing*, pages 851–862. Springer, 2009.

[22] Jorge G. Barbosa and Belmiro Moreira. Dynamic scheduling of a batch of parallel task jobs on heterogeneous clusters. *Parallel Computing*, 37(8):428–438, 2011.

[23] M. M. Baskaran, J. Ramanujam, and P. Sadayappan. Automatic C-to-CUDA code generation for affine programs. In *Compiler Construction*, pages 244–263. Springer, 2010.

[24] Andrew Baumann, Paul Barham, Pierre-Evariste Dagand, Tim Harris, Rebecca Isaacs, Simon Peter, Timothy Roscoe, Adrian Schüpbach, and Akhilesh Singhania.

The multikernel: a new OS architecture for scalable multicore systems. In *Proceedings of the ACM SIGOPS 22nd symposium on Operating systems principles*, SOSP '09, pages 29–44, New York, NY, USA, 2009. ACM.

[25] Keren Bergman, Shekhar Borkar, Dan Campbell, William Carlson, William Dally, Monty Denneau, Paul Franzon, William Harrod, Kerry Hill, Jon Hiller, et al. Exascale computing study: Technology challenges in achieving exascale systems. *Defense Advanced Research Projects Agency Information Processing Techniques Office (DARPA IPTO), Tech. Rep*, 15, 2008.

[26] Neil W. Bergmann, John A. Williams, Jie Han, and Yi Chen. A process model for hardware modules in reconfigurable system-on-chip. In *ARCS Workshops'06*, pages 205–214, 2006.

[27] S. Blackford, G. Corliss, J. Demmel, J. Dongarra, I. Duff, S. Hammarling, G. Henry, M. Heroux, C. Hu, W. Kahan, L. Kaufmann, B. Kearfott, F. Krogh, X. Li, Z. Maany, A. Petitet, R. Pozo, K. Remington, W. Walster, C. Whaley, V. Wolff, J. Gudenberg, and A. Lumsdaine. Basic linear algebra subprograms technical (BLAST) forum standard. *Int. J. High Perform. Comput.*, 15, 2001.

[28] Filip Blagojevic, Costin Iancu, Katherine Yelick, Matthew Curtis-Maury, Dimitrios S Nikolopoulos, and Benjamin Rose. Scheduling dynamic parallelism on accelerators. In *Proceedings of the 6th ACM conference on Computing frontiers*, pages 161–170. ACM, 2009.

[29] OpenMP Architecture Review Board. OpenMP application program interface, version 4.0. July 2013.

[30] M. Bohr. The evolution of scaling from the homogeneous era to the heterogeneous era. In *Electron Devices Meeting (IEDM), 2011 IEEE International*, pages 1.1.1–1.1.6, Dec. 2011.

[31] Shekhar Borkar and Andrew A. Chien. The future of microprocessors. *Commun. ACM*, 54(5):67–77, May 2011.

[32] George Bosilca, Aurelien Bouteiller, Anthony Danalis, Thomas Herault, Pierre Lemarinier, and Jack Dongarra. DAGuE: A generic distributed DAG engine for high performance computing. *Parallel Computing*, 38(1):37–51, 2012.

[33] Inc Bright Computing. Bright Cluster Manager. http://www.brightcomputing.com, 2015.

[34] Andre R. Brodtkorb, Christopher Dyken, Trond R. Hagen, Jon M. Hjelmervik, and Olaf O. Storaasli. State-of-the-art in heterogeneous computing. *Scientific Programming*, 18(1):1–33, 2010.

[35] Jeffrey Cassidy, Lothar Lilge, and Vaughn Betz. Fast, power-efficient biophotonic simulations for cancer treatment using FPGAs. In *Field-Programmable Custom Computing Machines (FCCM), 2014 IEEE 22nd Annual International Symposium on*, pages 133–140, May 2014.

[36] S. Cesare. Shared library call redirection using ELF PLT infection. *Phrack Magazine*, 10, 1999.

[37] Shuai Che, Jie Li, Jeremy W Sheaffer, Kevin Skadron, and John Lach. Accelerating compute-intensive applications with gpus and fpgas. In *Application Specific Processors, 2008. SASP 2008. Symposium on*, pages 101–107. IEEE, 2008.

[38] Kuan-Chung Chen and Chung-Ho Chen. An OpenCL runtime system for a heterogeneous many-core virtual platform. In *Circuits and Systems (ISCAS), 2014 IEEE International Symposium on*, pages 2197–2200, June 2014.

[39] Sangyeun Cho and Rami G Melhem. On the interplay of parallelization, program performance, and energy consumption. *Parallel and Distributed Systems, IEEE Transactions on*, 21(3):342–353, 2010.

[40] Hong Jun Choi, Dong Oh Son, Seung Gu Kang, Jong Myon Kim, Hsien-Hsin Lee, and Cheol Hong Kim. An efficient scheduling scheme using estimated execution time for heterogeneous computing systems. *The Journal of Supercomputing*, pages 1–17, 2013.

[41] ClearSpeed Technology, Inc. *CSXL User Guide*, 2007.

[42] ClearSpeed Technology Ltd. Clearspeed. http://www.clearspeed.com.

[43] João Colaço, Adrian Matoga, Aleksandar Ilic, Nuno Roma, Pedro Tomás, and Ricardo Chaves. Transparent application acceleration by intelligent scheduling of shared library calls on heterogeneous systems. In *Parallel Processing and Applied Mathematics*, volume 8384 of *Lecture Notes in Computer Science*, pages 693–703. Springer Berlin Heidelberg, 2014.

[44] International Roadmap Committee. International technology roadmap for semiconductors, 2011 edition. *Semiconductor Industry Association*, 2011.

[45] LLC CompuGreen. Green500 list november 2014. http://www.green500.org/lists/green201411, 2014.

[46] Altera Corporation. Altera SDK for OpenCL. http://www.altera.com/products/software/opencl/opencl-index.html, 2014.

[47] Intel Corporation. Intel math kernel library (Intel MKL). http://software.intel.com/en-us/intel-mkl.

[48] Intel Corporation. Intel threading building blocks (Intel TBB). `https://www.threadingbuildingblocks.org/`.

[49] Intel Corporation. Intel re-architects the fundamental building block for high-performance computing. `http://newsroom.intel.com/community/intel_newsroom/blog/2014/06/23/intel-re-architects-the-fundamental-building-block-for-high-performance-computing`, June 2014.

[50] NVIDIA Corporation. Nvidia introduces Cg – C for graphics. `http://www.nvidia.com.br/object/IO_20020612_6724.html`, June 2002.

[51] NVIDIA Corporation. NVIDIA unveils CUDA - the GPU computing revolution begins. `http://www.nvidia.com/object/IO_37226.html`, Nov. 2006.

[52] T.W. Curry. Profiling and tracing dynamic library usage via interposition. In *Proc. Summer USENIX'94*, 1994.

[53] Marvin Damschen, Christian Plessl, Andreas Agne, Markus Happe, Ariane Keller, Enno Lübbers, Bernhard Plattner, Marco Platzner, Sebastian Meisner, Hendrik Hangmann, et al. Transparent offloading of computational hotspots from binary code to Xeon Phi.

[54] Klaus Danne and Marco Platzner. An EDF schedulability test for periodic tasks on reconfigurable hardware devices. *SIGPLAN Not.*, 41(7):93–102, June 2006.

[55] R.H. Dennard, V.L. Rideout, E. Bassous, and A.R. LeBlanc. Design of ion-implanted MOSFET's with very small physical dimensions. *Solid-State Circuits, IEEE Journal of*, 9(5):256–268, Oct 1974.

[56] Matthew DeVuyst, Ashish Venkat, and Dean M. Tullsen. Execution migration in a heterogeneous-ISA chip multiprocessor. In *Proceedings of the Seventeenth International Conference on Architectural Support for Programming Languages and Operating Systems*, ASPLOS XVII, pages 261–272, New York, NY, USA, 2012. ACM.

[57] Gregory Diamos and Sudhakar Yalamanchili. Harmony: Runtime techniques for dynamic concurrency inference, resource constrained hierarchical scheduling, and online optimization in heterogeneous multiprocessor systems. Technical report, Georgia Institute of Technology, Computer Architecture and Systems Lab, 2008.

[58] die.net. dlopen(3) - Linux man page. `http://linux.die.net/man/3/dlopen`.

[59] Jack Dongarra, Pete Beckman, Terry Moore, Patrick Aerts, Giovanni Aloisio, Jean-Claude Andre, David Barkai, Jean-Yves Berthou, Taisuke Boku, Bertrand Braunschweig, et al. The international exascale software project roadmap. *International Journal of High Performance Computing Applications*, 25(1):3–60, 2011.

[60] Glenn A Elliott and James H Anderson. Globally scheduled real-time multiprocessor systems with GPUs. *Real-Time Systems*, 48(1):34–74, 2012.

[61] H. Esmaeilzadeh, E. Blem, R. St.Amant, K. Sankaralingam, and D. Burger. Dark silicon and the end of multicore scaling. In *Computer Architecture (ISCA), 2011 38th Annual International Symposium on*, pages 365–376, June 2011.

[62] Hadi Esmaeilzadeh, Emily Blem, Renée St. Amant, Karthikeyan Sankaralingam, and Doug Burger. Power challenges may end the multicore era. *Commun. ACM*, 56(2):93–102, 2013.

[63] Wu-chun Feng, Heshan Lin, Thomas Scogland, and Jing Zhang. OpenCL and the 13 dwarfs: a work in progress. In *Proceedings of the third joint WOSP/SIPEW international conference on Performance Engineering*, pages 291–294. ACM, 2012.

[64] Wu-chun Feng and Dinesh Manocha. High-performance computing using accelerators. *Parallel Computing*, 33(10):645–647, 2007.

[65] Message Passing Interface Forum. Document for a standard message-passing interface. Technical Report CS-93-214, University of Tennessee, Oct. 1993.

[66] HSA Foundation. HSA foundation launches new era of pervasive, energy-efficient computing with HSA 1.0 specification release, Mar. 2015.

[67] R. Gad, T. Suss, and A. Brinkmann. Compiler driven automatic kernel context migration for heterogeneous computing. In *Distributed Computing Systems (ICDCS), 2014 IEEE 34th International Conference on*, pages 389–398, June 2014.

[68] Marc Gonzalez, Albert Serra, Xavier Martorell, Jose Oliver, Eduard Ayguade, Jesus Labarta, and Nacho Navarro. Applying interposition techniques for performance analysis of OpenMP parallel applications. *Intl. Symp. on Parallel and Distributed Processing*, page 235, 2000.

[69] K. Goto. GotoBLAS. http://www.tacc.utexas.edu/tacc-projects/#blas.

[70] Brian Gough. *GNU Scientific Library Reference Manual - 3rd Edition*, 2009.

[71] Chris Gregg, Michael Boyer, Kim Hazelwood, and Kevin Skadron. Dynamic heterogeneous scheduling decisions using historical runtime data. In *Proceedings of the 2nd workshop on applications for multi-and many-core processors*, 2011.

[72] D. Grewe, Zheng Wang, and M.F.P. O'Boyle. Portable mapping of data parallel programs to OpenCL for heterogeneous systems. In *Code Generation and Optimization (CGO), 2013 IEEE/ACM International Symposium on*, pages 1–10, Feb. 2013.

[73] Dominik Grewe and M.F.P. O'Boyle. A static task partitioning approach for heterogeneous systems using OpenCL. In *Compiler Construction*, pages 286–305. Springer, 2011.

[74] ITRS Working Group. International technology roadmap for semiconductors. http://www.itrs.net.

[75] Khronos OpenCL Working Group. OpenCL 2.0 API specification. Oct. 2014.

[76] Vishakha Gupta, Ada Gavrilovska, Karsten Schwan, Harshvardhan Kharche, Niraj Tolia, Vanish Talwar, and Parthasarathy Ranganathan. GViM: GPU-accelerated virtual machines. In *Proceedings of the 3rd ACM Workshop on System-level Virtualization for High Performance Computing*, pages 17–24. ACM, 2009.

[77] Vishakha Gupta, Karsten Schwan, Niraj Tolia, Vanish Talwar, and Parthasarathy Ranganathan. Pegasus: Coordinated scheduling for virtualized accelerator-based systems. In *2011 USENIX Annual Technical Conference (USENIX ATC'11)*, page 31, 2011.

[78] T. Hamano, T. Endo, and S. Matsuoka. Power-aware dynamic task scheduling for heterogeneous accelerated clusters. In *Parallel Distributed Processing, 2009. IPDPS 2009. IEEE International Symposium on*, pages 1–8, May 2009.

[79] Paul H Hargrove and Jason C Duell. Berkeley lab checkpoint/restart (BLCR) for Linux clusters. In *Journal of Physics: Conference Series*, volume 46, page 494. IOP Publishing, 2006.

[80] J.L. Hennessy and D.A. Patterson. *Computer Architecture: A Quantitative Approach*. Morgan Kaufmann/Elsevier, 5th edition, 2012.

[81] John L Henning. SPEC CPU2006 benchmark descriptions. *ACM SIGARCH Computer Architecture News*, 34(4):1–17, 2006.

[82] IEEE. IEEE standard VHDL language reference manual. Technical report, 1988.

[83] Advanced Micro Devices Inc. AMD core math library for graphic processors (ACML-GPU). `http://developer.amd.com/tools-and-sdks/cpu-development/amd-core-math-library-acml/`.

[84] Advanced Micro Devices Inc. AMD drives adoption of industry standards in GPGPU software development, Aug. 2008.

[85] Advanced Micro Devices Inc. AMD paves ease-of-programming path to heterogeneous system architecture with new APP SDK 2.8 and unified developer tool suite, Dec. 2012.

[86] Xilinx Inc. SDAccel development environment.

[87] Xilinx Inc. Xilinx introduces ultrascale multi-processing architecture for the industry's first all programmable MPSoCs, Feb. 2014.

[88] Open SystemC Initiative. Functional specification for SystemC 2.0. 2001.

[89] Intel. Intel VTune performance analyzer. `https://software.intel.com/en-us/intel-vtune-amplifier-xe`, 2015.

[90] R. Janka, R. Judd, J. Lebak, Richards M., and D. Campbell. VSIPL: An object-based open standard API for vector, signal, and image processing. In *Proc. of Intl. Conf. on Acoustics, Speech, and Signal Processing*, volume 2, pages 949–952, 2001.

[91] Lennart Johnsson. Efficiency, energy efficiency and programming of accelerated hpc servers: Highlights of prace studies. In David A. Yuen, Long Wang, Xuebin Chi, Lennart Johnsson, Wei Ge, and Yaolin Shi, editors, *GPU Solutions to Multi-scale Problems in Science and Engineering*, Lecture Notes in Earth System Sciences, pages 33–78. Springer Berlin Heidelberg, 2013.

[92] J. A. Kahle, M. N. Day, H. P. Hofstee, C. R. Johns, T. R. Maeurer, and D. Shippy. Introduction to the cell multiprocessor. *IBM J. Res. Dev.*, 49(4/5):589–604, July 2005.

[93] Shinpei Kato, Karthik Lakshmanan, Ragunathan Raj Rajkumar, and Yutaka Ishikawa. TimeGraph: GPU scheduling for real-time multi-tasking environments. In *2011 USENIX Annual Technical Conference (USENIX ATC'11)*, page 17, 2011.

[94] Shinpei Kato, Michael McThrow, Carlos Maltzahn, and Scott Brandt. Gdev: first-class GPU resource management in the operating system. In *Proceedings of the 2012 USENIX conference on Annual Technical Conference*, USENIX ATC'12, pages 37–37, Berkeley, CA, USA, 2012. USENIX Association.

[95] S.W. Keckler, W.J. Dally, B. Khailany, M. Garland, and D. Glasco. GPUs and the future of parallel computing. *Micro, IEEE*, 31(5):7–17, Sept. 2011.

[96] Jungwon Kim, Seyong Lee, and Jeffrey S. Vetter. An OpenACC-based unified programming model for multi-accelerator systems. In *Proceedings of the 20th ACM SIGPLAN Symposium on Principles and Practice of Parallel Programming*, PPoPP 2015, pages 257–258, New York, NY, USA, 2015. ACM.

[97] Sangman Kim, Indrajit Roy, and Vanish Talwar. Evaluating integrated graphics processors for data center workloads. In *Proceedings of the Workshop on Power-Aware Computing and Systems*, HotPower '13, pages 8:1–8:5, New York, NY, USA, 2013. ACM.

[98] Dirk Koch, Christian Haubelt, and Jürgen Teich. Efficient hardware checkpointing: concepts, overhead analysis, and implementation. In *Proceedings of the 2007 ACM/SIGDA 15th international symposium on Field programmable gate arrays*, pages 188–196. ACM, 2007.

[99] Krzysztof Kosciuszkiewicz, Fearghal Morgan, and Krzysztof Kepa. Run-time management of reconfigurable hardware tasks using embedded Linux. In *Field-Programmable Technology, 2007. ICFPT 2007. International Conference on*, pages 209–215. IEEE, 2007.

[100] Benjamin A. Kuperman and Eugene Spafford. Generation of application level audit data via library interposition. Technical report, COAST Laboratory, Purdue University, West, 1999.

[101] Supada Laosooksathit, Nichamon Naksinehaboon, Chokchai Leangsuksan, Apurba Dhungana, Clayton Chandler, Kasidit Chanchio, and Amir Farbin. Lightweight checkpoint mechanism and modeling in GPGPU environment. *Computing (HPC systems)*, 12:13, 2010.

[102] Chris Lattner and Vikram Adve. LLVM: A compilation framework for lifelong program analysis & transformation. In *Code Generation and Optimization, 2004. CGO 2004. International Symposium on*, pages 75–86. IEEE, 2004.

[103] C. L. Lawson, R. J. Hanson, D. R. Kincaid, and F. T. Krogh. Basic linear algebra subprograms for Fortran usage. *ACM Trans. Math. Softw.*, 5(3):308–323, September 1979.

[104] Seyong Lee and Rudolf Eigenmann. OpenMPC: Extended OpenMP programming and tuning for GPUs. In *Proceedings of the 2010 ACM/IEEE International Conference for High Performance Computing, Networking, Storage and Analysis*, SC '10, pages 1–11, Washington, DC, USA, 2010. IEEE Computer Society.

[105] Teng Li, Vikram K Narayana, and Tarek El-Ghazawi. A static task scheduling framework for independent tasks accelerated using a shared graphics processing unit. In *Parallel and Distributed Systems (ICPADS), 2011 IEEE 17th International Conference on*, pages 88–95. IEEE, 2011.

[106] Michael D Linderman, Jamison D Collins, Hong Wang, and Teresa H Meng. Merge: a programming model for heterogeneous multi-core systems. In *ACM SIGOPS Operating Systems Review*, volume 42, pages 287–296. ACM, 2008.

[107] Cong Liu, Jian Li, Wei Huang, Juan Rubio, Evan Speight, and Xiaozhu Lin. Power-efficient time-sensitive mapping in heterogeneous systems. In *Proceedings of the 21st International Conference on Parallel Architectures and Compilation Techniques*, PACT '12, pages 23–32, New York, NY, USA, 2012. ACM.

[108] Yongchao Liu and Bertil Schmidt. Faster GPU-accelerated smith-waterman algorithm with alignment backtracking for short DNA sequences. In *Parallel Processing and Applied Mathematics*, volume 8385 of *Lecture Notes in Computer Science*, pages 247–257. Springer Berlin Heidelberg, 2014.

[109] Enno Lübbers and Marco Platzner. ReconOS: Multithreaded programming for reconfigurable computers. *ACM Trans. Embed. Comput. Syst.*, 9(1):8:1–8:33, 2009.

[110] Chi-Keung Luk, Robert Cohn, Robert Muth, Harish Patil, Artur Klauser, Geoff Lowney, Steven Wallace, Vijay Janapa Reddi, and Kim Hazelwood. Pin: building

customized program analysis tools with dynamic instrumentation. In *Proc. of the ACM SIGPLAN Conf. on Programming language design and implementation*, pages 190–200, 2005.

[111] Chi-Keung Luk, Sunpyo Hong, and Hyesoon Kim. Qilin: exploiting parallelism on heterogeneous multiprocessors with adaptive mapping. In *Microarchitecture, 2009. MICRO-42. 42nd Annual IEEE/ACM International Symposium on*, pages 45–55. IEEE, 2009.

[112] Kai Ma, Xue Li, Wei Chen, Chi Zhang, and Xiaorui Wang. Greengpu: A holistic approach to energy efficiency in GPU-CPU heterogeneous architectures. In *Parallel Processing (ICPP), 2012 41st International Conference on*, pages 48–57, Sept 2012.

[113] C.A. Mack. Fifty years of Moore's law. *Semiconductor Manufacturing, IEEE Transactions on*, 24(2):202–207, May 2011.

[114] James Manyika, Michael Chui, Brad Brown, Jacques Bughin, Richard Dobbs, Charles Roxburgh, Angela Hung Byers, and McKinsey Global Institute. Big data: The next frontier for innovation, competition, and productivity. 2011.

[115] Artur Mariano, Ricardo Alves, Joao Barbosa, Luis Paulo Santos, and Alberto Proenca. A (ir) regularity-aware task scheduler for heterogeneous platforms. In *International Conference on High Performance Computing*, 2012.

[116] Giuseppe Massari, Chiara Caffarri, Patrick Bellasi, and William Fornaciari. Extending a run-time resource management framework to support OpenCL and heterogeneous systems. In *Proceedings of Workshop on Parallel Programming and Run-Time Management Techniques for Many-core Architectures and Design Tools and Architectures for Multicore Embedded Computing Platforms*, PARMA-DITAM '14, pages 21:21–21:26, New York, NY, USA, 2014. ACM.

[117] A. Matoga, R. Chaves, P. Tomas, and N. Roma. A flexible shared library profiler for early estimation of performance gains in heterogeneous systems. In *High Performance Computing and Simulation (HPCS), 2013 International Conference on*, pages 461–470, July 2013.

[118] Maxeler Technologies Inc. https://www.maxeler.com.

[119] E. Mollick. Establishing Moore's law. *Annals of the History of Computing, IEEE*, 28(3):62–75, July 2006.

[120] Ingo Molnar. Modular scheduler core and completely fair scheduler [CFS]. *Linux-Kernel mailing list*, 2007.

[121] Gordon E. Moore. Cramming more components onto integrated circuits. *Electronics*, 38(8):114–117, Apr. 1965.

[122] Gordon E Moore. Lithography and the future of Moore's law. In *SPIE's 1995 Symposium on Microlithography*, pages 2–17. International Society for Optics and Photonics, 1995.

[123] Gordon E. Moore et al. Progress in digital integrated electronics. *IEDM Tech. Digest*, 11, 1975.

[124] Nicholas Moore, Albert Conti, Miriam Leeser, and Laurie Smith King. VForce: an extensible framework for reconfigurable supercomputing. *Computer*, 40(3):39–49, 2007.

[125] Kevin Morris. Xilinx vs. Altera - calling the action in the greatest semiconductor rivalry. http://www.eejournal.com/archives/articles/20140225-rivalry/.

[126] San Murugesan. Harnessing green IT: Principles and practices. *IT professional*, 10(1):24–33, 2008.

[127] Nicholas Nethercote and Julian Seward. Valgrind: A framework for heavyweight dynamic binary instrumentation. In *Proceedings of the 2007 ACM SIGPLAN Conference on Programming Language Design and Implementation*, PLDI '07, pages 89–100, New York, NY, USA, 2007. ACM.

[128] Netlib. Netlib repository. www.netlib.org/blas/.

[129] John Nickolls and William J Dally. The GPU computing era. *IEEE micro*, 30(2):56–69, 2010.

[130] Edmund B Nightingale, Orion Hodson, Ross McIlroy, Chris Hawblitzel, and Galen Hunt. Helios: heterogeneous multiprocessing with satellite kernels. In *Proceedings of the ACM SIGOPS 22nd symposium on Operating systems principles*, pages 221–234. ACM, 2009.

[131] NVIDIA Corporation. *CUDA CUBLAS Library*, 2008.

[132] Oak Ridge Leadership Computing Facility (OLCF). Titan. https://www.olcf.ornl.gov/titan/.

[133] OpenACC-Standard.org. The OpenACC application programming interface, version 2.0. June 2013.

[134] Sankaralingam Panneerselvam and Michael M Swift. Operating systems should manage accelerators. In *Proceedings of the 4th USENIX conference on Hot Topics in Parallelism*, pages 4–4. USENIX Association, 2012.

[135] R. Pellizzoni and M. Caccamo. Adaptive allocation of software and hardware real-time tasks for FPGA-based embedded systems. In *Real-Time and Embedded Technology and Applications Symposium, 2006. Proceedings of the 12th IEEE*, pages 208–220, Apr. 2006.

[136] Jacques A. Pienaar, Anand Raghunathan, and Srimat Chakradhar. MDR: Performance model driven runtime for heterogeneous parallel platforms. In *Proceedings of the International Conference on Supercomputing*, ICS '11, pages 225–234, New York, NY, USA, 2011. ACM.

[137] Judit Planas, Rosa M Badia, Eduard Ayguadé, and Jesus Labarta. Hierarchical task-based programming with StarSs. *International Journal of High Performance Computing Applications*, 23(3):284–299, 2009.

[138] John Reiser. rtldi – indirect runtime loader. http://www.bitwagon.com/rtldi/rtldi.html.

[139] Christopher J. Rossbach, Jon Currey, Mark Silberstein, Baishakhi Ray, and Emmett Witchel. PTask: operating system abstractions to manage GPUs as compute devices. In *Proceedings of the Twenty-Third ACM Symposium on Operating Systems Principles*, SOSP '11, pages 233–248, New York, NY, USA, 2011. ACM.

[140] Kyle Rupnow, Wenyin Fu, and Katherine Compton. Block, drop or roll (back): Alternative preemption methods for rh multi-tasking. In *Field Programmable Custom Computing Machines, 2009. FCCM'09. 17th IEEE Symposium on*, pages 63–70. IEEE, 2009.

[141] Santonu Sarkar and Mageri Filali Maltouf. Identifying hotspots in a program for data parallel architecture: An early experience. In *Proceedings of the 5th India Software Engineering Conference*, ISEC '12, pages 131–137, New York, NY, USA, 2012. ACM.

[142] R.R. Schaller. Moore's law: past, present and future. *Spectrum, IEEE*, 34(6):52–59, June 1997.

[143] Andrew G Schmidt, Bin Huang, Ron Sass, and Matthew French. Checkpoint/restart and beyond: resilient high performance computing with FPGAs. In *Field-Programmable Custom Computing Machines (FCCM), 2011 IEEE 19th Annual International Symposium on*, pages 162–169. IEEE, 2011.

[144] T.R.W. Scogland, H. Lin, and W. Feng. A first look at integrated GPUs for green high-performance computing. *Computer Science - Research and Development*, 25(3-4):125–134, 2010.

[145] Lin Shi, Hao Chen, and Ting Li. Hybrid CPU/GPU checkpoint for GPU-based heterogeneous systems. In Kenli Li, Zheng Xiao, Yan Wang, Jiayi Du, and Keqin Li, editors, *Parallel Computational Fluid Dynamics*, volume 405 of *Communications in Computer and Information Science*, pages 470–481. Springer Berlin Heidelberg, 2014.

[146] Lin Shi, Hao Chen, Jianhua Sun, and Kenli Li. vCUDA: GPU-accelerated high-performance computing in virtual machines. *Computers, IEEE Transactions on*, 61(6):804–816, June 2012.

[147] Harald Simmler, Lorne Levinson, and Reinhard Männer. Multitasking on FPGA coprocessors. In *Field-Programmable Logic and Applications: The Roadmap to Reconfigurable Computing*, pages 121–130. Springer, 2000.

[148] Satnam Singh. Computing without processors. *Commun. ACM*, 54(8):46–54, 2011.

[149] W. Stallings. *Operating Systems: Internals and Design Principles*. Pearson Prentice Hall, 6th edition, 2009.

[150] Garrick Staples. TORQUE resource manager. In *Proceedings of the 2006 ACM/IEEE Conference on Supercomputing*, SC '06, New York, NY, USA, 2006. ACM.

[151] Bjarne Steensgaard. Object and native code thread mobility among heterogeneous computers. In *In Proceedings of the 15th ACM Symposium on Operating Systems Principles*, pages 68–78, 1995.

[152] Elizer Sternheim, Rajvir Singh, and Yatin Trivedi. *Digital Design with Verilog HDL*. Automata Publishing Company, 1991.

[153] Jeff A. Stuart, Pavan Balaji, and John D. Owens. Extending MPI to accelerators. In *Proceedings of the 1st Workshop on Architectures and Systems for Big Data*, ASBD '11, pages 19–23, New York, NY, USA, 2011. ACM.

[154] Henry Styles and Wayne Luk. Customizing graphics applications: Techniques and programming interface. *Symp. on Field-Programmable Custom Computing Machines*, page 77, 2000.

[155] Enqiang Sun, Dana Schaa, Richard Bagley, Norman Rubin, and David Kaeli. Enabling task-level scheduling on heterogeneous platforms. In *Proceedings of the 5th Annual Workshop on General Purpose Processing with Graphics Processing Units*, GPGPU-5, pages 84–93, New York, NY, USA, 2012. ACM.

[156] Weibin Sun and Robert Ricci. Augmenting operating systems with the GPU. 2011.

[157] Hiroyuki Takizawa, Kentaro Koyama, Katsuto Sato, Kazuhiko Komatsu, and Hiroaki Kobayashi. CheCL: Transparent checkpointing and process migration of OpenCL applications. In *Parallel & Distributed Processing Symposium (IPDPS), 2011 IEEE International*, pages 864–876. IEEE, 2011.

[158] Hiroyuki Takizawa, Katsuto Sato, Kazuhiko Komatsu, and Hiroaki Kobayashi. CheCUDA: A checkpoint/restart tool for CUDA applications. In *Parallel and Distributed Computing, Applications and Technologies, 2009 International Conference on*, pages 408–413. IEEE, 2009.

[159] T. Tamasi. Evolution of computer graphics. In *Proc. NVISION 08*, 2008.

[160] Ivan Tanasic, Isaac Gelado, Javier Cabezas, Alex Ramirez, Nacho Navarro, and Mateo Valero. Enabling preemptive multiprogramming on GPUs. In *Proceeding of the 41st annual international symposium on Computer architecuture*, pages 193–204. IEEE Press, 2014.

[161] Ayman Tarakji, Niels Ole Salscheider, and David Hebbeker. OS support for load scheduling on accelerator-based heterogeneous systems. *Procedia Computer Science*, 29(0):231 – 245, 2014. 2014 International Conference on Computational Science.

[162] Douglas Thain, Todd Tannenbaum, and Miron Livny. Distributed computing in practice: the Condor experience. *Concurrency and Computation: Practice and Experience*, 17(2-4):323–356, 2005.

[163] Philippe Tillet, Karl Rupp, and Siegfried Selberherr. An automatic OpenCL compute kernel generator for basic linear algebra operations. In *Proceedings of the 2012 Symposium on High Performance Computing*, HPC '12, pages 4:1–4:2, San Diego, CA, USA, 2012. Society for Computer Simulation International.

[164] TOP500.org. Tianhe-2 supercomputer takes no. 1 ranking on 41st TOP500 list, 2013.

[165] TOP500.org. Top500 list November 2014. http://www.top500.org/lists/2014/11/, 2014.

[166] Haluk Topcuoglu, Salim Hariri, and Min-you Wu. Performance-effective and low-complexity task scheduling for heterogeneous computing. *Parallel and Distributed Systems, IEEE Transactions on*, 13(3):260–274, 2002.

[167] Gavin Vaz, Heinrich Riebler, Tobias Kenter, and Christian Plessl. Deferring accelerator offloading decisions to application runtime. In *Proc. Int. Conf. on ReConFigurable Computing and FPGAs (ReConFig)*. IEEE Computer Society, 2014.

[168] A. Venkat and D.M. Tullsen. Harnessing ISA diversity: Design of a heterogeneous-ISA chip multiprocessor. In *Proc. Int. Symp. on Computer Architecture (ISCA)*, pages 121–132, June 2014.

[169] Herbert Walder and Marco Platzner. Non-preemptive multitasking on FPGAs: Task placement and footprint transform. In *Proceedings of the 2nd International Conference on Engineering of Reconfigurable Systems and Architectures (ERSA)*, pages 24–30, 2002.

[170] Guibin Wang and Xiaoguang Ren. Power-efficient work distribution method for CPU-GPU heterogeneous system. In *Parallel and Distributed Processing with Applications (ISPA), 2010 International Symposium on*, pages 122–129, Sept 2010.

[171] Haifeng Wang and Qingkui Chen. An energy consumption model for GPU computing at instruction level. *International Journal of Advancements in Computing Technology*, 4(2), 2012.

[172] Yue Wang and Nagarajan Ranganathan. An instruction-level energy estimation and optimization methodology for GPU. In *Computer and Information Technology (CIT), 2011 IEEE 11th International Conference on*, pages 621–628. IEEE, 2011.

[173] Zheng Wang, Dominik Grewe, and Michael F. P. O'Boyle. Automatic and portable mapping of data parallel programs to OpenCL for GPU-based heterogeneous systems. *ACM Trans. Archit. Code Optim.*, 11(4):42:1–42:26, 2014.

[174] Yuan Wen, Zheng Wang, and Michael F.P. O'Boyle. Smart multi-task scheduling for OpenCL programs on CPU/GPU heterogeneous platforms. 2014.

[175] John R. Wernsing and Greg Stitt. Elastic computing: A portable optimization framework for hybrid computers. *Parallel Computing*, 2012.

[176] R. Clint Whaley and Jack J. Dongarra. Automatically tuned linear algebra software. In *Proceedings of the 1998 ACM/IEEE Conference on Supercomputing*, SC '98, pages 1–27, Washington, DC, USA, 1998. IEEE Computer Society.

[177] Wm. A. Wulf and Sally A. McKee. Hitting the memory wall: Implications of the obvious. *SIGARCH Comput. Archit. News*, 23(1):20–24, 1995.

[178] Shucai Xiao, P. Balaji, J. Dinan, Qian Zhu, R. Thakur, S. Coghlan, Heshan Lin, Gaojin Wen, Jue Hong, and Wu chun Feng. Transparent accelerator migration in a virtualized GPU environment. In *Cluster, Cloud and Grid Computing (CCGrid), 2012 12th IEEE/ACM International Symposium on*, pages 124–131, May 2012.

[179] J.H.C. Yeung, C.C. Tsang, K.H. Tsoi, B.S.H. Kwan, C.C.C. Cheung, A.P.C. Chan, and P.H.W. Leong. Map-reduce as a programming model for custom computing machines. In *Field-Programmable Custom Computing Machines, 2008. FCCM '08. 16th International Symposium on*, pages 149–159, Apr. 2008.

[180] Luna Mingyi Zhang, Keqin Li, and Yan-Qing Zhang. Green task scheduling algorithms with speeds optimization on heterogeneous cloud servers. In *Proceedings of the 2010 IEEE/ACM Int'L Conference on Green Computing and Communications & Int'L Conference on Cyber, Physical and Social Computing*, GREENCOM-CPSCOM '10, pages 76–80, Washington, DC, USA, 2010. IEEE Computer Society.